Steven

The Family Law Trial Evidence Handbook

Rules and Procedures for Effective Advocacy

Defending Liberty
Pursuing Justice

SECTION OF
FAMILY LAW

© 2013 American Bar Association. All rights reserved.

No part of this publication may be reproduced, stored in a retrieval system, or transmitted in any form or by any means, electronic, mechanical, photocopying, recording, or otherwise, without the prior written permission of the publisher. For permission contact the ABA Copyrights & Contracts Department, copyright@americanbar.org, or complete the online form at http://www.americanbar.org/utility/reprint/html.

Printed in the United States of America.

17 16 15 14 13   5 4 3 2

Library of Congress Cataloging-in-Publication Data on File

ISBN: 978-1-62722-003-3

Discounts are available for books ordered in bulk. Special consideration is given to state bars, CLE programs, and other bar-related organizations. Inquire at Book Publishing, ABA Publishing, American Bar Association, 321 N. Clark Street, Chicago, Illinois 60654-7598.

www.ShopABA.org

Dedication

To my father David P. Peskind (1935-1991) who, by his example, taught me goodness is more important than greatness.

Contents

About the Author

Steven Peskind is the principal of the Peskind Law Firm based in St. Charles, Illinois. He graduated from Tulane University and DePaul University College of Law. He is a Fellow of the American Academy of Matrimonial Lawyers and is an elected member of the American Law Institute and the American Bar Foundation. He recently served on the Illinois Family Law Study Committee working to improve Illinois family laws.

Mr. Peskind is a faculty member of the Family Law Trial Advocacy Institute presented annually in Boulder, Colorado by the ABA Family Law Section in conjunction with the National Institute for Trial Advocacy. In addition, he serves on the Publication Board of the ABA Family Law Section and the Editorial Board of the AAML Journal.

Mr. Peskind speaks nationally on a variety of family law topics ranging from taxation to evidence. In April 2012 he presented on effective trial techniques at the ABA Family Law Section Spring CLE. In October 2011 he presented at the AAML Columbus Day seminar in Chicago on the topic of authenticating digital evidence in family law cases. In 2010, he was the keynote speaker for the Oklahoma Bar Association Family Law Section annual meeting, and at a 2009 CLE Conference for the ABA Section of Family Law held in Montreal he spoke about the future of family law.

In addition to multiple bar journal articles, he has also published three law review articles. One article examined redefining parentage in the age of assisted reproductive technology and another explored the origin and utility of the best interest standard in determining child custody. A law review article published in 2013 focused on hearsay evidence in child custody proceedings. In 2005 he was inducted into Scribes, a legal writing honor society.

Mr. Peskind has been recognized as one of the Best Lawyers in America. The Leading Lawyers Network has designated Mr. Peskind a Leading Lawyer since 2003 and the Super Lawyers has recognized him as a Super Lawyer since 2008. Steven and his wife Susan live in Batavia, Illinois. They have three children and two grandchildren.

Acknowledgments

I want to recognize a number of people who helped me throughout the process of formulating and writing this book. This book was conceived on a walk in New Orleans in January 2010. A friend and fellow family lawyer, Lonnie Balbi, challenged me to write a book, and this is the result. Besides Lonnie, many have inspired and assisted me, and I want to acknowledge them:

- Thanks to the librarians at the Kane County Law Library (Halle Cox and Nancy Lee Browne) for helping me find articles and resources during my research;
- Thanks to my ABA editor Jeff Salyards whose kindness and guidance was integral to making this project happen;
- Thanks to my personal assistant Michelle Alexander for her support and helping me, as always, to keep all of the balls in the air;
- Thanks to Joe Howie in Tulsa, an e-discovery expert, who gave me insights into the evidentiary issues involving digital photography;
- Thanks to Professor Colin Miller at Chicago's John Marshall Law School and Editor of the Evidence Prof Blog for letting me pick his brain;
- Thanks to Gail Baker and the entire ABA Family Law Section Publication Board for their encouragement and guidance;
- Thanks to my friends and colleagues at the ABA/NITA Family Law Trial Institute, in Boulder, Colorado, where I had a laboratory for many of the concepts addressed in this book;

- Thanks to the entire Peskind Law team who stepped up during my frequent writing absences.

There are a couple of people I particularly want to acknowledge. Linda Ravdin from Bethesda, Maryland was my lay editor on this project. She and her team spent countless hours reviewing the manuscript and suggesting numerous changes to help make this a more readable and cogent book. I am forever indebted for her wisdom and friendship. This book would have been much different without her guidance.

Ann Fick, a paralegal at Peskind Law Firm and law student at DePaul University College of Law reviewed my draft as well. She also helped me research and edit large portions of the book. I am grateful to her for her hard work and patience. It's not easy telling the boss when one of his sentences sucked, and she did so tactfully and gracefully.

Anita Ventrelli and Mark Caldwell from the Trial Institute helped me clarify many of the concepts addressed in the book. Anita also spent much of 2012 speaking with me on advanced family law evidence and I have incorporated many of her evidentiary insights. I thank them for their virtuosity and passion for trial advocacy.

Also, I would like to specially thank my grandson Oliver Adams, my Wednesday morning buddy, who helped me write and edit in between reading Winnie the Pooh.

Finally, to my family who supported me during this process: Susan, Jenna, Dave, Mollie, and John. Their confidence in me never wavered and propelled me onward. In particular, to my wife and best friend Susan, who spent two years looking at the back of my head while I worked at my home computer. I hope this effort is worthy of her encouragement and patience. Her certainty sustained me.

Foreword

In hindsight, it makes perfect sense for Steve Peskind to have written a definitive work on evidence for the family law practitioner. Seldom does a book offer the promise that this one does of making one a better trial lawyer for having read it and keeping it close while preparing for any evidentiary proceeding. I met Steve in 1994 when we attended the American Bar Association Family Law Section's Trial Advocacy Institute as students. For those who have not attended, this Institute, now presented in partnership with the National Institute of Trial Advocacy, is an unparalleled experience for turning the collection of facts and documents we assemble into a persuasive presentation for judge or jury. The collective experience of Institute attendance or, as some would say, survival creates bonds that last a lifetime. Since our attendance at the Institute, Steve and I have both been fortunate enough to be included in the faculty so once each year, we take a deep breath and plunge into 8 days of intensive trial training for lawyers who have practiced anywhere from 2 months to 20 years. Their common denominator is the desire to take their family law trial skills and their communications skills up a notch.

Steve's book is unique as "handbooks" go because, unlike most, it is organized in a format that can work for all family law trial lawyers regardless of whether they practice in a state that uses a variation on the Federal Rules or a common law body of rules on evidence. It is reminiscent of tried and true evidence handbooks, my personal favorite from law school being Thomas Mauet. The superlative ones enable the reader to quickly turn to the rules that pertain to particular types of evidence with ease for reference during a trial. However, as I read this book, I decided that it sells the book short to call it a handbook on evidence because it is so very much more. It clearly articulates the philosophy and method we teach at the Trial Advocacy Institute and inspires anyone who reads the preface and introductory chapters to want to put cases together in a way that commands interest in the listener and in the style of great trial lawyers. By reminding all of us who practice family law that we are no less trial lawyers than those in other practice areas, Steve gives us the reasoning we need to work out our own evidentiary issues for the areas that will most certainly develop as the world evolves.

When Steve and I lecture on evidence, we remind students of the rule that everyone seems to overlook, namely, Federal Rule 901. We affectionately refer to this as the "It is What it Is" Rule. Steve reminds us in his chapters on Cutting Edge Digital and Electronic Evidence that because there is no Rule for them, we simply need to follow the tenets of Rule 901 and be in a position to demonstrate to the court that a text is a text and an e-mail is an e-mail. By getting us back to basics in a terse and organized way, a first reading of Steve's book will make anyone a better trial lawyer whether they have been in practice for 2 months or 20 years.

I have seen the evidence of Steve's particular brand of enlightenment in the associates he sends to the Institute and in the eyes of those to whom he lectures. His approach to all things legal inspires passion and thoughtfulness. He doesn't take the reasons why we do things for granted. Since Steve undertook to write this book, he has risen through the leadership of the ABA Family law Section to be a leader on the Publications Board. For that, the Section is truly lucky. This book combines the substantive knowledge critical to making the reader facile with the concepts of evidence with a format that insures that anything the family law trial lawyer could want is easily found at a moment's notice. Boiled down to its essence, Steven Peskind's Family Law Trial Evidence Handbook is the next best thing to attending the ABA FLS/NITA Trial Advocacy Institute. He is a gentleman and a scholar in the truest sense of those words, and I am privileged to count him among my dearest friends.

Anita M. Ventrelli
ABA Family Law Section Delegate & Former Chair
Member ABA/FLS Trial Advocacy Institute Board
Member ABA/FLS NITA Trial Advocacy Institute Faculty

Preface

Today, people with matrimonial conflict frequently look to mediation and collaborative law to avoid the cost and anxiety of traditional litigation. While these alternative dispute resolution systems (ADR) benefit many families, many others still need help from the courts. Family law matters involve painful emotions, and certain litigants are unable to discuss the issues—much less settle them. We often see people with personality disorders and other disordered thinking. Some people have legitimate disagreements about their children's best interests or thorny financial issues that need to be resolved by a judge. Not every case can be concluded at the conference table. Even in this era of ADR, complete family lawyers still need the skills to resolve their cases in court.

I conceptualized this book while serving on the faculty of the American Bar Association Family Law Trial Advocacy Institute. The institute instructs lawyer-students in the art and science of trial advocacy in a divorce case. While participating, I realized that there was no reference book or guide for the effective use of evidence in a divorce case. This book is an effort to fill that gap. While the rules of evidence are not applied differently in a divorce case, there are evidentiary issues that divorce lawyers regularly see, and this reference book provides a helpful resource for both novice and experienced family lawyers.

At the core of being a trial lawyer is a working knowledge of the rules of evidence—how to get evidence admitted or kept out in a contested trial or hearing. Procedures to authenticate exhibits are the building blocks of any case, and objections and their responses are the mortar. I have designed this book as a commonsense guide to these fundamentals of family law trial practice and a trial companion for contested family law matters. While the rules of evidence are state specific, the goal of this guidebook is to point lawyers in the right direction; and to help them develop their cases for trial.

Judges identify lawyers who can try cases well and appreciate their skill. And good settlements come from superior trial skills. A lawyer who knows how to try a case can often secure a better settlement than the lawyer who is less comfortable in the courtroom. Lawyers who do not recognize their limitations will try cases unsuccessfully against opponents who know the rules and can apply them. It is axiomatic, but knowledge is power. This book is the starting point for lawyers pursuing excellence in family law trial advocacy.

A Note about Primary Sources

I have relied on a variety of sources in researching and writing this book. My primary resource was *McCormick on Evidence*, sixth edition, Practitioner Treatise series published by Thomson West. The answer to every question I had was ultimately found in this marvelous resource. I also leaned heavily on Edward J. Imwinkelried's text *Evidentiary Foundations*, seventh edition, published by LexisNexis Publishing. This was a great practical complement to the *McCormick* book. Additionally, I relied on *Trial Evidence*, fourth edition, by Thomas Mauet and Warren Wolfson, published by Wolters Kluwer. I am proud to say that Dean Wolfson was the former dean of the DePaul Law School, my alma mater. Finally, I drew substantially from *Modern Trial Advocacy*, fourth edition, by Professor Steven Lubet, published by the National Institute for Trial Advocacy. I relied to a lesser extent on a variety of other resources, which are referenced in the footnotes throughout the book.

Trial Process and Procedure

The Role of the Trial Judge in a Family Law Proceeding

The vast majority of family law matters are tried without a jury, so this book focuses on the application of the rules in trials where the judge is the trier of fact. In a typical family law case, the trial judge serves as the referee, settlement coach, fact finder, determiner of the applicable law, and overseer of all aspects of the dispute. The judge's role is expansive and substantial, and that role is referenced in various provisions of the rules of evidence. The trial judge must ensure that the proceedings are fair and orderly. For example, Federal Rule of Evidence (FRE) 611 requires the court to control the order and interrogation of witnesses. FRE 614 allows the court, on its own motion, to call and interrogate witnesses as necessary.

The rules of evidence are designed to ensure fair trials. Judges in bench trials must protect the integrity of the proceeding and efficiently manage it. Without application of the rules of evidence, a trial can rapidly become a brawl. By using the rules of relevance, the court can maintain order and control over the evidence, limiting the case to germane and important information.

One could argue that the role of the trial judge in a family court proceeding is unique compared to judges in other civil and criminal proceedings. Because of the emotional subject matter and the nature of the proceedings, family court trial judges must be equal parts sage and babysitter. These judges must monitor and resolve disputes from the truly insignificant (division of the forks and knives) to the vitally important—custodial arrangements that will influence the futures of children. Not unlike other judges, however, the family court trial judge must act as a case manager: exploring settlement opportunities, determining the schedule for discovery, and adjudicating unresolved issues. Family court trial judges may not be able to solve all of the family's problems, but they must resolve those problems to the extent possible. Ultimately, it is the judge's foremost responsibility to see that justice is done for the litigants.

Trial judges possess great latitude with respect to their evidentiary rulings. And for the most part, appellate courts defer to the trial court's evidentiary rulings.[1] FRE 103 (a) specifically provides that "[A] party may claim error in a ruling to admit or exclude evidence only if the error affects a substantial right of the party." Not only must the error affect the substantial right of a party, but that party must also call the error to the attention of the judge so the judge can correct the mistake.[2] The lawyer must successfully offer or defend evidence in the trial court, as there will not likely be a second chance in the appellate court.

---

1.   *See, e.g.*, Kotteakos v. United States, 328 U.S. 750 (1946).
2.   FED. R. EVID. 103(a)(1). Preservation of error is discussed in detail in Chapter 15.

Format of a Family Law Trial

Some lawyers do not try matrimonial cases as they would an ordinary civil case. The rules become relaxed. They waive their opening statement. They do not conduct examinations of witnesses in an orderly fashion. These lawyers do not properly prepare witnesses and are often unprepared themselves. The trial proceeds haphazardly. This is not the way to handle a family law matter.

If lawyers do not take family law matters seriously, neither will litigants nor the public. Rulings concerning children profoundly affect their welfare, both short and long term. Children certainly deserve the same attention that a commercial case commands. Lawmakers codified the Federal Rules of Evidence and the Federal Rules of Civil Procedure because they recognized that clearly defined rules produce more just results. Lawyers need to learn and apply trial advocacy skills in family court with the same earnestness as trial lawyers in other courts. Family lawyers should not define themselves as highly paid brawlers; rather, they should be skilled advocates using the rules and art of advocacy. There are many resources to help family lawyers refine their trial skills, including the American Bar Association's Family Law Trial Advocacy Institute, presented annually.[3] In the remainder of this chapter, I briefly review the specific components of a family law trial.

---

3.   27th Annual Family Law Trial Advocacy Institute (ABA/NITA) <http://www2. americanbar.org/calendar/aba-section-of-family-law-advanced-trial-advocacy-institute-held-jointly-with-nita/Pages/default.aspx>; National Institute for Trial Advocacy <http:// www.nita.org/>;

Gallagher Law Library, University of Washington School of Law, Trial Advocacy Resources <http://lib.law.washington.edu/ref/trialad.html>

Theories and Themes

Understanding the theory of your case is the starting point for all matters that proceed to a trial or hearing. A case theory is "the adaptation of a factual story to the legal issues in the case. Your theory must contain a simple, logical, provable account of facts which, when viewed in light of the controlling law, will lead to the conclusion that your client should win."[4] What facts, applied to the existing law, warrant the relief you seek?

The theory is the skeleton of the case. What are the particular facts supporting a claim for alimony? Why should the court award custody of the children to your client? Was she the primary caretaker of the children, who have thrived in her care? Again, the theory is the facts as applied to the law that supports the desired result. The theme, on the other hand, is the persuasive basis for why the theory should prevail.

The theme is a short statement designed to grab the judge's attention with a moral hook on which the relief should be granted. A theme appeals to common values and cultural beliefs. A good theme artfully encapsulates the core principle of the case with a phrase or parable that will resonate with the judge. The theme is not designed to appeal to judges' logic, but rather their sentiments. Neuroscience proves that decision makers rely (often unconsciously) on feelings more than on reason. If advocates can associate the client's cause with a powerful phrase, story, or cultural reference, they are on their way to a successful result.

Literary archetypes are useful sources. For example, if the issue involves one party's disciplined money management contrasted against the spouse's frivolous spending, an appropriate theme might reference Aesop's "Ant and the Grasshopper" fable. Or, more simplistically, perhaps the theme could be "givers and takers." If a

---

4.   STEVEN LUBET, MODERN TRIAL ADVOCACY 380 (4th ed. 2009).

theory is the basis for the relief, the theme is the reason why your requested relief is the righteous thing for the judge to do. In biological terms, if the theory is the skeleton, the theme is the pumping heart of your case.

Thread the theme throughout the entire hearing or trial. Reference it in the opening statement, in the closing argument, and at all times in between. Use the language from your theme when you question witnesses. Repetition is powerful: regular references to your theory and theme make for a more effective presentation.

Opening Statement

Regrettably, many trial judges and family law attorneys dismiss the necessity of an opening statement. In all fairness, when judges nurse a particular case from file to trial, they may not think they need a road map to start the trial. But framing the issues and the evidence is always helpful, if for no other reason than to give the court the context before the evidence is presented. From the lawyers' perspective, the opening statement is vital. It is their first opportunity to advocate for their client: to identify the primary facts, issues, and theories and to tie them together with a compelling thematic thread.

First impressions stick, and the opening statement gives the court a background against which to better understand the evidence when it ultimately is offered. For a court to determine materiality and relevance, it must have a context, and the opening statement provides that context. While the opening statement must be free from argument, one can nevertheless persuade by effectively organizing the facts. The opening statement is a vital opportunity for lawyers to focus the dialogue on their theory and theme, directing the court's attention in favor of their client. Never waive an opening statement.

Tell a story in the opening statement. Stories are the most effective way to persuade. I personally start the opening statement with the theme, referencing a parable, simple story, or hook phrase: "Your honor, this case is about givers and takers," for example. From there, I summarize the issues that need to be resolved. Next, I state the salient facts in a story format, trying to sequence them in the most logical and persuasive way. There are no rules requiring a chronological presentation of the facts, as long as the facts make sense in the overall scheme of the case. Confront any problems with the case as well. Discussing your weaknesses softens their impact, so preemptively explain issues of concern. I conclude by summarizing what the client will be requesting and then provide a final reference back to the theme. Repetition is a fundamental principle of effective trial advocacy.

Direct Examination

Direct examination is one of the most underrated trial advocacy skills. Lawyers rarely devote enough time to preparing their clients for their direct examination, despite the fact that the client is usually the most important witness in the case. Seminars abound on effective cross-examination, but few instructors spend much energy on direct examination. Conducting an effective direct examination of a witness is more challenging than a cross-examination. On cross, the lawyer, through properly phrased questions, has total control over the testimony. Direct examination cedes control to the witness. In a divorce case, when the underlying subject matter is often emotionally compelling, direct examination is vital to a successful result. Have clients tell their stories, and make them interesting.

Gold-Bikin and Kolodny, in their book, *The Divorce Trial Manual*, describe the fundamentals of an effective direct examination:

The keys to an effective direct examination are well-planned, non-leading open-ended questions. The questions will begin with the "w" words—*who, why, what, where, when*—and the "h" word, *how.* Occasionally, a question may begin with "Describe." These words allow the witness to do the talking.[5]

Leading your witness on direct is unproductive and often ineffective. It is the witness's own words that will move the judge, not the lawyer's partisan "testimony" through leading questions.

Direct examination serves two purposes. First, as mentioned above, direct examination gives witnesses an opportunity to tell their story. Second, direct examination lays the foundation for important evidence. One needs to authenticate documents, photographs, and other tangible exhibits as a prerequisite to their admission, and direct testimony by a witness is the most common method of doing so.[6] Do not treat direct examination as an afterthought. Thorough preparation is necessary for an effective result.

Cross-Examination

If direct examination is the stepchild of trial advocacy, cross-examination must be the golden child; most people think it generates the most excitement in any trial. Fictionalized lawyers regularly achieve some winning insight during cross-examination. But as most practicing lawyers know, dramatic "gotchas" rarely happen in real life. Cross-examination actually serves the mundane purpose of accumulating evidence that supports the theory or the

---

5.   LYNNE Z. GOLD-BIKIN & STEPHEN KOLODNY, THE DIVORCE TRIAL MANUAL: FROM INITIAL INTERVIEW TO CLOSING ARGUMENT 59 (ABA ed., 2004).
    6.   I address the topics of foundation and authentication in Chapter 9.

theme. Home runs rarely happen during cross-examination; the important thing is to get on base.

A focused cross-examination may achieve some or all of the following objectives:

- To impeach the testimony of an adverse witness
- To impugn the credibility of a particular witness, particularly an expert witness testifying on behalf of an opponent
- To challenge the observations or conclusions of an adverse witness
- To acquire facts or admissions to support the theory and the theme of the case
- To lay a foundation or authenticate a document or other item of tangible evidence

Plan the cross examination in advance and make sure it is goal oriented. Reactive battering of an adverse witness wastes time and is often dangerous. While many clients love seeing righteous indignation by their lawyer, not every witness warrants this treatment. And when the judge sees a witness treated unfairly, the lawyer risks alienating the judge. Cross-examination is not for your client's entertainment; it is to help win the case.

Cross-examination does not need to be cross to be effective. Identify your precise goals prior to cross-examination and methodically set out to achieve them. Law schools and trial advocacy clinics may teach the principles of cross-examination, but the only real way to become an effective cross-examiner is by actually trying cases and examining witnesses. Law students are taught never to ask a question if they do not already know the answer. This is a good rule, but in practice, a calculated risk is sometimes appropriate. A trial lawyer's instinct is honed through practice and experience. And it is this instinct that makes a great cross-examiner.

Control of the witness is vital. The best way to do this is by asking tight leading questions and maintaining eye contact. Most witnesses want to tell *their* story, and the examiner must make sure that they are denied the opportunity to do so. Ask precise questions that advance the theory and theme. Address only one fact per question. A wily witness will exploit any ambiguity in the question. Avoid adverbs—they are deadly. A witness will toy with questions that include words like *slowly* or *quickly*. Likewise, certain adjectives allow for hedging and invite problems: "Wasn't she a good mom?" Adverbs and adjectives allow the witness to qualify their answer. They should be avoided.

Closing Argument

Closing argument is where all the pieces are put together; it is where everything should make sense to the judge. The opening provides the context and tells judges what they are going to hear, the trial tells the story, and the closing ties it all up. Repetition is a powerful ally in the courtroom. Unlike the opening statement, the closing is the place where lawyers can argue the significance of the evidence, emphasizing their clients' strengths and the opponents' weaknesses. Lawyers can also address the application of the facts to the law at this time.

Each lawyer's style is different—some are thespians and others are accountants. The important thing is to recount the evidence in a way that resonates with the judge. Gold-Bikin and Kolodny outline the elements of a successful closing argument:

- Follow a logical sequence.
- Reiterate the theory and the theme.
- Use introduced exhibits.
- Raise rhetorical questions.

- Use analogies.
- Argue the proven facts, not counsel's opinions.
- Argue strengths.
- Explain weaknesses.
- Be cogent, concise, and clear.
- Keep it short, make the point, and sit down.
- Speak without notes.7

Lawyers should consider these guidelines when preparing for closing argument. It is the last word. And it must be potent.

Ethical Considerations

Lawyers are officers of the court. We have an ethical duty to the court to behave in a manner befitting our education and influence in society. The passionate nature of the proceedings sometimes invites unscrupulousness, but we must remember to keep those impulses in check. Rule 3.3 of the ABA Model Rules of Professional Conduct provides:

(a) A lawyer shall not knowingly:
    (1) make a false statement of fact or law to a tribunal or fail to correct a false statement of material fact or law previously made to the tribunal by the lawyer;
    (2) fail to disclose to the tribunal legal authority in the controlling jurisdiction known to the lawyer to be directly adverse to the position of the client and not disclosed by opposing counsel; or
    (3) offer evidence that the lawyer knows to be false. If a lawyer, the lawyer's client, or a witness called by the lawyer,

---

7. Lynne Z. Gold-Bikin & Stephen Kolodny, *supra* note 5 at 42.

has offered material evidence and the lawyer comes to know of its falsity, the lawyer shall take reasonable remedial measures, including, if necessary, disclosure to the tribunal. A lawyer may refuse to offer evidence, other than the testimony of a defendant in a criminal matter that the lawyer reasonably believes is false.[8]

The Model Rules of Professional Conduct are not aspirational: they *require* us to behave appropriately.

Family law litigation can be brutal, and the level of competition between the lawyer combatants is oftentimes ferocious. Litigants sometimes become emotionally disabled or become unable to function because of their situation. They make demands that we must sometimes refuse. Some lawyers want to please their client at all costs, but they need to know when to draw the line. Trial lawyers by temperament and wiring love to win; but winning at all costs impugns the system and corrodes the lawyer's soul. Playing by the rules maintains the integrity of the system and, frankly, our lives. No client is worth compromising your integrity.

---

8. Model Rules of Professional Conduct Rule 3.3 (2010).

The Fundamentals of Evidence | 2

In the later chapters of this book, I address many evidentiary concepts in detail, including the policy reasons behind the various rules as well as examples of the rules in application. In this chapter, I give an overview of common principles of evidence and discuss the effective use of evidence in a divorce trial.

What Is Evidence?

As lawyers, we use the word evidence every day. But how do we define this ubiquitous word? Evidence is simply any information, whether written, verbal, or physical, that a trial court may properly consider in a contested proceeding. Commonly, we present evidence by the testimony of a witness. Also, we offer exhibits, that is, documents or things. The evidence ultimately admitted in any case comprises the facts that a court can consider in rendering a ruling.

We investigate our cases and undertake discovery to analyze settlement options or to accumulate information for use at trial. While information is often broadly collected throughout the case, not every piece of information can or should be used as evidence. Skilled trial lawyers understand what they are trying to prove and gather the appropriate evidence to achieve their goals. You do not win cases by the volume of evidence presented; you win by the precision and craftsmanship of its presentation. Throwing large amounts of paper at a judge does not guarantee good results any more than haphazardly ignoring valuable information. The lawyer must determine if potential evidence is

(a) admissible—is the information reliable and relevant, and does it meet the substantive rules of admissibility?
(b) persuasive—does the information advance the theme or a particular argument?
(c) cumulative—does the court already have the information through other evidence admitted in the case?

Lawyers must start by determining whether the potential evidence is admissible under the applicable rules of evidence of the jurisdiction.

History of the Federal Rules of Evidence

In American jurisprudence, the rules of evidence originated with the common law. Judicial decisions established the rules concerning the admissibility of evidence in civil and criminal trials. During the twentieth century, certain projects were undertaken to codify the law of evidence. The California Evidence Code and the Uniform Rules of Evidence were two such projects that strove to summarize, in one source, all of the appropriate common law rules of evidence.

The Federal Rules of Evidence originated in 1961. At that time, U.S. Supreme Court Chief Justice Earl Warren appointed a commission of lawyers and scholars to craft proposed rules of evidence for use in federal courts. The rules were an attempt to codify the substantial body of case law that addressed evidentiary issues up until that time. The Supreme Court circulated drafts of the rules in 1969 and 1971. In 1972, the Court approved the Federal Rules of Evidence, effective July 1, 1973. Congress, however, exercising its powers under the Rules Enabling Act,[1] refused to authorize the rules until it had the opportunity to review them. The Federal Rules of Evidence became law on January 2, 1975, when the President Ford signed the Act to Establish Rules of Evidence for Certain Courts and Proceedings.[2] Effective December 2011, the Federal Rules of Evidence were reconstituted to make them more readable and clear. The substance of the rules was not changed, however.

Each jurisdiction has its own rules of evidence that lawyers must know. However, many jurisdictions have adopted the Federal Rules of Evidence in whole or in part. Even if they have not adopted the federal rules verbatim, most jurisdictions follow their policies and principles. Also, most law school evidence courses focus on the federal rules. For those reasons, this book primarily references the Federal Rules of Evidence. Each chapter provides an overview of the rules pertinent to family law trials, along with practical examples of the rules in action.

Purpose of the Rules

FRE 102 defines the purpose of the rules generally:

---

1. Rules Enabling Act, ch. 651, 73 Stat. 1064 (1934) (codified as amended at 28 U.S.C. §§ 331, 2071–2073 (2006)).
2. Act of Jan. 2, 1975, Pub. L. No. 93-595, § 2 (a)(1)–(2), 88 Stat. 1948 (repealed by Pub. L. No. 100-702, § 401 (a)–(d), 102 Stat. 4648 (1988)).

These rules should be construed so as to administer every proceeding fairly, eliminate unjustifiable expense and delay, and promote the development of evidence law, to the end of ascertaining the truth and securing a just determination.

Broadly speaking, the purpose of the rules is to provide "uniformity, improvement and simplification," in trial advocacy and a fair proceeding.[3] Particularly in an area of law as passionate and volatile as family law, the rules of evidence allow the court to maintain the integrity of the legal process itself.

Rules of Admissibility

Potential evidence must satisfy three criteria: Is the evidence relevant? Is the evidence reliable? Does the evidence meet the substantive requirements set forth in the Federal Rules of Evidence (e.g., hearsay, privilege, etc.)? These three questions need to be answered (hopefully well in advance of the trial!) before the court can properly admit and consider any potential evidence. Sometimes evidence is presented to the court by a stipulation between the parties, including stipulations concerning the authenticity of exhibits or other undisputed matters. Another consideration is the distinction between the issue of admissibility and the weight of the evidence. Some evidence, while technically admissible, may not carry much weight if its probative value is small. Courts in nonjury trials will often allow admission of evidence but discount its value after hearing the totality of the case.

---

3.   Edward W. Cleary, *Preliminary Notes on Reading the Rules of Evidence*, 57 NEB. L. REV. 908, 912 (1978).

Direct versus Circumstantial Evidence

Evidence can be either direct or circumstantial. Direct evidence is conclusive proof of a proposition. For example, ordinarily a pay stub or a W-2 form for an employee conclusively proves his or her income from that job. Circumstantial evidence, on the other hand, contributes toward proof of a fact but is insufficient alone to prove it—it is one brick in the wall. For example, the amount of money the business owner deposits into a bank account circumstantially contributes toward the ultimate determination of the owner's income.

Relevance

Whether offering direct or circumstantial evidence, the lawyer must first determine if it is relevant. If something is irrelevant or not germane to any of the issues in the case, the lawyer need not consider the other questions of admissibility. For a piece of evidence to be considered relevant, it must be material and have probative value. Materiality involves the context: Does the proposed evidence address a matter that is at issue? Does it relate to matters that are germane and important for the ultimate determination by the court? If not, it is considered immaterial and inadmissible. Evidence must also be probative of an issue in the case: Does the proposed evidence more probably than not prove a point in controversy? Does the evidence help the judge draw reasonable conclusions? While materiality looks at the evidence in the larger context of the whole case, probative value is ascribed to evidence that is a piece of the puzzle worth considering. For example, the color of the babysitter's hair would be immaterial to a custody determination. The babysitter's plans to retire in five years, while arguably material, would not likely have any probative value at the present time.[4]

Reliability of the Evidence

Assuming evidence is relevant, it must also be reliable in order for the court to consider it. According to *McCormick*[5], the value of all testimony depends on the presence of the following core elements:

- Perception
- Memory
- Narration
- Sincerity

Did the witnesses accurately perceive what they are describing? Have they accurately remembered their initial perception? Does their narrative accurately describe the perception? Is the testimony sincere—is it truthful? For testimonial evidence to have any value, it must have these four elements.

Witness Testimony

Witnesses must be qualified as competent before they testify. A competent witness is one who is reliable and can testify based on sensory observations or personal knowledge. An incompetent witness, in contrast, lacks one of the critical components of reliability (perception, memory, the ability to narrate, or sincerity)

---

4.   I address the topic of relevance in Chapters 3–5.
5.   2 McCormick on Evidence § 245 at 125 (Kenneth S. Broun, ed., Thomson West 6th ed. 2006).

necessary for the testimony to be considered. For example, incompetent witnesses might include a young child who is incapable of understanding the oath or a witness who is speculating or guessing. Ordinarily, a witness may not give opinions or speculate. This type of testimony is considered unreliable because it is not based on firsthand observations; rather it is based on a witness's subjective opinions, which lack any meaningful probative value.

Tangible Evidence (Exhibits)

A lawyer who introduces tangible evidence such as documents, photographs, or physical objects must establish that the evidence is authentic. An inauthentic exhibit lacks any probative value. To prove authenticity, the proponent must preliminarily show that the potential evidence is what it claims to be—not a difficult burden, but it requires a rudimentary showing that the exhibit is legitimate. Ordinarily, a lawyer establishes authenticity through a witness testifying to the origin of the exhibit, establishing that the item presented is what it claims to be. Exhibits can also be authenticated by admissions or stipulations. Some exhibits are self-authenticating under the rules; if an item qualifies as self-authenticating, it does not need to be authenticated by a witness for admission into evidence.[6]

Other Considerations of Admissibility: Hearsay

Assuming evidence is both relevant and reliable, it still must satisfy the other substantive requirements of admissibility. An out-of-court statement offered to prove the truth of the matter asserted is inadmissible as hearsay without a proper exemption or exception.

---

6.   I discuss the topic of authentication of exhibits in Chapter 9.

Party admissions (and prior inconsistent statements) are exempt from the hearsay rule; they are not considered hearsay.

In contrast, an exception allows admission of certain kinds of hearsay evidence considered reliable enough for admission. Exceptions derive from an implicit balancing test: while some concerns exist about the reliability of the evidence, those concerns are outweighed by the harm of entirely disallowing the evidence. Whether an out-of-court statement is exempt from the hearsay rule or is admissible as an exception to the rule, the result is the same—the evidence is admitted. Family lawyers frequently rely on these exceptions:

- FRE 803(1)—present sense impression
- FRE 803(2)—the excited utterance
- FRE 803(3)—then existing mental, emotional, or physical condition
- FRE 803(4)—statement made for the purpose of medical diagnosis or treatment
- FRE 803(5)—recorded recollection

An out-of-court statement or writing that fits within one of the exceptions is admissible and the court may consider it.[7]

Privilege

Another substantive matter to consider is the evidentiary privileges, such as the privilege against self-incrimination or the attorney-client privilege. A privilege protects rights or relationships deemed more important than a party's right to have the court hear the evidence. For example, the preservation of the right to confidential

---

7.   I explore the topic of hearsay in detail in Chapters 6 and 7.

communication between lawyers and their clients is deemed sac-
rosanct, and this larger policy trumps an opponent's right to force
disclosure of this information. Privileges generally protect information from involuntary disclosure, even if it is otherwise considered
relevant and reliable.[8]

Original Writing Rule

The original writing rule (also known as the best evidence rule)
governs admission of a document or recording offered to prove its
contents, preferring an original over secondary evidence. This rule
was originally formed before the availability of exact reproductions,
and today, the federal rules allow duplicates under most circumstances. The rule recognizes the importance of a judge considering
a document's exact words when the case hinges on the document's
terms. A witness paraphrasing the document from memory or other
secondary sources to prove its contents is considered unreliable
when the original is available to examine. A related rule, the rule
of completeness, seeks to avoid misleading the judge through the
introduction of select parts of a document, without a full disclosure of all of its contents.[9]

Objections to Evidence

To recap, for admissibility, all evidence, whether testimonial or
an exhibit, must be relevant, reliable, and authentic and must not
violate any of the substantive rules of evidence. The goal of the
proponent is to establish that the evidence meets these requirements.

---

8.   I discuss privileges applicable to family law cases in Chapter 12.
9.   I discuss these rules in Chapter 10.

On the other side, the party seeking to keep out information has certain tools at its disposal. The most commonly used method is an objection to the evidence made at trial. When an examiner asks a witness a question or offers an exhibit, the opponent may object based on the lack of relevance or reliability of the evidence or the fact that the evidence violates a substantive rule such as hearsay. Objections also apply to the procedural aspects of a trial. If, for example, a question improperly leads a witness on direct examination, a timely objection can prevent the witness from being allowed to answer the question as framed.

Besides using objections, a lawyer may challenge the opponent's evidence by a motion, either pretrial or during the trial. For example, the lawyer can present a pretrial motion in limine to bar a witness's testimony if the opponent failed to meet proper disclosure requirements under the discovery rules. Such a motion could also challenge certain anticipated prejudicial testimony as irrelevant before a live witness tells his or her story. Both during and after the trial, a lawyer may use a motion to challenge evidentiary admissions as improper, even after the admissions are made.

If certain evidence needs a foundation prior to its admission—for example, proof of an exhibit's authenticity—the opponent has a right to challenge the foundation prior to the exhibit's admission. This procedure, known as voir dire, allows the adverse party to examine the witness out of order, during the proponent's direct examination, for the purpose of challenging the legitimacy of the offered exhibit.[10]

---

10. I address the topic of objections to evidence in Chapter 15.

Effective Use of Evidence

Trial advocacy is both an art and a science. If effectively knowing and applying the rules of evidence is the science of trial advocacy, persuasively packaging and presenting the evidence is the art. For example, a summary can be vital to an effective presentation of a quantity of raw data. Demonstrative aids can help experts and lay witnesses better explain their testimony. Demonstrative aids are also effective tools during opening statements and closing arguments. Show *and* tell should be the mantra of all trial lawyers.[11]

Consider creative ways to use exhibits to tell your story. Some judges are more persuaded by visual rather than auditory stimuli. While a witness's testimony may communicate the basic facts, the key to effective advocacy is to register with the court's heart zone, to make the court feel inclined to help your client. The evidence must be memorable and impel the court to act in favor of the client. Abraham Lincoln, when he was a lawyer in Springfield, Illinois, would read the newspaper aloud to himself. When asked why, he responded that if he could read the paper and hear it at the same time, he would be more likely to remember it. The same applies here. Pictures help illustrate testimony. Both showing and telling is more memorable.

Physical objects can also be effective. Documents can sometimes be used in lieu of laborious testimony. Showing a bank statement is more compelling that a witness's testimony concerning the balance in the account. Knowing how to take all of these tools and use them to effectively support your theme or argument is the art of trial advocacy.

---

11. I discuss summaries and demonstrative exhibits in Chapter 9.

Planning

The important decisions concerning the use of evidence should not be made on the day of trial. Instead, decisions should be made weeks and months before the trial. Obviously, not all cases go to trial, but effective case management should contemplate that possibility. From the time of retention, the lawyer should be formulating the various issues, theories, and possible themes of the case. Thoughtful analysis early serves two valuable purposes. First, by understanding the ultimate proofs necessary for the case, the lawyer can focus discovery and investigation. Particularly when parties have limited resources, a focused and precise approach to discovery is welcome.

Second, by analyzing the ultimate proof early, the lawyer can properly prepare for the admission of the key evidence to support the theory and theme. As the court in *United States v. Safavian* noted, failure to authenticate an exhibit is usually a self-inflicted injury.[12] Few things slow down a trial as much as laborious authentication questions. As always, plan ahead. Many jurisdictions' rules of discovery allow a party to serve a request for admission of the genuineness of documents. An admission of genuineness authenticates the document or thing, enabling its admission subject to relevance and any other evidentiary rules. A party who unreasonably refuses to admit the genuineness of a particular document may be sanctioned.

Use the pretrial conference to discuss the authenticity of your exhibits, as well as admissibility of exhibits in general. Seek stipulations if possible. Assuming there is a stipulation concerning a particular exhibit, prepare a court order confirming the stipulation to avoid a later change of heart or claim of confusion. Even if local rules or custom and practice do not ordinarily require it, ask the

---

12. United States v. Safavian, 644 F.Supp.2d 1 (2009).

court to conduct an exhibit conference before the trial to discuss any contested evidentiary issues. This is particularly important with digital evidence, which requires preparation for authentication.

Use of a Proof Chart

A proof chart is a form that gives the lawyer a central forum in which to accumulate potential evidence and anticipate possible evidentiary hurdles. To obtain admission of most evidence, the lawyer must prepare in advance to lay the foundation. The lawyer may need legal authority to support the admission. A proof chart is invaluable in organizing the evidence and preparing for trial. Early groundwork allows time to prepare for anticipated objections and other obstacles to the admission. A proof chart form is included in the Appendix.

Relevance | 3

Relevance is the threshold requirement for admissibility of all evidence, regardless of the type. Is the evidence material and probative of an issue in the case? No other rules matter if the evidence is not relevant. All discussions of admissibility of evidence start with the subject of relevance.

Rules to consider:

Rule 401. Test for Relevant Evidence

Evidence is relevant if:

(a)   it has any tendency to make a fact more or less probable than it would be without the evidence; and
(b)   the fact is of consequence in determining the action.

Rule 402. General Admissibility of Relevant Evidence

Relevant evidence is admissible unless any of the following provides otherwise:

- the United States Constitution;
- a federal statute;
- these rules; or
- other rules prescribed by the Supreme Court.
- Irrelevant evidence is not admissible.

Rule 403. Excluding Relevant Evidence for Prejudice, Confusion, Waste of Time, or Other Reasons

The court may exclude relevant evidence if its probative value is substantially outweighed by a danger of one or more of the following: unfair prejudice, confusing the issues, misleading the jury, undue delay, wasting time, or needlessly presenting cumulative evidence.

Rule 104. Preliminary Questions

(a) *In General.* The court must decide any preliminary question about whether a witness is qualified, a privilege exists, or evidence is admissible. In so deciding, the court is not bound by evidence rules, except those on privilege.

(b) *Relevance That Depends on a Fact.* When the relevance of evidence depends on whether a fact exists, proof must be introduced sufficient to support a finding that the fact does exist. The court may admit the proposed evidence on the condition that the proof be introduced later.

(c) *Conducting a Hearing So That the Jury Cannot Hear It.* The court must conduct any hearing on a preliminary question so that the jury cannot hear it if:
  (1) the hearing involves the admissibility of a confession;
  (2) a defendant in a criminal case is a witness and so requests; or
  (3) justice so requires.
(d) *Cross-Examining a Defendant in a Criminal Case.* By testifying on a preliminary question, a defendant in a criminal case does not become subject to cross-examination on other issues in the case.
(e) *Evidence Relevant to Weight and Credibility.* This rule does not limit a party's right to introduce before the jury evidence that is relevant to the weight or credibility of other evidence.

Relevance Defined

In order for evidence to be relevant, it must be "of consequence," or material, *and* have probative value. Both elements are required for admissibility. *McCormick* defines materiality as contextual:

> Materiality concerns the fit between the evidence and the case. It looks to the relation between the propositions that the evidence is offered to prove and the issues in the case. If the evidence is offered to help prove a proposition that is not a matter in issue, the evidence is immaterial.[1]

For example, if a wife offered evidence that her husband regularly smoked marijuana, the husband could argue it is not material to the division of assets. However, she could argue that it is relevant

---

1. 1 McCormick on Evidence § 185 at 729 (Kenneth S. Broun, ed., Thomson West 6th ed. 2006).

if he squandered assets in support of his hobby. Context is everything when the discussion involves materiality. Pot smoking may be material in a child custody case if the parent used drugs while a child was in his or her care, but it may not be material if the parent's use was occasional and never around the child.[2] Materiality of the evidence depends on the issues being litigated.

The evidence also must more probably than not prove or disprove a point of contention. Put another way, does this item of evidence make it more or less likely that the fact asserted is true? If it does not, it is not probative and is thus irrelevant. As the Advisory Committee Notes to the Federal Rules of Evidence observe, "Problems of relevancy call for an answer to the question whether an item of evidence, when tested by the processes of legal reasoning, possesses sufficient probative value to justify receiving it in evidence."[3] The court must evaluate the evidence, using common sense to determine whether it advances the argument or is just background noise.

For example, a party may offer evidence of her spouse's financial indiscretions dating back several years. The proponent of the evidence may argue that the transactions are relevant because the marital estate was improperly depleted by the misbehavior. Relevance may be supported by proof that the squandering spouse was contemplating a divorce. In contrast, the other party could argue that the transactions are too remote in time to have any bearing on present circumstances and that numerous transactions after those events marginalized the transactions from years ago. Again, consider the context. If a million dollars disappeared five years ago, it would be hard to argue the evidence of its disappearance is irrelevant based on remoteness. On the other hand, it may be hard to argue $200 spent at a casino five years ago is material.

---

2.   Starck v. Starck, 133 Ill. App. 3d 35; 299 N.E.2d 605.
3.   FED. R. EVID. 401 Advisory Committee's Note.

Proposed testimony about future events also illustrates this principle: if superseding events could alter the outcome, then the testimony may not have the necessary probative value to be admitted as relevant at the hearing. For example, assume a wife indicates a desire to become a physical therapist after the divorce but has not started college yet. The husband could argue the relevance of evidence of her future earning ability in an attempt to deny her alimony. He could attempt to quantify that future income as evidence of her ability to support herself in the future. The wife could argue that evidence of her future income lacks probative value because too many factors could intervene. Remoteness of evidence does not refer merely to lapses in time; it also relates to the variables that could intervene. The wife could discover that she hates physical therapy and change her major to social work, she could drop out, she could become ill, or the job market may become flush with physical therapists, thus limiting wages and employment opportunities.

Circumstantial Evidence

Circumstantial evidence contributes toward the proof of a fact in issue; it is not dispositive by itself. It should be distinguished from direct evidence that proves a fact (if believed) without more substantiation. The relevance of one piece of circumstantial evidence must be considered in light of the totality of the evidence. *McCormick* illustrates this principle:

> An item of evidence, being but a single link in the chain of proof, need not prove conclusively the proposition for which it is offered. It need not even make that proposition appear more probable than

not. . . . It is enough if the item could reasonably show that a fact is slightly more probable than it would appear without the evidence.[4]

Circumstantial evidence can be relevant as one of the links in the chain of evidence. As *McCormick* observes, "A brick is not a wall."[5] To stay with the metaphor, the individual bricks used to build the wall of the case are properly admissible.

The rules allow circumstantial evidence if it is relevant. The Advisory Committee comments reflect the drafters' clear intent to permit this type of evidence: "Dealing with probability in the language of the rule has the added virtue of avoiding confusion between questions of admissibility and questions of the sufficiency of the evidence."[6] In other words, an individual piece of evidence need not independently prove a fact in controversy. This point needs to be kept in mind when defending relevancy objections. One need not prove an ultimate fact with each piece of evidence. Circumstantial evidence is appropriate, and if it is probative of a relevant topic, admissible.

For example, assume the wife seeks to offer a check evidencing the husband's consultation fee with an attorney four years ago. The husband objects, arguing the check is not relevant, as it has no probative value. The wife could argue that the check is relevant as circumstantial evidence of intentional dissipation (i.e., divorce planning) because the marital estate started depleting at or about that time. If a relevance objection is made to circumstantial evidence, be prepared to respond to how the piece of evidence fits into the ultimate theory of the case. A response to a relevancy objection can be advantageous; it may give you an opportunity to educate the judge concerning the theory of the case. The opposite is true

---

4.   1 McCormick on Evidence, *supra* note 1, at 733.
5.   *Id.*
6.   Fed. R. Evid. 401 advisory committee's notes.

as well: be careful about making relevancy objections, which give your opponent the opportunity to enlighten the court.

Conditional Relevance of Circumstantial Evidence

When the relevance of a piece of circumstantial evidence depends on evidence to be offered later, it may be conditionally admitted. For example, if a wife testifies that her husband frequently travelled to Wyoming, the husband could argue that fact is not probative of any issue in the case. The wife could respond that a later witness will testify that the husband was a silent partner in a Wyoming real estate venture, and this travel is probative of the husband's ownership of a marital asset. FRE 104(b) provides,

> Relevance That Depends on a Fact. When the relevance of evidence depends on whether a fact exists, proof must be introduced sufficient to support a finding that the fact does exist. The court may admit the proposed evidence on the condition that the proof be introduced later.

In our example, the later proof of the partnership establishes the probative value of the earlier evidence. If later evidence is not admitted, or was insufficient to tie up the ownership interest, the husband could make a motion to strike the earlier conditionally relevant evidence, removing it from the record.

In movies and television dramas, relevancy objections are made and lawyers ask for latitude, arguing they will tie it up. This is a dramatization of the concept of conditional relevance. In reality, if the relevance of a piece of evidence depends on admission of evidence to be offered later, the lawyer should cite FRE 104(b) and request that the court conditionally admit the testimony or exhibit until the later evidence is presented.

Relevance of Background Information

Prefatory questions that set the scene are allowed as a matter of course. Background information helps the court get a context, to understand some background about the witness. For example, an attorney may ask general questions about an individual's education and profession, despite the marginal relevance of the testimony. Occasionally these questions will draw an objection and the court should be advised that you are eliciting some preliminary background information from the witness. Of course, these questions must be reasonable, related in time and subject matter to the purpose of the witness's testimony.

The Relevancy-Balancing Test

FRE 403 limits the admissibility of relevant evidence if its probative value is "substantially outweighed by a danger of one or more of the following: unfair prejudice, confusing the issues . . . undue delay, wasting time, or needlessly presenting cumulative evidence." In practice, most family court judges recognize the need to err on the side of caution and hear evidence whose admissibility may be in dispute. In a bench trial, the judge is the finder of fact and is not likely to be influenced by inflammatory evidence. It is rare in a bench trial that a lawyer could convince a trial judge that the evidence is too prejudicial for admission. But an objection under FRE 403 is still valid, and this rule is particularly helpful when an opposing attorney offers cumulative and redundant evidence. The lawyer can seek to persuade the judge as the evidence gatekeeper to balance the probative value of the potential evidence against delays caused by a particular line of questions. A poorly prepared lawyer aimlessly fishing for information or tactically running the clock can be contained under this rule.

Tactically, the lawyer should be careful making this type of objection based on prejudice. First, the objection itself suggests that the evidence is important enough to try to bar. The objection is a neon sign screaming that the evidence hurts your case. And, in any event, the objection is not likely to be sustained. Sometimes, it is better to silently allow the admission instead of bringing attention to it.

Practice Points

- Know the preferences of your judge. Constant relevance objections may annoy some judges and infuriate others. Still, some judges may welcome them as a way to limit the proofs. Determine the temperament of your judge.
- Use the relevancy objection sparingly. If irrelevant evidence is offered that does not hurt, it frequently makes sense to let it go for the sake of moving things along. Well-timed relevancy objections are sometimes helpful to discover what the court considers important. They also can tactically throw opponents off their rhythm.
- *Listen!* Do not be so absorbed in your own internal dialogue that you forget to pay attention to what the judge is telling you, either indirectly or directly. If the judge continuously grants your opponent's relevancy objections as to a particular subject, the judge may not want to hear any more about it. Move on or risk further alienating the judge.
- Be wary of FRE 403 objections based on prejudice. If the judge is dozing through the evidence, an objection based on prejudice will certainly wake the judge up and get his or her attention. Objecting acknowledges the importance of the evidence, and you will likely lose the objection anyway.

- FRE 403 can be used to contain clock burners. Remind the court of this rule when your opponent presents redundant or cumulative evidence.
- If the judge denies your repeated relevancy objections and allows your opponent to go on, do not press further. Ask for a continuing objection to the line of questions.[7]

---

7. This procedure is discussed in Chapter 14.

Evidence of Character and Habit | 4

Character evidence can be a type of circumstantial evidence helpful to family lawyers in appropriate circumstances—particularly in custody cases where a person's character is integral to the ultimate issue. When offering character evidence, one must still show that the evidence is relevant to an issue in the case. Character may also be a stand-alone criterion, for example, where the jurisdiction's custody law makes character one of the criteria for determining the best interests of the child. Habit evidence, while distinguished from character evidence, illustrates how past conduct may prove current behavior.

Rules to consider:

Rule 404. Character Evidence; Crimes or Other Acts

(a) Character Evidence.

(1)   Prohibited Uses. Evidence of a person's character or character trait is not admissible to prove that on a particular occasion the person acted in accordance with the character or trait.

(2)   Exceptions for a Defendant or Victim in a Criminal Case. . . . .[1]

(3)   Exceptions for a Witness. Evidence of a witness's character may be admitted under Rules 607, 608, and 609.

(b)   Crimes, Wrongs, or Other Acts.

(1)   Prohibited Uses. Evidence of a crime, wrong, or other act is not admissible to prove a person's character in order to show that on a particular occasion the person acted in accordance with the character.

(2)   Permitted Uses; Notice in a Criminal Case.

Rule 405. Methods of Proving Character

(a)   By Reputation or Opinion. When evidence of a person's character or character trait is admissible, it may be proved by testimony about the person's reputation or by testimony in the form of an opinion. On cross-examination of the character witness, the court may allow an inquiry into relevant specific instances of the person's conduct.

(b)   By Specific Instances of Conduct. When a person's character or character trait is an essential element of a charge, claim, or defense, the character or trait may also be proved by relevant specific instances of the person's conduct.

---

1.   See Appendix for the full text of Rule 404.

Rule 406. Habit; Routine

Evidence of a person's habit or an organization's routine practice may be admitted to prove that on a particular occasion the person or organization acted in accordance with the habit or routine practice. The court may admit this evidence regardless of whether it is corroborated or whether there was an eyewitness.

Character Evidence Defined

By its definition, character evidence relies on a person's character for its probative value. "Character is the nature of a person, his disposition generally, or his disposition in respect to a particular trait such as honesty, peacefulness, or truthfulness." [2] Character is an individual's personality or demeanor—his or her essential nature. Professor Irving Younger defined character as "anything that cannot be photographed."[3]

The factual and legal issues of a case determine whether character evidence is relevant. In a proceeding where character is integral to the case (a custody dispute, for example), character evidence is allowed. *McCormick* provides the rationale:

> The hazards of prejudice, surprise and time-consumption implicit in this manner of proof are more tolerable when character is itself in issue than when this evidence is offered as a mere indication that the defendant committed the acts that are the subject of the suit.[4]

---

2. MICHAEL H. GRAHAM, CLEARY & GRAHAM'S HANDBOOK OF ILLINOIS EVIDENCE § 404.1 at 181 (8th ed. 2004).

3. Irving Younger, *Three Essays on Character and Credibility under the Federal Rules of Evidence*, 5 HOFSTRA L. REV. 7 (1976–1977).

4. 1 McCORMICK ON EVIDENCE, *supra* note 1, § 187 at 746 (Kenneth S. Broun, ed., Thomson West 6th ed. 2006).

For example, in the world of no-fault divorce, the issue of character rarely is relevant to the division of assets. In child custody proceedings, in contrast, the character of the battling litigants may be relevant.[5] This principle may also extend to the character of a parent's new spouse.[6] Here, a parent's character may be integral to the ultimate determination and thus may be allowed into evidence. In fact, many statutes direct the court to consider character factors in determining custody. For example, Illinois' statute directs the court to consider "the willingness and ability of each parent to facilitate and encourage a close and continuing relationship between the other parent and the child."[7] This factor invites character evidence.

In contrast, a lawyer prosecuting a contempt petition cannot use character evidence to prove what the alleged contemnor may have done on a particular occasion. For example, assume the wife is prosecuting a petition for contempt of a court order because the husband has failed to pay child support. Assume further that she attempts to offer evidence of multiple unpaid parking tickets to prove that as a parking scofflaw, he is likely to disregard the court's orders here as well. The husband would argue relevance: the prejudice outweighs any probative value—the value of the evidence is slight compared to the possibility of prejudice arising from the testimony. He would further argue this was an impermissible use of character evidence to prove behavior in conformance with the earlier arguable misconduct.

Rule 404(b) provides that evidence of a crime, wrong, or other act is not admissible to prove character in order to infer conduct on a later occasion. The lawyer may, however, offer the character evidence for another purpose, for example, to show motive,

---

5.   1 McCormick on Evidence, *supra* note 4, §187 at 745; *see also* McCullough v. McCullough, 52 So. 3d 373 (Miss. Ct. App. 2009).
6.   Leisure v. Wheeler, 828 N.E.2d 409 (Ind. Ct. App. 2005).
7.   750 Ill. Comp. Stat. 5/602-(a)(8) (2011).

opportunity, notice, and so on. For instance, assume Betty, a home-maker of 25 years wanted to go to college to reeducate herself. Assume further that she asked her husband, Bob, to assist with her tuition and he refused. Betty would like to offer the fact that Bob refused to assist her with her reeducation. Bob would argue that this evidence is an improper use of character evidence and is irrelevant and prejudicial. In response, Betty could argue that the evidence is not offered to show that he was stingy or to show a bad character; rather it was offered to show he had notice that Betty wanted to go to college. The Advisory Committee acknowledges the difficulty of this rule in application:

> No mechanical solution is offered. The determination must be made whether the danger of undue prejudice outweighs the probative value of the evidence in view of the availability of other means of proof and other factors appropriate for making decisions of this kind under Rule 403.[8]

A party may offer evidence of another's past bad acts when the conduct is directly related to the issue being adjudicated—when it is intrinsic to the event in dispute. Intrinsic conduct is "part of the episode being tried. It is linked in time and circumstance to the crime or event at issue." [9] For example, assume that several years before trial, the husband had induced his employer to reduce his wages and compensate him in perquisites or time off. Assume further that he did this to reduce child support to his first wife. The issue before the court is his current income. The husband would argue that this earlier conduct is irrelevant to his current income and that any past misconduct is irrelevant under Rule 404(b)(1). The wife would argue that since the evidence of her husband's

---

8.   FED. R. EVID. 403, 56 F.R.D. 183, 219.
9.   THOMAS A. MAUET & WARREN D. WOLFSON, TRIAL EVIDENCE 99 (4th ed. 2009).

past attempts to induce his employer to manipulate his income was intrinsic to the determination of his current income for the purposes of support, Rule 404(b)(1) is inapplicable. Remember, though, the general relevancy rules still apply.

Methods of Proving Character

If character evidence is relevant, FRE 405 outlines how one may prove it. Character may be proven either by reputation or opinion testimony or by specific acts in which character is integral to the action. For example, character is integral in a custody case and thus could be proven by specific acts.

FRE 405(a) states, in reference to character evidence, "[I]t may be proved by testimony about the person's reputation or by testimony in the form of an opinion." For example, witnesses could testify to a parent's reputation as an effective or responsible parent. The rule also allows opinions concerning character. Custody evaluators and guardians ad litem frequently express opinions concerning a parent's character. As noted above, FRE 404 generally disallows evidence of specific acts to establish propensity to behave in a certain way. In contrast, FRE 405(b) allows evidence of specific instances of conduct if character is at the heart of the case (such as in a custody case).

Keep in mind the trial court's continuing obligation to monitor the evidence. While certain conduct may be technically relevant and allowable under FRE 405, the trial court still may limit the testimony pursuant to FRE 403 if the probative value of the evidence is outweighed by considerations of fairness, waste of time, or prejudice. For instance, otherwise admissible character evidence may be irrelevant because it is too remote to the present parenting circumstances.[10] The trial court remains the gatekeeper for what character evidence it will allow based on the circumstances of the case.

Admissibility of Habit Evidence

FRE 406 provides that evidence of habit or routine may be used to prove conduct consistent with the regular practice. This is a species of circumstantial evidence. *McCormick* distinguishes habit evidence from character evidence:

> Character is a generalized description of a person's disposition, or of the disposition in respect to a general trait, such as honesty, temperance or peacefulness. Habit, in the present context, is more specific. It denotes one's regular response to repeated situations. If we speak of a character for care, we think of a person's tendency to act prudently in all the varying situations of life—in business, at home, in handling automobiles and in walking across the street. A habit, on the other hand, is the person's regular practice of responding to a particular kind of situation with a specific type of conduct. . . . Habits that come within this definition have greater probative value than do general traits of character. Furthermore, the potential for prejudice is substantially less. By and large, the detailed patterns of situation-specific behavior that constitute habits are unlikely to provoke such sympathy or antipathy as would distort the process of evaluating the evidence.[11]

For example, a party accused of domestic violence might offer testimony of the petitioner's regular overreaction to slight provocation

---

10. Roeh v. Roeh, 113 Idaho 557, 746 P.2d 1016 (Idaho Ct. App. 1987).
11. 1 McCORMICK ON EVIDENCE, *supra* note 4, § 195 at 782-83.

to corroborate a claim that she exaggerated in her testimony. Questions to the alleged abuser would seek to elicit instances of the alleged victim's past conduct with examples of how she consistently blew any slights out of proportion. The victim's lawyer would object, arguing the victim's past conduct was irrelevant to the facts in dispute. The counter argument would be that this pattern of behavior was habitual under Rule 406 and could be considered by the court.

Foundationally, there must be evidence that the behavior was indeed habitual—one or two occasions does not make a habit. The proponent of the evidence needs to elicit enough foundational testimony reflecting the habit:

- On April 5, 2010, how did your wife react when you told her that she looked tired? (She ranted that I told her she was ugly and became hysterical.)
- Have you ever observed her react to observations about her appearance before this occasion? (Yes.)
- What did you observe? (Violent reaction)
- Can you provide other examples when this occurred? (Five examples of exaggerated responses to perceived criticism within the last four years)
- In the past five years, are you aware of any occasion where she reacted differently to your negative comments about her appearance? (No.)

More broadly, one can use habit evidence to prove facts related to matters such as acquisition of assets, prudence in managing money and homemaker contributions. While FRE 406 addresses the use of habit evidence to prove a particular act in conformance with the habit, nothing would prohibit testimony establishing habits for other purposes: habitual contributions by a homemaker or wage earner or habitual sloth, for example. As always, the rules of relevance apply and, in particular, the provisions of Rule 403, which weighs the probative value of the evidence against other considerations.

Practice Points

- When the central issue involves character—for example, in a contested custody case—a party may offer specific acts illustrating a particular character trait to establish conduct consistent with that character trait.
- Use habit evidence to circumstantially show behavior in conformance with past conduct.
- Some family law lawyers attempt to turn a divorce trial into a morality play. They attempt to slip in character evidence as a means to inflame the judge. Stay awake and be prepared to respond with a reference to the particular rules prohibiting its use when such evidence is offered against your client.
- Do not forget about Rule 403. Character evidence, while technically relevant, may be excluded if it is prejudicial, cumulative, or marginally probative.
- Use the discovery process to determine the scope of a witness's testimony in advance. Where it appears that improper character evidence or inadequate habit testimony will be offered, use a pretrial motion in limine to exclude it before the witness testifies.

Other Miscellaneous Relevancy Issues 5

The federal rules also address the relevance of certain specific types of conduct. Evidence of settlement negotiations, withdrawn guilty pleas, and past sexual conduct are considered irrelevant except in certain clearly defined circumstances. This chapter addresses these situations in the context of a family law case.[1]

Rules to consider:

Rule 408. Compromise Offers and Negotiations

(a)   Prohibited Uses. Evidence of the following is not admissible—on behalf of any party—either to prove or disprove the validity or amount of a disputed

---

1.   Other rules of relevancy, for example, restricting evidence of subsequent remedial measures (FRE 407) and payment of medical bills (FRE 409), are beyond the scope of this book.

claim or to impeach by a prior inconsistent statement or a
contradiction:

(1)   furnishing, promising, or offering—or accepting,
promising to accept, or offering to accept—a valuable
consideration in compromising or attempting to compromise the claim; and

(2)   conduct or a statement made during compromise negotiations about the claim—except when offered in a
criminal case and . . .

(b) Exceptions. The court may admit this evidence for another
purpose, such as proving a witness's bias or prejudice, negating a contention of undue delay, or . . .

Rule 410. Pleas, Plea Discussions, and Related Statements

(a)   Prohibited Uses. In a civil . . . case, evidence of the following
is not admissible against the defendant who made the plea
or participated in the plea discussions:

(1)   a guilty plea that was later withdrawn;

(2)   a nolo contendere plea;

(3)   a statement made during a proceeding on either of those
pleas under Federal Rule of Criminal Procedure 11 or a
comparable state procedure; or

(4)   a statement made during plea discussions with an attorney for the prosecuting authority if the discussions did
not result in a guilty plea or they resulted in a later-
withdrawn guilty plea.

(b) Exceptions. The court may admit a statement described in
Rule 410(a)(3) or (4):

(1)   in any proceeding in which another statement made
during the same plea or plea discussions has been

introduced, if in fairness the statements ought to be considered together; or
(2) in a criminal proceeding. . . .

Rule 412. Sex-Offense Cases: The Victim's Sexual Behavior or Predisposition

(a) Prohibited Uses. The following evidence is not admissible in a civil . . . proceeding involving alleged sexual misconduct:
   (1) evidence offered to prove that a victim engaged in other sexual behavior; or
   (2) evidence offered to prove a victim's sexual predisposition.
(b) Exceptions.
   (1) Criminal Cases . . .
   (2) Civil Cases. In a civil case, the court may admit evidence offered to prove a victim's sexual behavior or sexual predisposition if its probative value substantially outweighs the danger of harm to any victim and of unfair prejudice to any party. The court may admit evidence of a victim's reputation only if the victim has placed it in controversy.
(c) Procedure to Determine Admissibility.
   (1) Motion. If a party intends to offer evidence under Rule 412(b), the party must:
     (A) file a motion that specifically describes the evidence and states the purpose for which it is to be offered;
     (B) do so at least 14 days before trial unless the court, for good cause, sets a different time;
     (C) serve the motion on all parties; and
     (D) notify the victim or, when appropriate, the victim's guardian or representative.
   (2) Hearing. Before admitting evidence under this rule, the court must conduct an in camera hearing and give the victim and parties a right to attend and be heard. Unless

the court orders otherwise, the motion, related materials, and the record of the hearing must be and remain sealed.

(d)   Definition of "Victim." In this rule, "victim" includes an alleged victim.

Rule 415. Similar Acts in Civil Cases Involving Sexual Assault or Child Molestation

(a)   Permitted Uses. In a civil case involving a claim for relief based on a party's alleged sexual assault or child molestation, the court may admit evidence that the party committed any other sexual assault or child molestation. The evidence may be considered as provided in Rules 413 and 414.

(b)   Disclosure to the Opponent. If a party intends to offer this evidence, the party must disclose it to the party against whom it will be offered, including witnesses' statements or a summary of the expected testimony. The party must do so at least 15 days before trial or at a later time that the court allows for good cause.

(c)   Effect on Other Rules. This rule does not limit the admission or consideration of evidence under any other rule.

Settlement Offers and Negotiations

FRE 408 prohibits putting into evidence an offer of settlement or a statement of fact made in settlement negotiations to prove the validity, invalidity, or amount of a disputed claim. The traditional rule allowed evidence of a party's admission of fact made in a settlement dialogue unless the statement was clearly demarked as "hypothetical" or "without prejudice." FRE 408 alters the common law rule and denies admission to all statements made in settlement negotiations—both offers of compromise and statements of fact made in the settlement discussions. This evidence is not considered relevant: an offer of compromise may be motivated by numerous reasons, and one can draw no conclusions from a party's willingness to negotiate. Allowing settlement negotiations into evidence would have a chilling effect on negotiations, and any potential probative value must yield to the public policy favoring the amicable resolution of disputes. Allowing settlement negotiations into evidence would also give rise to the practical problem of disqualification of lawyers, since a lawyer may be called to testify to the negotiations.[2]

For example, a husband's settlement offer to pay alimony could not be used against him as an admission of the wife's need for financial assistance. Likewise, a mother's offer to agree to joint custody could not be used as an admission of the father's propriety as a potential custodian. FRE 408 precludes a party from putting his or her own offer to compromise into evidence as well as a party's evidence of the other party's offer to compromise.

Permissible Uses of Settlement Negotiations

There are exceptions to the rule precluding admissibility of an offer to compromise. An offer to compromise is admissible if it relates to a collateral issue. For example, evidence of an offer to divide property that identifies an asset to be included in the property division could be admissible if the party who made the offer later denied the existence of the asset. In such a case, the settlement offer is not offered to prove the existence of the offer; rather, it is offered to prove something unrelated: the existence of the asset.

Also, if a party tries to avoid a previously accepted settlement, the existence of the agreement can be proven through evidence

---

2. Pierce v. F.R. Tripler & Co., 955 F.2d 820 (2d Cir. 1992).

of the offer and acceptance.[3] A party cannot object on relevance grounds to admission of evidence of negotiations of an alleged settlement, when the settlement itself is the ultimate issue.

The rule itself provides specific examples of permissible uses of settlement discussions: "proving a witness's bias or prejudice, [or] negating a contention of undue delay." Another example is evidence of a party's good faith attempts to settle as relevant in a fee dispute. For instance, a party seeking fees could tender evidence of repeated efforts to solicit a response to a settlement proposal as proof of bad faith. A party could also offer a fraudulent statement made during settlement negotiations in a case challenging validity of an agreement on the grounds of fraud.[4] Additionally, if a party challenges a marital settlement agreement or a premarital agreement based on duress or coercion, the defending party may offer evidence of settlement negotiations to disprove the claim.

Withdrawn Plea or Plea of No Contest

Ordinarily, a plea of guilty is deemed an admission in a civil case.[5] FRE 410 governs the admissibility of a withdrawn guilty plea or a no-contest plea. Generally, a withdrawn guilty plea or a plea of no contest (nolo contendere), whether withdrawn or not, is inadmissible against the defendant in a civil proceeding. The rule also excludes discussions during plea bargaining and any admissions made as part of the plea agreement. The primary focus of this rule is on criminal proceedings, but it does apply to civil proceedings as well, including divorce and other family law cases.[6]

---

3.   1 McCormick on Evidence, § 266 (Kenneth S. Broun, ed., Thomson West 6th ed. 2006).

4.   Uforma/Shelby Bus. Forms, Inc. v. NLRB, 111 F.3d 1284 (6th Cir. 1997).

5.   Spircoff v. Stranski, 703 N.E.2d 431, 435 (Ill. App. Ct. 1998).

6.   2 McCormick on Evidence, *supra* note 3, § 266 at 237.

The Rape Shield Rule

FRE 412 bars evidence of a victim's prior sexual behavior in a proceeding involving sexual misconduct. The rule is not limited to criminal prosecutions; it provides only that the proceeding involves "sexual misconduct." FRE 412(b)(2) provides that the sexual conduct of one alleging a sexual assault may be admitted if "its probative value substantially outweighs the danger of harm to any victim and of unfair prejudice to any party." This rule also provides that evidence of the victim's reputation is relevant only if the victim places his or her reputation into controversy. Divorce and domestic violence cases sometimes involve a sexual assault claim. This rule allows a court to potentially consider the victim's behavior in appropriate circumstances.

The exceptions under 412(b)(2) must still contend with Rule 404, which generally disallows evidence of character. Ultimately, the court must invoke a balancing test to determine whether the probative value of the alleged victim's sexual conduct substantially outweighs the risk of harm to the victim. Rule 403 (Exclusion of Relevant Evidence on Grounds of Prejudice, Confusion, or Waste of Time) also invokes a balancing test—allowing relevant evidence to be excluded if the probative value is outweighed by danger of prejudice or other good cause. The Advisory Committee notes distinguish the two rules:

> This test for admitting evidence offered to prove sexual behavior or sexual propensity in civil cases differs in three respects from the general rule governing admissibility set forth in Rule 403. First it reverses the usual procedure spelled out in 403 by shifting the burden to the proponent to demonstrate admissibility rather than making the opponent justify exclusion of the evidence. Second the standard expressed in subdivision (b)(2) is more stringent than in the original rule; it raises the threshold for admission by requiring

that the probative value of the evidence *substantially* outweigh the specified dangers. Finally the Rule 412 test puts "harm to the victim" on the scale in addition to prejudice to the parties.[7]

Policy limits this type of evidence to extraordinary circumstances. For example, in a domestic violence case in which the wife accuses her husband of improper sexual advances, the husband may use this rule to seek the admission of evidence of the wife's prior sexual behavior with the husband. He bears the burden of showing that the value of that evidence substantially outweighs the risk of harm to his wife—a mighty hurdle under the framework of this rule.

To avoid surprise, the rule requires a party seeking to offer evidence of sexual misconduct under Rule 412(b) to file a written motion at least 14 days before trial— specifically describing the proposed evidence and the purpose of its admission. The court then conducts an in-camera hearing, allowing both the victim and the other party to be heard. This proceeding is sealed unless ordered otherwise.

FRE 412(b) does not apply to evidence of sexual conduct generally. For example, if a custody claim were based in part on a parent's sexual indiscretions, the rule would not apply since the proffered evidence does not involve the conduct of a victim.

As always, the general rules of relevancy (Rules 403 and 404) still apply.

Evidence of Sexual Misconduct in a Civil Proceeding

FRE 415 provides that when relief in a civil case is predicated on a party's alleged sexual assault or child molestation, evidence of the party's commission of similar offenses is admissible. This rule

7. *Id.* §§ 43, 44, and 193 app. at 604.

contravenes the usual notion that similar offenses are not necessarily probative of whether one engaged in the behavior on this particular occasion. Thus, in a hearing to restrict a parent's visitation, the court could consider prior sexual abuse of a child as proof of the parent's propensity to engage in the behavior now.

This rule reflects the policy of erring on the side of caution when it comes to children's safety. But it is not without controversy. The Judicial Conference of the United States "observed the opposition of an 'overwhelming majority of judges, lawyers, law professors and legal organizations' to the proposed rules."[8] Nevertheless, Congress adopted Rule 415 allowing this type of evidence.

In the event a party seeks to offer evidence of prior sexual misconduct toward a child, the party must notify the adverse party 15 days in advance, to give the latter an opportunity to seek a protective order or file a motion to limit the proofs. FRE 415 also reiterates that all other rules of evidence remain in effect (rules pertaining to relevance, for example) and that it in no way limits their applicability.

Practice Points

- Beware of the exceptions to nonadmissibility of settlement negotiations. Recognize the possibility that an opposing party may attempt to admit a written settlement offer into evidence under an alternative theory. When writing a settlement letter or e-mail, keep in mind the possibility that the court may see it.
- Become familiar with FRE 412 and 415 and their interplay with the other character evidence rules. Evidence of a party's promiscuity or sexual conduct is rarely relevant in a divorce

---

8.   THOMAS A. MAUET & WARREN D. WOLFSON, TRIAL EVIDENCE (4th ed. 2009), at 117.

proceeding. Research local case law. For example, Illinois prohibits evidence of any sexual conduct unless it directly affects the child.[9] Evidence of sexual conduct outside the presence of the child is irrelevant unless one can show harm to the child.

- As always, consider the judge. Will he or she want to hear about evidence of sexual conduct? Will the judge be offended? Is the evidence so marginally relevant that it appears as a transparent attempt to inflame the court? Your job is not to satisfy the client's desire to humiliate the spouse; rather, it is to advance realistic arguments to a receptive court.
- Notify the client early in the case that this type of evidence is irrelevant and protected by the rules of evidence so the client understands why it is not being pursued. Good client management involves educating clients about the rules of evidence and how they apply.
- Make sure to comply with the notice requirements of Rules 412 and 415 if you intend to use evidence of sexual misconduct.

---

9. *In re* Marriage of Radae, 208 Ill. App. 3d 1027, 567 N.E.2d 760 (1991).

Hearsay 6

Hearsay is defined as an out-of-court statement used to prove the truth of the matter asserted. This chapter explores the subtleties of what is and is not hearsay. It addresses the exemptions to the hearsay rule, including use of admissions by a party opponent. The hearsay rules deal with three kinds of out-of-court statements: (1) inadmissible hearsay; (2) admissible hearsay (exceptions); (3) out-of-court statements that are not considered hearsay for a variety of reasons, for example, admissions of a party opponent and prior inconsistent statement under oath.

Rule to consider:

Rule 801. Definitions That Apply to This Article; Exclusions from Hearsay

(a)   Statement. "Statement" means a person's oral assertion, written assertion, or nonverbal conduct, if the person intended it as an assertion.

(b) Declarant. "Declarant" means the person who made the statement.

(c) Hearsay. "Hearsay" means a statement that: (1) the declarant does not make while testifying at the current trial or hearing; and (2) a party offers in evidence to prove the truth of the matter asserted in the statement.

(d) Statements That Are Not Hearsay. A statement that meets the following conditions is not hearsay:

    (1) *A Declarant-Witness's Prior Statement.* The declarant testifies and is subject to cross-examination about a prior statement, and the statement:

        (A) is inconsistent with the declarant's testimony and was given under penalty of perjury at a trial, hearing, or other proceeding or in a deposition;

        (B) is consistent with the declarant's testimony and is offered to rebut an express or implied charge that the declarant recently fabricated it or acted from a recent improper influence or motive in so testifying; or

        (C) identifies a person as someone the declarant perceived earlier. . . .

    (2) *An Opposing Party's Statement.* The statement is offered against an opposing party and:

        (A) was made by the party in an individual or representative capacity;

        (B) is one the party manifested that it adopted or believed to be true;

        (C) was made by a person whom the party authorized to make a statement on the subject;

        (D) was made by the party's agent or employee on a matter within the scope of that relationship and while it existed; or

(E) was made by the party's coconspirator during and
     in furtherance of the conspiracy. . . .

The statement must be considered but does not by itself establish
the declarant's authority under (C); the existence or scope of the
relationship under (D); or the existence of the conspiracy or participation in it under (E). . . .

Rule 802. The Rule against Hearsay

Hearsay is not admissible unless any of the following provides
otherwise:

- a federal statute;
- these rules; or
- other rules prescribed by the Supreme Court.

The Prohibition Against Using Out-of-Court Statements as Evidence

The rule against hearsay evidence evolved from English common
law.[1] "[Dean] Wigmore calls the rule against hearsay 'that most
characteristic rule of the Anglo-American Law of Evidence—a rule
which may be esteemed, next to jury trial, the greatest contribution
of that eminently practical legal system to the world's methods of
procedure.'"[2] Pragmatism is at the heart of this rule. It took root
in England in the seventeenth century, originating as a practical
mechanism to keep unreliable evidence away from juries.

---

1. 2 McCORMICK ON EVIDENCE, § 244 (Kenneth S. Braun, ed., Thomson West 6th
ed. 2006).
2. *Id.* at 122.

McCormick discusses the origin of the rule prohibiting hearsay as a means of insuring reliability of evidence:

> The Anglo-American tradition evolved three conditions under which the witnesses ordinarily are required to testify; oath, personal presence at the trial, and cross-examination. The rule against hearsay is designed to insure compliance with these ideal conditions, and when one of them is absent, the hearsay objection becomes pertinent.[3]

The hearsay rule minimizes the likelihood that the fact finder will be influenced by unreliable evidence. The originators of this rule considered an unsworn statement made outside the presence of the court and not subject to cross-examination inherently unreliable and thus ordinarily inadmissible.

Hearsay Defined

Hearsay is an out-of-court statement offered to prove the truth of the matter asserted. FRE 801 defines hearsay as "a statement that: (1) the declarant does not make while testifying at the current trial or hearing; and (2) a party offers in evidence to prove the truth of the matter asserted in the statement." In order to qualify as hearsay, the evidence must be considered a statement.

According to Rule 801(a), a statement is "a person's oral assertion, written assertion, or nonverbal conduct, if the person intended it as an assertion." The rule uses the term *assert* but does not define it. This omission has caused confusion. According to *McCormick*, "the word simply means to say that something is so, e.g., that an event happened or that a condition existed."[4] Assertions can include

---

3.   2 McCormick on Evidence, *supra* note 1, § 245 at 125 (footnote omitted).
4.   2 McCormick on Evidence, *supra* note 1, § 246 at 129.

questions (Why do you have a knife in your pocket?) or imperative statements (Take off those bloody clothes!).

Nonverbal Communication as Hearsay

Nonverbal conduct intended as communication may also be subject to the hearsay rule if it is considered an assertion. Examples of nonverbal conduct that may be intended as a communication include rolling of eyes, a thumbs-up sign, and pointing. Sometimes, nonverbal communication is stronger than words, such as when a child points to a doll to describe where on her body she was touched. These examples illustrate deliberate nonverbal conduct intended as a communication.

In some instances, people may not intend their nonverbal conduct as a communication. When someone faints after hearing bad news, the reaction (fainting) is a form of involuntary nonverbal conduct. The rule distinguishes this type of nonverbal conduct and excludes it from the hearsay rule since it is not an intended communication. Such conduct is not assertive and thus not hearsay.

The trial court must decide whether nonverbal conduct is intentional or unintentional, that is, whether the actor intended to communicate a message by the conduct. According to the Advisory Committee Notes, "The rule is so worded as to place the burden on the party claiming that the intention existed; ambiguous and doubtful cases will be resolved against him and in favor of admissibility."[5] Thus, if a party seeks to exclude nonverbal conduct as an intentional assertion of fact (and thus hearsay), the party has the burden to establish that the declarant's conduct intentionally communicated, rather than involuntarily responded, to a stimulus.

---

5. *See* FED. R. EVID. 801 Advisory Committee's Notes.

Who Is the Declarant?

FRE 801(b) defines a declarant as "the person who made the statement." Rule 801(c) defines as hearsay all statements made by a declarant, except those made while testifying at the trial.[6]

Hearsay involves two actors. The *declarant* is the actor who makes the out-of-court statement. The *witness* is the actor who testifies in court to the declarant's out-of-court statement. When the declarant and the witness are the same person, and the witness seeks to testify to his or her earlier out-of-court statement, the statement is still hearsay if offered for its truth. Courts and lawyers frequently confuse this principle. Why would an out-of-court statement made by a declarant who is now present in court and subject to cross-examination be defined as hearsay? There is no satisfactory explanation but the Federal Rules of Evidence do not allow such a deviation. They strictly define the out-of-court statement as hearsay, even if the declarant later testifies as a witness.

Nonassertive Out-of-Court Statement

A nonassertive out-of-court statement is not hearsay. Common circumstances where an out-of-court statement is not hearsay because it is not offered for its truth include:

- *Verbal acts.* A statement made in a negotiation leading up to the execution of a contract is not an assertion. Rather, such a statement is considered a verbal act, giving rise to the legal determination of whether a document is enforceable. The negotiations leading up to the agreement are not offered for their

---

6.   An exception exists for a sworn statement made by the witness in an earlier court proceeding, and that is discussed below.

truth but rather to show the words were spoken. For example, the husband says, "I will transfer my Swiss bank account to you." The wife says, "I accept." These words are not offered to prove the oral contract and are thus not considered hearsay. When certain words or verbal conduct are integral to the substantive legal claim, the out-of-court statement or conduct, as the case may be, is not hearsay.

- *Verbal parts of acts.* McCormick defines this rule: "Explanatory words which accompany and give character to the transaction are not hearsay when under the substantive law the pertinent inquiry is directed only to objective manifestations rather than the actual intent or other state of mind of the actor."[7] If the inquiry is focused on some objective act, for example, whether a deed was executed, the commentary related to that act is not hearsay. For example, a husband executes a deed conveying his individual property into joint tenancy. The deed itself objectively evidences the conveyance, and any commentary surrounding the transaction is not hearsay. Instead, such commentary is considered nonassertive since the deed conclusively resolves the question of the conveyance. For example, if the lawyer who prepared the deed said to the husband while he was signing, "You know you are making a gift to her of your interest?" the statement is not hearsay.

- *Communication offered to show the effect on the observer.* An out-of-court statement offered to show the impact on an observer is not hearsay. For example, a parent in a relocation case could offer into evidence a brochure about schools in the new location to show how the parent weighed the benefits of prospective schools for the children. The materials are not offered to show the truth contained in the text but to show the impact on the parent who evaluated the materials.

---

7.   2 MCCORMICK ON EVIDENCE, *supra* note 1, § 249 at 134.

In these categories, the oral or written statement is not offered to prove the truth of a factual assertion, but merely to show that something was said or written. The assertions are not hearsay.

Prior Inconsistent Statement Made under Oath Is Not Hearsay

FRE 801(d)(1) provides that a prior inconsistent statement by a declarant-witness made under oath in an earlier proceeding is not hearsay, meaning it is admissible as substantive proof of the fact asserted. To qualify, the earlier statement must have been given under oath and at a proceeding such as a trial, hearing, or deposition. This rule allows the trier of fact to hear the circumstances of both statements. By contrast, when the prior statement is unsworn, the earlier statement is only admissible to impeach the witness by showing the inconsistency, and not as substantive proof of the fact asserted in the earlier statement.

Where the earlier statement is sworn, it is incumbent on the party seeking to rely on an earlier statement to provide the statement itself. The sworn statement or transcript can be offered as an exhibit as substantive proof of the facts asserted therein.

Prior Consistent Statement Admissible as Not Hearsay

The general rule is that a declarant-witness's prior consistent statement is not admissible as substantive evidence, that is, as proof of the matter asserted therein. However, under certain circumstances, the earlier consistent statement may be admissible. Rule 801(d)(1)(B) allows admission of a prior consistent statement that "is consistent with the declarant's testimony and is offered to rebut an express or implied charge that the declarant recently fabricated it or acted from a recent improper influence or motive in so testifying." Rule 801(d)(1)(B) permits a party to rehabilitate the party's witness by offering the witness's out-of-court statement consistent with his or her trial testimony. To be admissible for this purpose, the witness need not have made the prior consistent statement under oath. For example, assume the wife's lawyer challenges an accountant's testimony or opinion based upon the fact that the husband pays a substantial annual fee to the accountant for business services. The husband's lawyer might offer a prior consistent statement found in an article the accountant wrote for a CPA journal. The rule allows the admission of the earlier statement by the witness consistent with his or her trial testimony, to rebut the improper influence charge.

FRE 801(d)(2) also allows admission of a prior consistent statement to rehabilitate a witness accused of prior inconsistent statements. Take, for example, a custody case in which a witness testifies that the mother is ever vigilant and focused on her children's welfare. On cross, a question insinuates that the witness never expressed this admiration to anyone. A proper question on redirect may point to a statement that the witness made to someone that is consistent with the testimony. While this statement would not be admissible as substantive proof, it could be used to rehabilitate the impugned witness.[8]

Admissions of a Party Opponent

Rule 801(d)(2) defines an admission by a party opponent as not hearsay. The parties themselves provide most of the testimony in divorce cases. Any out-of-court statement made by a party is an

---

8. I discuss use of prior consistent statements for impeachment in Chapter 14.

admission, and the other party may offer the admission as an exemption to the hearsay rule. *McCormick* defines an admission as "words or acts of a party or a party's representative that are offered as evidence by the opposing party."[9] Unlike the constraints of other rules regarding testimony, an admission can consist of an opinion. *Any* statement made by the opponent—whether oral or written, under oath or not, consistent or inconsistent with his or her testimony in the current proceeding—can be admitted (subject to relevancy) as substantive evidence.[10]

McCormick explains the reasoning behind the admission exemption:

> The admissibility of an admission made by the party himself rests not upon any notion that the circumstances in which it was made furnish the trier means of evaluating it fairly, but upon the adversary theory of litigation. A party can hardly object that he had no opportunity to cross-examine himself or that he is unworthy of credence save when speaking under sanction of an oath.[11]

Do not confuse hearsay *exemptions* with the rule's *exceptions*. Unlike exceptions to the hearsay rule (to be discussed in the next chapter), admissions and certain prior statements of a declarant-witness are exempt from the hearsay rule; they are not considered hearsay because "no guarantee of trustworthiness is required."[12] In contrast, an exception allows the admission for the truth of the matter asserted of certain hearsay evidence that is considered sufficiently reliable for admission. Ultimately, whether an out-of-court

9. 2 MCCORMICK ON EVIDENCE, *supra* note 1, § 254 at 178.

10. *See, e.g.,* United States v. Reed, 227 F. 3d 763,770 (7th Cir. 2000) noted in 2 MCCORMICK ON EVIDENCE, *supra* note 1, § 254 at 181 n.14.

11. 2 MCCORMICK ON EVIDENCE, *supra* note 1, § 254 at 179 (quoting EDMUND MORRIS MORGAN, BASIC PROBLEMS OF EVIDENCE 265–66 (1963)).

12. 56 F.R.D. 183, 296 (1973).

statement is admitted into evidence under an exemption or an exception, the result is the same—the evidence is allowed in.

Judicial Admissions Distinguished from Evidentiary Admissions

Evidentiary admissions must be distinguished from judicial admissions. A judicial admission is not evidence; it is a legal construct designed to remove a fact or issue from contention. A judicial admission is a contention made in a pleading that conclusively resolves a particular issue.[13] In her answer to a pleading, if Sally admits that she is healthy and capable of self-support, she has made a judicial admission, binding her to the acknowledgment. Evidentiary admissions, in contrast, may be controverted.[14]

A judicial admission in a pleading is conclusive until the pleading is amended or withdrawn. If a party withdraws a pleading containing the admission, the allegations in the withdrawn pleading become an evidentiary admission, allowing the party to offer evidence to explain or refute the admission. Also, a party may use a statement of fact in a pleading as an evidentiary (as opposed to judicial) admission against an opposing party in another lawsuit.[15]

The judicial admission is substantive evidence: the party seeking to enforce the admission could offer the pleading containing the admission into evidence as an exhibit or read it into the record. The admission is not merely an opportunity for impeachment.

---

13. 2 McCormick on Evidence, *supra* note 1, § 254 at 181.
14. *Id.*
15. *See* Foster v. State, 157 Ga. App. 554, 555 (1981) ("When such admissions in pleadings are introduced as evidence in a later and different action, they no longer operate as admissions in judicio, but rather, as evidentiary admissions").

Testimonial Admissions by a Party Opponent

A family law case may have one or more preliminary hearings prior to the final trial, such as a hearing on temporary alimony or child support. At trial, the opponent can offer any admissions made by the other party during testimony in one of these preliminary matters. Prepare for preliminary evidentiary proceedings with this in mind. Offensively, ensure that a court reporter is present to preserve the testimony for later use. Defensively, prepare your client for pretrial hearings at which the client may testify to ensure that no surprises come out of his or her mouth during testimony. Although a party can contradict or explain earlier testimonial admissions at trial, the admission can still carry significant weight, is difficult to defend, and will affect their credibility with the court. Avoid the need to justify an inconsistency by preventing an inadvertent or mistaken admission in the first place.

Statement of Third Person Imputed to Party

An admission of a party opponent can include a statement made by a third person with authority to bind the party, including a lawyer. FRE 801(d)(2)(C) and (D). Generally, a statement by a lawyer in a pleading or in an opening statement, not specifically withdrawn, is a conclusive *judicial* admission.[16] For example, if a lawyer states in an opening, "The evidence will show that my client is capable of paying support at any amount the court deems just," the client cannot later claim he or she cannot afford to pay a particular sum. In contrast, an out-of-court statement by a lawyer on the client's behalf is an *evidentiary* admission and thus controvertible.

---

16. Konstant Products, Inc. v. Liberty Mutual Fire Ins. Co., 929 N.E.2d 1200, 1203 (Ill. App. Ct. 2010).

For example, assume a lawyer writes a letter in response to an assertion about his or her client failing to honor a court order to pay certain bills: "My client has the money to pay these bills but refuses because of her interference with his parenting time." That statement could be offered as an evidentiary admission of the client's ability to pay in a contempt proceeding. While the client can explain or rebut this type of evidentiary admission, that may require the lawyer to testify, creating other problems for the client. Think about the possibility of binding your client when you send correspondence. Your words may be used against your client.

Adoptive Admissions

A party may adopt the statement of another person as an admission. In order for the adoptive statement to qualify as an admission, there must be clear proof that the party accepted the statement as his or her own. For example, assume that a husband owns a business and the value of the business is an issue. During a meeting where the husband is present, a trade organization representative indicates that the husband's industry is moving in a good direction and the health of this industry is great. The husband hears the statement and tells the assembled group that he agrees. The trade representative's statement is not hearsay—it is an adoptive admission by the husband.[17]

In order to prove an adoptive admission, the offering party must offer proof of the original statement as well as its ultimate adoption by the other party. The mere act of hearing a statement is insufficient to constitute a party's adoptive admission of the statement. The evidence must reveal a clear acceptance of the fact communicated in the statement. The court needs to consider all of

---

17. 2 McCormick on Evidence, *supra* note 1, § 261 at 209.

the circumstances to determine if a statement was actively adopted, rather than passively acknowledged.

Admission by Silence

Silence can be an admission when a party hears and fails to deny a particular statement. The statement itself must be such that it would, if untrue, call for the party to have denied it under the circumstances.[18] Courts are generally reluctant to let the act of being silent qualify as an admission. A number of reasons could explain a party's failure to respond to a statement made by another person: the party was not paying attention, was distracted, or was confused. Nevertheless, according to *McCormick*, a court may allow silence to serve as an adoptive admission if the offering party proves

- "The statement was heard by the party claimed to have acquiesced.
- The statement was understood by the party.
- The subject matter was within the party's knowledge.
- There were no physical or emotional impediments to responding.
- The personal makeup of the speaker (e.g., young child) or the person's relationship to the party or the event (e.g., a bystander) was not such as to make it unreasonable to expect a denial.
- The statement itself was such as would, if untrue, call for the party to have denied it under the circumstances."[19]

The court needs to consider these nonexclusive criteria to evaluate the propriety of an inference from silence. After weighing these

---

18. 2 McCORMICK ON EVIDENCE, *supra* note 1, § 262 at 213–14.
19. 2 McCORMICK ON EVIDENCE, *supra* note 1, § 262 at 213–14.

criteria, if the court determines that the lack of a response is meaningful as it relates to the initial assertion, the court can consider the silence or absence of a response as probative of the disputed issue. Take this example: Betty is in the backyard when the next-door neighbor, Linda, frantically yells that she just saw Betty's husband, Bob, striking their child with a stick. Betty and Linda find Bob on the other side of the house and confront him about this. He says nothing. Betty offers his silence in response to the accusation as an admission of the alleged behavior. In response, Bob may argue his silence was not an admission; rather, it was indicative of his shock at the claim.

Admission by Conduct

Failing to produce evidence or a witness in a party's control may allow the trier of fact to draw a negative inference. This principle is known as an "admission by omission" or an "admission by conduct." Take the example of a wife who claims that she executed a note promising to pay back her mother money that the mother advanced for the purchase of a house. The husband disputes the claim and alleges that the mother made a gift. The wife claims both she and her mother have copies of the note. The note is requested in discovery and never produced, nor is it produced at trial and the mother does not testify. The court could construe the absence of the note as well as the absence of the mother's testimony as an admission that no note actually exists.

McCormick observes that courts should use this type of admission and the inferences that come from it sparingly:

> The appellate courts often counsel caution. A number of factors support a conservative approach. Conjecture or ambiguity of inference is often present. The possibility that the inference may be

drawn invites waste of time in calling unnecessary witnesses or in presenting evidence to explain why they were not called. Failure to anticipate that the inference may be invoked entails substantial possibilities of surprise. Finally the availability of modern discovery procedures serves to diminish both its justification and the need for the inference.[20]

Generally, where there is no jury, this issue is less important. Within reason, judges draw their own conclusions from the evidence or lack thereof. If a party argues the significance of an omitted witness, the judge can either consider the omission or disregard it. Maybe it would be extraordinarily inconvenient or expensive to use the witness. Maybe the witness's testimony—while marginally helpful— would be time-consuming or the opposing party could have called the witness. To rebut charges of an admission by omission, a party may need to show the court that there were legitimate reasons for not presenting evidence within the party's control. Ultimately, the judge weighs the totality of circumstances to determine the significance of absent evidence.

A litigant's improper conduct during a proceeding can also be an admission by conduct.[21] If wrongdoing amounts to an obstruction of the process, the other party can argue that the behavior is an admission by conduct. A party's misconduct arguably reflects an acknowledgement of the party's weak position and implicitly recognizes the improper conduct can be construed against him or her. The misconduct must rise to the level of bad faith—mere negligence is not enough to create an admission because it does not reflect conscious recognition of the case's deficiencies.

Examples of conduct that may warrant this treatment include spoliation of evidence, failure to produce evidence, perjury, falsification

---

20. 2 McCormick on Evidence, *supra* note 1, § 264 at 222–23 (footnotes omitted).
21. 2 McCormick on Evidence, *supra* note 1, § 265 at 226–231.

of documents or evidence, subornation of perjury, and other conduct that is improper. When a party seeks information from the opponent's computer, only to discover that the hard drive has been scrubbed, the court can draw a conclusion that the hard drive contained information adverse to the owner-party. For example, assume the wife tells her lawyer that the business-owner husband has a second set of records reflecting all of his income that he keeps on his laptop. A letter to preserve the laptop for inspection is sent by the wife's lawyer to the husband's lawyer. When contacted a week later, the husband's lawyer indicates the hard drive crashed on the computer and that his client destroyed the computer. A judge could treat this conduct as an admission that the second set of books existed and that his claimed income was inaccurate.

Some controversy exists concerning whether such conduct constitutes an admission. Earlier decisions reflect courts' unwillingness to consider this type of conduct as proof of a fact in controversy. The modern trend, however, reflects courts' intolerance for this type of conduct, shifting the burden to the transgressor to provide proof to avoid a negative inference. [22]

Practice Points

- First, evaluate whether evidence is hearsay. If not, no hearsay exception is even necessary for admissibility.
- Most family law cases rely heavily on the testimony of the parties. Become familiar with the concept of admissions of a party opponent, including adoptive admission, admission by silence, and the other types of party admissions discussed above.

---

22. *See* Walters v. Walters, 249 P.3d 214, 218 (Wyo. 2011) (stating that it is well-settled law that destroying or altering evidence in bad faith gives rise to the presumption that the evidence destroyed would have been unfavorable to the party who destroyed it).

- Defensively, remember that even if a statement is admissible as nonhearsay, ordinary relevancy principles still apply. Be prepared to argue relevancy if a hearsay objection fails.
- Consider sending a letter at the beginning of the case advising the opponent of specific evidence that will be sought in discovery and admonishing the opponent that you will argue to the court that the spoliation or destruction of that evidence is an admission of facts in controversy. While this is not binding on the court, the judge may take notice if a hard drive is scrubbed or important evidence becomes unavailable due to the acts of the opposing party.
- Think before you respond (or fail to respond) to letters from your opponent. Silence or an affirmative statement may be an admission. Think before you write!

Hearsay Exceptions 7

In the last chapter I defined hearsay and discussed those out-of-court statements not considered hearsay. In this chapter I examine the exceptions to the hearsay rule. Some exceptions apply to any out-of-court statement, and others apply only where the declarant is unavailable to testify. Most commonly, when a hearsay exception is properly raised to preclude admission, the lawyer will need to look to the exceptions for a way to get the out-of-court statement admitted.

Rules to consider:

Rule 803. Exceptions to the Rule against Hearsay—Regardless of Whether the Declarant Is Available as a Witness

(a) The following are not excluded by the rule against hearsay, regardless of whether the declarant is available as a witness:

(1) *Present Sense Impression.* A statement describing or explaining an event or condition, made while or immediately after the declarant perceived it.

(2) *Excited Utterance.* A statement relating to a startling event or condition, made while the declarant was under the stress of excitement that it caused.

(3) *Then-Existing Mental, Emotional, or Physical Condition.* A statement of the declarant's then-existing state of mind (such as motive, intent, or plan) or emotional, sensory, or physical condition (such as mental feeling, pain, or bodily health), but not including a statement of memory or belief to prove the fact remembered or believed unless it relates to the validity or terms of the declarant's will.

(4) *Statement Made for Medical Diagnosis or Treatment.* A statement that:

(A) is made for—and is reasonably pertinent to—medical diagnosis or treatment; and

(B) describes medical history; past or present symptoms or sensations; their inception; or their general cause.

(5) *Recorded Recollection.* A record that:

(A) is on a matter the witness once knew about but now cannot recall well enough to testify fully and accurately;

(B) was made or adopted by the witness when the matter was fresh in the witness's memory; and

(C) accurately reflects the witness's knowledge. If admitted, the record may be read into evidence but may be received as an exhibit only if offered by an adverse party.

(6) *Records of a Regularly Conducted Activity.* A record of an act, event, condition, opinion, or diagnosis if:

(A) the record was made at or near the time by—or from information transmitted by—someone with knowledge;

(B) the record was kept in the course of a regularly conducted activity of a business, organization, occupation, or calling, whether or not for profit;

(C) making the record was a regular practice of that activity;

(D) all these conditions are shown by the testimony of the custodian or another qualified witness, or by a certification that complies with Rule 902 (11) or (12) or with a statute permitting certification; and

(E) neither the source of information nor the method or circumstances of preparation indicate a lack of trustworthiness.

(7) *Absence of a Record of a Regularly Conducted Activity.* Evidence that a matter is not included in a record described in paragraph (6) if:

(A) the evidence is admitted to prove that the matter did not occur or exist;

(B) a record was regularly kept for a matter of that kind; and

(C) neither the possible source of the information nor other circumstances indicate a lack of trust-worthiness.

(8) *Public Records.* A record or statement of a public office if:

(A) it sets out:

(i) the office's activities;

(ii) a matter observed while under a legal duty to report, but not including, in a criminal case, a matter observed by law-enforcement personnel; or

        (iii) in a civil case or against the government in a criminal case, factual findings from a legally authorized investigation; and

   (B) neither the source of information nor other circumstances indicate a lack of trustworthiness.

(9) *Public Records of Vital Statistics.* A record of a birth, death, or marriage, if reported to a public office in accordance with a legal duty.

(10) *Absence of a Public Record.* Testimony—or a certification under Rule 902—that a diligent search failed to disclose a public record or statement if the testimony or certification is admitted to prove that:

   (A) the record or statement does not exist; or

   (B) a matter did not occur or exist, if a public office regularly kept a record or statement for a matter of that kind.

(11) *Records of Religious Organizations Concerning Personal or Family History.* A statement of birth, legitimacy, ancestry, marriage, divorce, death, relationship by blood or marriage, or similar facts of personal or family history, contained in a regularly kept record of a religious organization.

(12) *Certificates of Marriage, Baptism, and Similar Ceremonies.* A statement of fact contained in a certificate:

   (A) made by a person who is authorized by a religious organization or by law to perform the act certified;

   (B) attesting that the person performed a marriage or similar ceremony or administered a sacrament; and

   (C) purporting to have been issued at the time of the act or within a reasonable time after it.

(13) *Family Records.* A statement of fact about personal or family history contained in a family record, such as a

Bible, genealogy, chart, engraving on a ring, inscription on a portrait, or engraving on an urn or burial marker.

(14) *Records of Documents That Affect an Interest in Property.* The record of a document that purports to establish or affect an interest in property if:

(A) the record is admitted to prove the content of the original recorded document, along with its signing and its delivery by each person who purports to have signed it;

(B) the record is kept in a public office; and

(C) a statute authorizes recording documents of that kind in that office.

(15) *Statements in Documents That Affect an Interest in Property.* A statement contained in a document that purports to establish or affect an interest in property if the matter stated was relevant to the document's purpose—unless later dealings with the property are inconsistent with the truth of the statement or the purport of the document.

(16) *Statements in Ancient Documents.* A statement in a document that is at least 20 years old and whose authenticity is established.

(17) *Market Reports and Similar Commercial Publications.* Market quotations, lists, directories, or other compilations that are generally relied on by the public or by persons in particular occupations.

(18) *Statements in Learned Treatises, Periodicals, or Pamphlets.* A statement contained in a treatise, periodical, or pamphlet if:

(A) the statement is called to the attention of an expert witness on cross-examination or relied on by the expert on direct examination; and

(B) the publication is established as a reliable authority by the expert's admission or testimony, by another expert's testimony, or by judicial notice. If admitted, the statement may be read into evidence but not received as an exhibit.

(19) *Reputation Concerning Personal or Family History.* A reputation among a person's family by blood, adoption, or marriage—or among a person's associates or in the community—concerning the person's birth, adoption, legitimacy, ancestry, marriage, divorce, death, relationship by blood, adoption, or marriage, or similar facts of personal or family history.

(20) *Reputation Concerning Boundaries or General History.* A reputation in a community—arising before the controversy—concerning boundaries of land in the community or customs that affect the land, or concerning general historical events important to that community, state, or nation.

(21) *Reputation Concerning Character.* A reputation among a person's associates or in the community concerning the person's character.

(22) *Judgment of a Previous Conviction.* Evidence of a final judgment of conviction if:

(A) the judgment was entered after a trial or guilty plea, but not a nolo contendere plea;

(B) the conviction was for a crime punishable by death or by imprisonment for more than a year;

(C) the evidence is admitted to prove any fact essential to the judgment; and

(D) when offered by the prosecutor in a criminal case for a purpose other than impeachment, the judgment was against the defendant. The pendency of an appeal may be shown but does not affect admissibility.

(23) *Judgments Involving Personal, Family, or General History, or a Boundary.* A judgment that is admitted to prove a matter of personal, family, or general history, or boundaries, if the matter:
(A)   was essential to the judgment; and
(B)   could be proved by evidence of reputation.
(24) [*Other Exceptions.*] [Transferred to Rule 807.]

Rule 804. Exceptions to the Rule against Hearsay— When the Declarant Is Unavailable as a Witness

(a)   *Criteria for Being Unavailable.* A declarant is considered to be unavailable as a witness if the declarant:
(1)   is exempted from testifying about the subject matter of the declarant's statement because the court rules that a privilege applies;
(2)   refuses to testify about the subject matter despite a court order to do so;
(3)   testifies to not remembering the subject matter;
(4)   cannot be present or testify at the trial or hearing because of death or a then-existing infirmity, physical illness, or mental illness; or
(5)   is absent from the trial or hearing and the statement's proponent has not been able, by process or other reasonable means, to procure:
(A)   the declarant's attendance, in the case of a hearsay exception under Rule 804(b)(1) or (6); or
(B)   the declarant's attendance or testimony, in the case of a hearsay exception under Rule 804(b)(2), (3), or (4). But this subdivision (a) does not apply if the statement's proponent procured or wrongfully caused the declarant's unavailability as a witness in order to prevent the declarant from attending or testifying.

(b) *The Exceptions.* The following are not excluded by the rule against hearsay if the declarant is unavailable as a witness:

(1) *Former Testimony.* Testimony that:

(A) was given as a witness at a trial, hearing, or lawful deposition, whether given during the current proceeding or a different one; and

(B) is now offered against a party who had—or, in a civil case, whose predecessor in interest had—an opportunity and similar motive to develop it by direct, cross-, or redirect examination.

(2) *Statement under the Belief of Imminent Death.* In a prosecution for homicide or in a civil case, a statement that the declarant, while believing the declarant's death to be imminent, made about its cause or circumstances.

(3) *Statement against Interest.* A statement that:

(A) a reasonable person in the declarant's position would have made only if the person believed it to be true because, when made, it was so contrary to the declarant's proprietary or pecuniary interest or had so great a tendency to invalidate the declarant's claim against someone else or to expose the declarant to civil or criminal liability; and

(B) is supported by corroborating circumstances that clearly indicate its trustworthiness, if it is offered in a criminal case as one that tends to expose the declarant to criminal liability.

(4) *Statement of Personal or Family History.* A statement about:

(A) the declarant's own birth, adoption, legitimacy, ancestry, marriage, divorce, relationship by blood, adoption, or marriage, or similar facts of personal or family history, even though the declarant had no

way of acquiring personal knowledge about that
fact; or

(B) another person concerning any of these facts, as
well as death, if the declarant was related to the
person by blood, adoption, or marriage or was so
intimately associated with the person's family that
the declarant's information is likely to be accurate.

(5) [*Other Exceptions.*] [Transferred to Rule 807.]

(6) *Statement Offered against a Party That Wrongfully
Caused the Declarant's Unavailability.* A statement
offered against a party that wrongfully caused—or
acquiesced in wrongfully causing—the declarant's
unavailability as a witness, and did so intending that
result.

Rule 805. Hearsay within Hearsay

Hearsay within hearsay is not excluded by the rule against hearsay
if each part of the combined statements conforms with an exception to the rule.

Rule 806. Attacking and Supporting
the Declarant's Credibility

When a hearsay statement—or a statement described in Rule 801(d)
(2)(C), (D), or (E)—has been admitted in evidence, the declarant's
credibility may be attacked, and then supported, by any evidence
that would be admissible for those purposes if the declarant had
testified as a witness. The court may admit evidence of the declarant's inconsistent statement or conduct, regardless of when it
occurred or whether the declarant had an opportunity to explain
or deny it. If the party against whom the statement was admitted

calls the declarant as a witness, the party may examine the declarant on the statement as if on cross-examination.

Rule 807. Residual Exception

(a) *In General.* Under the following circumstances, a hearsay statement is not excluded by the rule against hearsay even if the statement is not specifically covered by a hearsay exception in Rule 803 or 804:

    (1) the statement has equivalent circumstantial guarantees of trustworthiness;

    (2) it is offered as evidence of a material fact;

    (3) it is more probative on the point for which it is offered than any other evidence that the proponent can obtain through reasonable efforts; and

    (4) admitting it will best serve the purposes of these rules and the interests of justice.

(b) *Notice.* The statement is admissible only if, before the trial or hearing, the proponent gives an adverse party reasonable notice of the intent to offer the statement and its particulars, including the declarant's name and address, so that the party has a fair opportunity to meet it.

FRE 803—Exceptions to the Hearsay Rule

The hearsay exceptions compiled in FRE 803 apply regardless of the declarant's availability as a witness. An out-of-court statement governed by FRE 803 carries enough indicia of reliability to be admissible, despite the declarant's absence. In contrast, FRE 804 applies *only* where the declarant is unavailable. Considered somewhat less reliable, the court may consider these out-of-court statements only when the declarant is unavailable to testify in person. The exceptions contained in these two rules originated in the common law. "The present rule is a synthesis of them, with revision where modern developments and conditions are believed to make that course appropriate."[1]

In offering an out-of-court statement into evidence, before considering whether an exception to the hearsay rule applies, first determine whether the out-of-court statement is hearsay in the first place. For example, an admission of a party opponent is not hearsay; see FRE 801(d). Also, remember that even if a statement is not hearsay or if it falls within a recognized exception, it still could be barred on other grounds, such as relevance or authenticity.

A declarant's out-of-court statement, whether admissible as non-hearsay or under an exception, must derive from the declarant's personal knowledge (admissions being an exception to this general rule). The court can determine the basis of the declarant's knowledge by the witness's testimony or can infer it from the circumstances surrounding the declarant's statement. Ordinarily and subject to some exceptions,[2] the declarant's opinions, secondhand observations, and statements not derived from personal observations or knowledge are inadmissible.[3]

Present Sense Impression

FRE 803(1) allows an out-of-court statement that expresses a present sense impression. The rule defines a present sense impression as "a statement describing or explaining an event or condition, made while or immediately after the declarant perceived it." Distinguished from the excited utterance exception, discussed below,

---

1. *See* 56 F.R.D. 183, 303 Advisory Committee's Notes.
2. For example, admissions by a party opponent can include opinion testimony and lay opinions are admissible under certain circumstances.
3. See Chapter 14 where I discuss the proper subject matter of witness testimony.

a mundane observation can be the basis of the testimony under this rule; the present sense impression exception is not limited to a description of an exciting event or circumstance. The out-of-court statement must describe or explain the event. A critical judgment about the event, even one contemporaneously made, is inadmissible as a present sense impression. Thus, while witnesses may testify to what declarants said they observed or heard, witnesses may not testify to what declarants said about how the observation made them feel or another subjective thought related to the observation. According to *McCormick*, "the lack of a startling event makes the assumption of spontaneity difficult to maintain unless the statements directly pertain to perception."[4]

The statement describing the event must have been made at the time of the event or immediately after. A description made days or weeks after the event does not qualify under this exception. Did the declarant have time for reflection? If not, the statement may be admissible. If too much time has elapsed, the observation becomes spoiled: the opportunity for reflection interferes with its spontaneity.

Consider this example: Sally's next-door neighbor observes Sally's three-year-old child running around the yard unattended. The neighbor immediately calls the child's father, Henry, and tells him what she saw. In court, the father seeks to testify to what the neighbor told him. Sally's lawyer objects that the neighbor's statement is hearsay because it is offered for the truth of the matter asserted. Henry's lawyer argues the neighbor's statement was of a present sense impression, that is, it describes the event she saw and she made it contemporaneously with her perception of it. Henry's reiteration of the neighbor's statement is limited to what the neighbor saw or perceived. The rules disallow Henry from reporting any subjective comments by the neighbor.

---

4. 2 McCormick on Evidence, § 271 at 253 (footnote omitted) (Kenneth S. Broun, ed., Thomson West 6th ed. 2006).

Excited Utterance

FRE 803(2) allows admission of a statement made by a declarant under the stress of a startling event. In order for a statement to qualify as an excited utterance,

- there must have been an occurrence or event sufficiently startling to render inoperative the normal reflective thought processes of the observer;
- the statement of the declarant must have been a spontaneous reaction to the occurrence or event and not the result of reflective thought;
- the statement must relate to the event.[5]

This exception relies on the belief that the stress of an exciting event ensures its veracity.

To decide if an event is sufficiently startling to qualify for admission under this exception, the court must determine the likely effect on the declarant. The rule does not require an earthquake or tsunami—a wide range of events can qualify as sufficiently startling, including seeing a photograph in a newspaper.[6] Also, the declarant need not be personally involved with the startling event: the person may be affected as a bystander.

As with the present sense impression exception, spontaneity is key to admissibility. The statement must have been made contemporaneously with the startling event and before the declarant had an opportunity to reflect. Passage of time imposes a higher burden on the party offering the statement to qualify it as admissible. *McCormick* provides a useful test: "where the time interval between the event and the statement is long enough to permit reflective thought,

---

5.   2 McCormick on Evidence, *supra* note 4, § 272 at 255 (footnote omitted).
6.   United States v. Napier, 518 F.2d 316 (9th Cir. 1975).

the statement will be excluded in the absence of some proof that the declarant did not engage in a reflective thought process."[7] For example, testimony that the declarant appeared to be bright red, hyperventilating, and upset when he or she made the out-of-court statement might constitute this proof. Also the court needs to consider the context of the statement. For example, a court held that a statement made by a petrified child (who was found cowering under her covers at her parents' home) twelve hours after a murder was admissible as an excited utterance despite the passage of time since the actual murder.[8]

The excited utterance exception is not limited to the declarant's description of the event. The declarant's conclusions and opinions are also admissible if they qualify as excited utterances under this exception. In this way, the rule distinguishes itself from the present sense impression exception, which limits admissibility of declarants' out-of-court statements to their observations and precludes admission of their judgments or opinions. Thus, if an event is sufficiently startling to the declarant, a witness can testify to the declarant's hearsay statement, even if that statement contains conclusions, opinions, or other critical commentary.

The witness must provide some context for the declarant's statement. In other words, the witness must be able to testify that the declarant had firsthand knowledge of the event described. Conclusive proof of the declarant's personal observation is unnecessary. It is sufficient if the witness provides evidence of the general circumstances of declarant's observation, so the court can weigh the reliability of the declarant's observation. When there is doubt about whether the declarant directly observed the event, a lawyer seeking admission, or one arguing against admissibility, will need to persuade the judge to balance the probative value of the out-of-court

---

7. 2 McCormick on Evidence, *supra* note 4, § 272 at 258 (footnote omitted).
8. Gross v. Greer, 773 F.2d 116 (7th Cir. 1985).

statement against the likelihood that the declarant did not directly observe the event.

Child custody cases sometimes involve sexual abuse claims. The excited utterance exception allows a witness to testify to a child's report of abuse. Again, the court's focus is on the spontaneity of the statement. Courts nationwide are accepting longer time periods between the trauma and the child's description of it.[9] Some courts focus on when the child first had the opportunity to report the trauma rather than the interval between the event and its report.[10] Because of the sensitivity to child abuse, many states have drafted special hearsay legislation to address these circumstances.[11]

In family court, a party may be able to offer reliable evidence of abuse without a child's live testimony. Courts are reluctant to compel their appearance. Legislative trends reflect heightened sensitivity to the child witness.[12] These trends balance the child witness's rights against due process considerations.

If the child reported the claim to a parent, the parent's lawyer could seek to elicit the child's report of the abuse through the parent under the excited utterance exception. However, the other parent may seek to attack the credibility of the parent witness as inherently suspect because of bias. If a child reveals that he or she has been abused, the child should be taken to a hospital or a pediatrician, who will likely report the abuse to authorities. While still subject to scrutiny, a disclosure by a child to medical personnel or an official investigator may allow a disinterested witness to testify to the child's report.

---

9.   2 McCormick on Evidence, *supra* note 4, § 272.1 at 263-64.

10.   United States v. Rivera, 43 F.2d 1291 (9th Cir. 1995). *See also* 2 McCormick on Evidence, *supra* note 4, § 272 at 263 n.9

11.   2 McCormick on Evidence, *supra* note 4, at 264 n.11.

12.   2 McCormick on Evidence, *supra* note 4, § 272 at 265.

Then-Existing Mental, Emotional, or Physical Condition (the "State of Mind Exception")

FRE 803(3) allows as an exception to the hearsay rule: "A statement of the declarant's then-existing state of mind (such as motive, intent, or plan) or emotional, sensory, or physical condition (such as mental feeling, pain, or bodily health . . .)." This broad exception is a useful tool in any family law case. Sometimes referred to as the "state of mind exception," a witness may testify to a declarant's out-of-court statement concerning how the declarant felt at the time the statement was made. For example, a witness may testify to a third party's out-of-court statement reflecting the third party's mental condition.

Immediacy is again vital: the declarant's statement about his or her condition must be spontaneous. Testimony reprising a declarant's reminiscence about an earlier condition is not admissible under this exception; only testimony reporting a declarant's statement about conditions at the time the statement is made is admissible.

Rule 803(3) does not require that the witness to a declarant's statement about his or her present medical condition be a physician or health care provider. Any person who heard the declarant's statement can testify to it.[13]

Some courts and commentators have voiced concerns about allowing admission of a self-serving statement made by a declarant who has an agenda.[14] This concern does not automatically invalidate the evidence, however. The rules provide remedies for illegitimate testimony beyond the hearsay rules. Rule 403, which prohibits statements with questionable probative value, allows a court to refuse admission of unreliable evidence. Moreover, the value of the evidence must be distinguished from its technical admissibility.

---

13. 2 McCormick on Evidence, *supra* note 4, § 273 at 265.
14. 2 McCormick on Evidence, *supra* note 4, § 274 at 267–68 n.8

The state of mind exception can be useful in family law cases to offer evidence of a child's feelings or what they have experienced; it is a way to present the child's perspective, without actually involving the child as a witness in the proceeding. A child's mental state is frequently relevant in a family court proceeding. In custody and visitation matters, the court may consider the child's wishes. A child's complaint that "I have a stomachache every time I visit daddy" is an example of a permissible statement under this exception, if made immediately after the child returns from a visit. Keep in mind, however, that the credibility of the witness reporting the out-of-court statement is always at issue, and a court will closely scrutinize a report by a parent.

A party may be able to prove a gift with the state of mind exception. Donative intent is a state of mind; an out-of-court statement by a donor as to their intent to make a gift can be admissible under this exception. Generally, whenever motive or intent is relevant, this exception serves as a basis to offer an out-of-court statement of intent.

Statement Made for Medical Diagnosis or Treatment

FRE 803(4) allows admission of a statement made by a patient to a physician, related to the patient's diagnosis or treatment. Such a statement is presumed reliable because the patient would not likely fabricate symptoms since that could hamper treatment. Under this exception, admission is not limited to a statement made to a treating physician. The court can admit a declarant's statement made to any person helping the declarant obtain treatment, such as a family member or admitting nurse. The declarant's intent is more important than to whom the statement is made. "The test for admissibility is whether the subject matter of the statements is reasonably pertinent to diagnosis or treatment—an apparently objective standard."[15]

This exception may be used to offer into evidence a statement made by a child to a physician, as long as the statement is relevant. A number of courts have allowed a third-party witness to testify to a statement of a child to identify the perpetrator of sexual abuse on the basis that the statement is necessary to treat the child's injury.[16] But use of statements for this purpose is controversial.[17] As always, check local statutes and case law.

Recorded Recollection

The recorded recollection exception allows witnesses to rely on a memorandum or record when a lack of memory limits their ability to testify with specificity. Rule 803(5) provides that a recorded recollection is a record that

> (A) is on a matter the witness once knew about but now cannot recall well enough to testify fully and accurately; (B) was made or adopted by the witness when the matter was fresh in the witness's memory; and (C) accurately reflects the witness's knowledge.

The rule is interpreted expansively; "memorandum" has been construed to include a videotape or audio recording.

Here are the requirements for admission of a recorded recollection:[18]

---

15. 2 MCCORMICK ON EVIDENCE, *supra* note 4, § 277 at 287 (footnote omitted).
16. *See, e.g.,* 2 MCCORMICK ON EVIDENCE, *supra* note 4, § 278 at 290 n.8.
17. *Id.*
18. 2 MCCORMICK ON EVIDENCE, *supra* note 4, §§ 279–82.

- The memorandum must be from the firsthand knowledge of the witness. While this requirement does not mean the witness prepared the memorandum, it does require the witness to acknowledge it as accurate and adopt it as true.
- The memorandum must have been close enough in time to a particular event to guarantee its accuracy. While it does not need to be made contemporaneously, the memorandum must have been prepared when the information was still fresh in the author's mind.
- The witness must testify to having an impaired memory, that he or she has an insufficient recollection of the event. The rule does not require absolute memory loss—it only requires a showing of deficient recollection that impairs the witness's ability to testify fully and accurately.

When all of these requirements are met, the witness may read the memorandum into the record. The adverse party has the choice to offer the memorandum itself into evidence. Rule 803(5) allows only the adverse party to offer the memorandum into evidence.

In practice, many courts allow the admission of a memorandum of recorded recollection at the request of the proponent. For example, a divorce or custody litigant may keep a calendar or journal that logs events as they occur. Assuming the other requirements of the rule are met, a party could offer the calendar as a past recollection recorded. It is not likely that an appellate court would reverse a trial court's admission of the calendar under these circumstances, despite the rule's specific prohibition.[19] As a practical tip, many lawyers may stipulate to the admission of the document rather than sit through laborious testimony itemizing each event.

---

19. 2 McCormick on Evidence, *supra* note 4, § 279 at 295 n.11 (cases allowing the admission of the past recollection recorded).

Records of Regularly Conducted Activity (Business Records Exception)

Created as a practical way for courts to receive into evidence business records in commercial disputes, FRE 803(6) allows the admission of records kept in the ordinary course of business. *McCormick* provides the perspective: "The impetus for receiving these hearsay statements at common law arose when the person or persons who made the entry, and upon whose knowledge it was based, were unavailable because of death, disappearance or other reason."[20] Since these records are kept to aid an enterprise, they are presumably accurate. Commonly known as the business records exception, this hearsay exception allows for admission of bank records, credit card statements, medical records, and other documents in a divorce case. This exception would also allow a lawyer to offer billing records into evidence to prove fees.

FRE 803(6) allows admission of a "record of an act, event, condition, opinion, or diagnosis" under the following circumstances:

- It must have been made contemporaneously or shortly after an event occurred.
- It must have been made by a knowledgeable person.
- The recorded information must have been kept in the ordinary course of business.
- It must be the regular practice of the business to make the type of report being offered.

The rule defines business broadly and applies to any "business, organization, occupation, or calling, whether or not for profit."

Frequently businesses run reports compiling individual transactions. These compilations are admissible under this rule. A

---

20. 2 McCormick on Evidence, *supra* note 5, ch. 2, § 285 at 304.

compilation may serve as evidence of the individual transactions, although the rule does not preclude admission of the records of the underlying transactions themselves. A monthly credit card statement is an example of a compilation. A party need not offer the individual charge receipts separately as exhibits.

FRE 803(7) addresses the absence of an entry to prove that a transaction did not occur. The rule allows the proponent to use the absence of an entry to prove it did not occur when it was the type of transaction ordinarily recorded.

As noted above, the definition of the word *business* for both FRE 803(6) and 803(7) is expansive. The types of records covered by these two rules generally include the following:

- Medical or hospital records
- Police reports or criminal records
- School records
- Administrative child support collection reports
- Child protective services reports
- Diaries, notes or journals kept in the ordinary course of business (but not a personal diary)

FRE 803(6) and FRE 803(7) also apply to illegal activities. The business records exception applies to both legitimate and illegitimate ventures. Consult your state rules to determine what records are admissible as business records.

Records created solely for litigation purposes are not business records as defined in Rule 803(6).

Falsified records, if proven to be false, are also inadmissible under this exception.

To be admissible as a business record, the record must be recorded at or near the time of the transaction. An entry made months after an event is suspect because of faded memories and questionable motives. The trial court must consider the totality of the circumstances when weighing the timeliness of a recorded transaction. The longer the interval is between the event and the recording of the entry, the more doubtful it becomes and less likely to qualify for admission under this rule.

FRE 803(6) and 803(7) require that the record keeper have personal knowledge of the matter being recorded. The rules do not require, however, that the record keeper actually observe the transaction firsthand. Another employee who does have firsthand knowledge could report the transaction to the person recording it. All participants in the chain of record keeping who observe, report, and ultimately record the data must be acting within the ordinary scope of their assigned roles in the process. This rule would thus exclude statements in police reports or other reports from persons who are interviewed and not themselves acting within the scope of the business. For example, the neighbor who is interviewed by the child protective service and gives a statement is not working for the agency. The neighbor's statement is thus not admissible under this rule.[21] However, if the neighbor's statement qualifies under some other exception, for example, a present sense impression, the business record, which includes the statement could be admissible.

McCormick explains, "If any person in the process is not acting in the regular course of business, then an essential link in the trustworthiness chain fails, just as it does when the person feeding the information does not have firsthand knowledge."[22]

FRE 803(6) and 803(7) do not require that each actor in the recording chain testify. The custodian of the records or another person who has knowledge about the entire process can qualify as a witness. The proponent of the evidence must elicit from the witness the predicate foundation for admission of the records. While the custodian of the records would qualify under the rule, so would

---

21. *See* Johnson v. Lutz, 253 N.Y. 124, 170 N.E. 517 (1930).
22. 2 MCCORMICK ON EVIDENCE, *supra* note 24, § 290 at 314.

any other person with knowledge concerning the routine or process. The Senate Judiciary Committee revealed its understanding of this requirement:

> It is the understanding of the committee that the use of the phrase 'person with knowledge' is not intended to imply that the party seeking to introduce the memorandum, report, record, or data compilation must be able to produce, or even identify, the specific individual upon whose first-hand knowledge the memorandum, report, record, or data compilation was based. A sufficient foundation for the introduction of such evidence will be laid if the party seeking to introduce the evidence is able to show that it was the regular practice of the activity to base such memorandums, reports, records or data compilation upon a transmission from a person with knowledge. . . . In short, the scope of the phrase, 'person with knowledge' is meant to be coterminous with the custodian of the evidence or other qualified witness. [23]

The following is an example of laying a foundation for the admission of business records:

- What is your position with ABC Corp.? (Comptroller)
- Is your position full time or part time? (Full time)
- As comptroller, what do you do? (Oversee the financial operations of ABC Corp.)
- As such, are you familiar with the company protocol for maintaining its records? (Yes)
- Generally, can you describe the process of logging entries of income and payment of expenses? (Yes)

---

23. REPORT OF THE SENATE COMMITTEE ON THE JUDICIARY. SENATE COMM. ON JUDICIARY, FED. RULES OF EVIDENCE, S. REP. NO. 1277, 93rd Cong., 2d Sess., p.16 (1974); 1974 U.S. Code Cong. & Ad. News 7051, 7063.

- Please describe the process. (When a check comes in, . . .)
- Does the company prepare income statements? (Yes)
- I want to show you what I have identified as the Plaintiff's Group Exhibit Number 27 for identification. What are these documents? (ABC Corp. monthly income statements)
- How does the company use these statements? (We prepare them monthly to track our income and expenses, profitability, etc.)
- Your honor, I move to admit Plaintiff's Exhibit 27.[24]

Consistent with efforts to facilitate the admission of business records, the rules permit the record keeper to certify in writing to the authenticity of the business records. Under this procedure, the record keeper need not testify in person to lay the foundation for their admission. FRE 803(6) incorporates the provisions of FRE 902, which allows the admission of certified business records if the custodian of the records or other appropriate authority certifies in writing that

(a) the record was made at or near the time by—or from information transmitted by—someone with knowledge;

(b) the record was kept in the course of a regularly conducted activity of a business, organization, occupation, or calling, whether or not for profit;

(c) making the record was a regular practice of that activity.

Self-authenticated records can be admitted under this procedure without further foundation. FRE 902 requires advance written notice to any adverse party, allowing each party an opportunity to challenge his or her admission.

---

24. Keep in mind that these records may also be admitted as adoptive admissions if the opponent is the business owner and approved the financial statements.

Frequently in family law cases, lawyers subpoena credit card statements, bank statements or other business records. Rule 902 authorizes the admission of those records without calling the record keeper. The lawyer issuing the subpoena should prepare a certification that complies with FRE 902, and send it with the subpoena. Ask the record keeper to execute it, advising the person that its execution will avoid the necessity of a court appearance. Assuming the record keeper executes the certification, the subpoenaed business records are self-authenticated and admissible under the business records exception.

Computer-Generated Business Records

Courts have distinguished two types of computer records. If the computer itself makes the statement, it is considered *computer-generated evidence*. For example, a phone company computer automatically records phone numbers called, and there is no human input beyond the initial programming. The computer itself generates the potential evidence. Conversely, if a human inputs the data into the computer, it is considered *computer-stored evidence*. Computer-stored evidence is hearsay; it is an assertion by the person inputting the data.[25] Computer-generated evidence, in contrast, is not considered hearsay. A computer cannot make an assertion—only a person can.[26]

Both computer-stored and computer-generated data can be admissible as business records under Rules 803(6) and 803(7). The business records exception is applied no differently for computer data (stored or generated) than ink and paper records. To

---

25. *See In re* Marriage of DeLarco, 313 Ill. App. 3d 107, 728 N.E.2d 1278 (2000).

26. *See, e.g.,* Tatum v. State, 17 Va. App. 585, 440 S.E.2d 133 (1994) (holding that caller ID records were not hearsay as they are computer generated). *See also* State v. Armstead, 432 So. 2d 837 (La. 1983).

be admissible, the computer records need to reflect data recorded at or near the time of the event and must be kept in the ordinary course of business. The date of the printout does not determine timeliness; the salient date is when the data was recorded. [27]

However, to get computer records admitted into evidence, the lawyer must establish the viability of the hardware, software, and system security. Courts have liberally allowed these requirements to be satisfied by testimony that the computers were accurate and that the company relied on them in conducting business.[28] Today, courts recognize that computer processing is generally reliable and trustworthy.[29] In an era where computers are pervasive in all aspects of business, the burden has effectively shifted to the opponent of the evidence to show that the records are unreliable or invalid. Here is a sample foundation for the admission of computer records:

- Please state your name. (John Jones)
- What is your occupation? (I am the CFO of Acme Products)
- What are your job responsibilities? (I oversee all aspects of the finances of the business)
- Does ABC Products use a computer to store or record data? (Yes)
- What type of software does the company use to keep track of financial data? (It is a Windows-based platform. We rely on

---

27. Brown v. J.C. Penney Co., 297 Ore. 695 at 703, 688 P.2d 811 at 816 (1984) ("The printout is not the record; the printout is the means of making the record available for perusal by human beings").

28. *See also* United States v. Vela, 673 F.2d 86 (5th Cir. 1982) (government is not required to present expert testimony as to the mechanical accuracy of the computer where it presented evidence that the computer was sufficiently accurate that the company relied on it in conducting its business).

29. 2 MCCORMICK ON EVIDENCE, *supra* note 4, § 294 at 325 (footnote omitted). ("However, the trend here is not to require the proponent of the statement to call the programmer to lay the foundation for the admission. With regard to questions of inaccuracy and data security, courts have not imposed rigid requirements.")

QuickBooks to record all inflow and outflow, pay our vendors, record transactions, etc.)

- Have computer security procedures been implemented? (Yes. We have strong password protections and anti-hacking measures are in place.)
- At Acme, who is responsible for inputting data? (We have two employees that input data. I oversee them and prepare all reports)
- Sir, I want to show you Defendant's Exhibit 4. Do you recognize this document? (Yes)
- What is it? (It is a QuickBooks income statement for Acme for the first quarter of this year)
- Did you review this report for accuracy after it was reported? (Yes)
- Did Acme rely on this report? (Yes)
- Judge, I move for admission of Defendant's Exhibit 4.

Public Records or Reports

Rule 803(8) allows admission of records of activities that a public agency engaged in during the ordinary course of business. This rule allows admission of governmental reports, such as reports by the U.S. Census Bureau, municipal or state crime studies, and cost of living research by the U.S. Department of Agriculture. These types of reports may be relevant in a family law case. The quality of a community where a parent lives may influence the court in a best interest hearing. Also, a child support claim may be assisted by studies showing national cost of living averages. Rule 803(8) allows the admission of these types of studies or reports if relevant.

Not all government reports or investigations are admissible. The report must be final; interim or partial studies are not admissible.[30]

---

30. Toole v. McClintock, 999 F.2d 1430, 1434–35 (11th Cir. 1993).

Also, courts have rejected governmental reports based on the lack of skill or expertise by the investigator.[31] If the report lacks trustworthiness, the court can properly reject it, regardless of whether it is a product of the government. In determining whether a report is trustworthy, courts consider the following: "the timeliness of the investigation, the skill or experience of the investigator, whether a formal hearing was held, and the bias of the investigator."[32] The court need not conduct a full hearing to determine these requirements; the general requirements of trustworthiness need only be satisfied facially. Assuming the judge finds the report trustworthy, the burden shifts to the opponent to establish that the report is untrustworthy.[33] Assuming a report is not challenged or the challenge is defeated, the exhibit would be admitted under this rule, allowing the court to consider the data. Ultimately, of course, the exhibit must also pass the relevancy test.

Another similar rule, FRE 803(9), provides a hearsay exception for public records related to births, deaths, and marriages "if reported to a public office in accordance with a legal duty." Vital statistics kept by a public agency fall within this rule. A marriage record submitted by a minister to a government agency and a hospital death record are admissible as hearsay exceptions under this rule. For the exception to apply, the record must be prepared as part of the *official duty* of the record keeper. A tax return prepared by a paid preparer is not considered a public record because the tax preparer is not an official of the government (although the return may be admissible under another rule).

Rule 803(10) speaks to the absence of a recorded entry in public documents. This rule mirrors the provision of Rule 803(7), which pertains to omissions in business records. Rule 803(10) provides

---

31. Matthews v. Ashland Chem., Inc., 770 F.2d 1303, 1309–10 (5th Cir. 1985).
32. 2 McCormick on Evidence, *supra* note 4, § 296 at 330 (footnote omitted).
33. Bridgeway Corp. v. Citibank, 201 F.3d 134, 143–44 (2d Cir. 2000).

that an omission in records regularly maintained by a public office or agency may be admitted through a certification of the absence of a particular record. Specifically the rule states, "Testimony—or a certification under Rule 902—that a diligent search failed to disclose a public record or statement if the testimony or certification is admitted to prove that: (A) the record or statement does not exist; or (B) a matter did not occur or exist, if a public office regularly kept a record or statement for a matter of that kind."[34]

Religious and Family Records

Rule 803(11) allows the admission of a religious organization's records relating to the following: births, marriages, divorces, deaths, legitimacy, ancestry, relationship by blood or marriage, and other similar facts of personal or family history.

Rule 803(12) allows as a hearsay exception a factual statement in a certificate to prove that the certificate's maker performed a ceremony, such as a marriage, baptism, or bar mitzvah. The certificate itself, without further evidence, proves the event. The maker of the certificate could include a clergyman, public official, or other person authorized by law to perform the act certified. When the maker of the certificate is not a public official, additional foundational proof is necessary to show that the maker was authorized and did make the certificate. The rule specifically requires that the certification be timely. It must be executed contemporaneously or shortly after the event.

Rule 803(13) allows the admission of hearsay statements about personal or family history found in family records, including family

---

34. FRE 902 pertains to self-authentication of documents, and that procedure is discussed in Chapter 9.

Bibles, genealogies, charts, engravings, or other statements made
in family heirlooms or other intergenerational memorabilia.

Records of Documents Affecting
an Interest in Property

Real estate transactions often need to be proven in family law cases.
Under FRE 803(14), a recorded document, such as a deed or a
car title, is admissible to prove the transaction. The rule assumes
the reliability of a properly recorded instrument. Additionally, the
recorded document evidences its execution and delivery. Obtain
a certified copy of the recorded document from the Recorder of
Deed's office or the Department of Motor Vehicles as the actual
exhibit, as opposed to a copy from your client's own file. Admission
of the document proves the transaction without additional evidence.
FRE 803(15) expands the preceding rule by allowing admission
of the recitals of fact in the deed. For example, a deed may recite
that the person executing the deed had power of attorney for the
record owner. The recital is admissible to prove the transferor did
in fact have a power of attorney without your having to put the
power of attorney in evidence or produce a live witness to prove
its existence.

Ancient Documents

Rule 803(16) excepts ancient documents from the hearsay rule.
An ancient document is a document that is at least 20 years old.
McCormick notes that, while the rule does not specifically require
it, the proponent must at least facially show that the declarant or
the author of the document had firsthand knowledge of the facts
stated in the document when the document was made. That the

declarant had such knowledge can be inferred from the circumstances. *McCormick* comments on this requirement, "Given the passage of time, proving personal knowledge will often be impossible and should not be imposed, but the proponent may properly be required to show from the circumstances that the declarant could have had firsthand knowledge."[35] Additionally, the evidence must not be suspicious in appearance and must be considered reliable by the court.

Family lawyers sometimes confront property classification issues involving transactions going back many decades. For example, a parent transfers property or cash to an adult child, and a question arises during the child's divorce about the nature of the conveyance, for example, whether it was a loan or a gift. This rule allows the admission of relevant documents that are at least 20 years old without also offering the testimony of the author of the document. Therefore, even if the parent has since died, the lawyer for a party could offer into evidence a letter written by the parent more than 20 years before, that discusses a loan to be repaid.

Market Reports and Similar Commercial Publications

"Market quotations, lists, directories, or other compilations that are generally relied on by the public or by persons in particular occupations" are admissible under FRE 803(17) as an exception to the hearsay rule. Stock market reports found in the *Wall Street Journal* are included in this exception, which is an easy and practical way to prove the value of securities on a particular day. But, in what other ways could a lawyer creatively employ this rule? Arguably data acquired by a Google search is a compilation. A party could argue that the rule applies to the real estate valuation

---

35. 2 McCormick on Evidence, *supra* note 4, § 323 at 402 n.15.

website Zillow or other similar websites that compile data, or that the public uses resources such as the Kelley Blue Book or Edmunds to value vehicles. A party can use this exception to seek admission of these records to prove the value of an automobile.[36] Help-wanted ads in a newspaper could be admissible under this rule to refute a chronically unemployed spouse's claim that there are no jobs available. A brochure published by a local chamber of commerce to induce potential residents to move to the area may be admissible under this exception in a relocation case. As *McCormick* observes,

> While the precise definition of this exception is somewhat difficult, other than by example, some of its basic characteristics are clear. The list must be published in written form and circulated for use by others; it must be relied upon by the general public or by persons in a particular occupation; and it must pertain to relatively straightforward objective facts.[37]

McCormick's comments suggest defenses to the admission of this data. A party may argue that the information contained in a report includes subjective assumptions by the publisher, and the policy behind the rule to admit "relatively straightforward objective facts" prohibits this particular report because it is not objective and thus unreliable.

The information allowed by this exception is the core of many simple divorce cases. Be prepared to cite it for the admission of routine financial information, including valuation of motor vehicles, interest rates, stock values, and so on. But as always, be prepared to address reliability and authentication concerns before admission.

---

36. *See, e.g.,* Grossman v. United States, 614 F.2d 295 (1st Cir. 1980) (where a company catalogue was admitted to prove the value and identity of stolen merchandise (cigarette lighters)).

37. 2 McCORMICK ON EVIDENCE, *supra* note 4, § 321 at 395 (footnotes omitted).

Learned Treatises

In formulating a report, an expert may rely on scholarly or scientific treatises or articles. The law allows an expert to consider source materials that are not in evidence. Rule 803(18) provides that if an expert relies on a statement contained in "treatises, periodicals, or pamphlets" and if the court considers the treatise reliable, the statement may be read into evidence. The substantive use of learned treatises is controversial. Some states have laws limiting the admission of a statement in a learned treatise to impeachment of the expert and disallowing admission of such a statement as substantive evidence, that is, for the truth of the matter asserted in the treatise.[38] The federal rules drafters disagreed with this limited approach; the federal rules allow such a statement as substantive evidence, as well as for impeachment. If an expert testifies on direct examination to information in a scholarly source, or if the opponent seeks to cross-examine the expert on information in such a source, the referenced statement may be read into the record as substantive evidence unless the court determines the reference unreliable.

FRE 803(18) applies to statements "contained in a treatise, periodical, or pamphlet." The rule is to be interpreted broadly.[39] Case law has extended the rule to include industry and other professional or governmental standards manuals.[40] At least one court has even qualified as a learned treatise a videotape prepared by a trade organization deemed reliable by the trial court.[41] It is the content that is important, not the medium.

---

38. 2 McCormick on Evidence, *supra* note 4, § 321 at 391 to 395.
39. 2 McCormick on Evidence, *supra* note 4, § 321 at 393 (quoting Fed. R. Evid. 803(18)).
40. *See, e.g.,* McKinnon v. Skil Corp., 638 F.2d 270 (1st Cir. 1981); Dawson v. Chrysler Corp., 630 F.2d 950 (3d Cir. 1980); Johnson v. William C. Ellis & Sons Iron Works, Inc., 609 F.2d 820 (5th Cir. 1980).
41. Costantino v. Herzog, 203 F.3d 164 (2d Cir. 2000).

This is an important rule for family lawyers. Family lawyers regularly rely on expert testimony. Cross-examining an opposing expert with a scholarly article that contradicts their testimony can impugn their credibility and, at the same time, enhance your expert's testimony. The rule also allows the out-of-court statement itself to serve as your expert by allowing the court to consider the learned treatise for the truth of the matters contained in it.

For example, assume two experts disagree on the interplay between depreciation and capital expenditures in a business valuation in the normalization process. One, in support of his or her argument, relies on a learned treatise by a nationally recognized expert on business valuation. The expert testifies that the treatise is well regarded in the valuation community and served as the "textbook" for the National Association of Certified Valuation Analysts. The opposing expert testifies the treatise lacks credibility, but without a competing treatise as authority, the court deems that this expert's testimony lacks weight. The treatise, in this example, became the third expert in the case.

If you intend to use a treatise to impeach an opposing expert, do not expect the expert to acknowledge the treatise's authority, particularly if the expert is going to be demolished by it. Develop alternative ways to lay the foundation for its authority. One option is to seek a stipulation prior to trial. Also consider using a request to admit that the desired source is authoritative in the field. But be careful: smart lawyers will check with their expert to see whether he or she ever cited or relied on the treatise before agreeing to its reliability as a treatise, and the expert may then have enough time to anticipate and fend off the attack. Other options include having your expert lay the foundation for the reliability of the impeaching treatise. Or, if an expert is not otherwise necessary for your case, one could be hired for the sole purpose of confirming the reliability of an impeachment source. During the discovery process, determine whether the opposing expert relied on any particular treatises and then plan how to impeach the expert with those sources. While it is possible that a court could judicially notice the reliability of a treatise, do not rely on judicial notice to support the admission of a crucial piece of evidence, particularly if it is academic or technical in nature.

Reputation Evidence

FRE 803(19), (20), and (21) address admissibility of reputation evidence as hearsay exceptions. Reputation evidence generally consists of testimony of a member of a community to another member's general reputation in that community. Certain facts, having become so ingrained in the community consciousness, are deemed trustworthy enough to be allowed into evidence, as the rule drafters note: "when the topic is such that the facts are likely to have been inquired about and that persons having personal knowledge have disclosed facts which have thus been discussed in the community; and thus the community's conclusion, if any has been formed, is likely to be a trustworthy one."[42] FRE 803(19) speaks to reputation regarding family relationships and FRE 803(20) addresses land boundaries. Rule 803(21) allows evidence of reputation of character.

FRE 803(19) allows reputation testimony concerning "the person's birth, adoption, legitimacy, ancestry, marriage, divorce, death, relationship by blood, adoption, or marriage, or similar facts of personal or family history." This rule is somewhat anachronistic in an era where DNA and other scientific evidence largely prove family relationships. And it is rare (outside of parentage court) that lawyers need to prove a family relationship as an element of a case.

---

42. *See* FED. R. EVID. 803 Advisory Committee's Note (citing 5 Wigmore, EVIDENCE § 1580 at 444).

The rule allows reputation evidence about family relationships or family history by the family members themselves, associates of the family, or a member of the community at large. Two other related rules are Rule 803(23), which allows admission of a judgment as proof of a family relationship, and Rule 804(b)(4), which permits testimony reporting an out-of-court statement about family history or relationships when the declarant is unavailable.[43]

FRE 803(20) allows reputation testimony concerning land boundaries. This rule may be invoked concerning disputes about the boundaries of the family farm/ranch where some of the land was premarital or inherited and some was bought and paid for during the marriage.

FRE 803(21) provides a hearsay exception for evidence concerning a person's reputation among associates in the community. This exception allows only general reputation testimony, not testimony of particular instances of conduct.[44] The evidence still must be relevant and conform with FRE 404 and FRE 405, the rules pertaining to character evidence.[45]

Judgments

FRE 803(22) provides a hearsay exception for a court judgment reflecting a previous criminal conviction, if the following conditions are met:

(1)   Only a prior criminal conviction or plea of guilty is allowed. A civil judgment, judgment of acquittal, or a plea of nolo contendere is excluded under this rule.

---

43.   FRE 804(b)(4) is addressed in the next chapter and applies only when the declarant is unavailable to testify.

44.   State v. Marshall, 312 Ore. 367, 823 P.2d 961 (1991).

45.   *See, e.g.,* Schweitzer-Reschke v. Avnet, Inc., 881 F. Supp. 530 (D. Kan. 1995).

(2) The rule only applies to a conviction of a serious crime (defined as a crime punishable by death or by imprisonment of over a year).

(3) In a civil case there are no restrictions on whom a criminal conviction can be used against.[46]

The above discussion only relates to admissibility of a criminal judgment as a hearsay exception. All other rules of relevance apply to the admission of judgments, and the evidence is still subject to limitations on the use of character evidence.[47]

Rule 803(23) applies to a judgment pertaining to "personal, family, or general history or boundaries." This rule allows admission of a court judgment as evidence, if the same fact could be proven by reputation testimony under Rule 803(20).

FRE 804—Hearsay Exceptions That Require Witness Unavailability

FRE 804 contains four hearsay exceptions for certain out-of-court declarations but only when the declarant is unavailable. These types of declarations are less reliable than those in Rule 803. Mauet and Wolfson observe, "All of the exceptions of FRE 804(b) reflect a strong preference for the in-court presence of the declarant. That is, testimony given on the witness stand is preferred over hearsay, but hearsay, if reliable, is preferred over a complete loss of the evidence."[48]

---

46. 2 McCormick on Evidence, *supra* note 4, § 298 at 339 ("When the judgment of conviction is offered in a civil case, however, it is treated as are investigative reports generally, and there is no restriction as to the parties against whom the evidence is admissible").

47. In chapter _____ on impeachment, I discuss the concept of using prior convictions to impeach a witness.

48. Thomas A. Mauet & Warren D. Wolfson, Trial Evidence 166 (4th ed. 2009).

Rule 804 permits admission of the following types of hearsay only when the proponent can prove that the declarant is unavailable to testify as a witness:

- Testimony from a former hearing or court proceeding
- Statement under the belief of impending death
- A statement against interest
- A statement of personal or family history
- A statement offered against a party that results in the witness's unavailability

Unavailability Defined

Unavailability is determined by the witness's availability to testify, rather than his or her physical absence from or presence at trial. "Witnesses may be physically present in court but their testimony nevertheless unavailable."[49] Rule 804(a) lists five examples of unavailability. A witness is unavailable if the witness

(1) is exempted from testifying about the subject matter of the declarant's statement because the court rules that a privilege applies;

(2) refuses to testify about the subject matter despite a court order to do so;

(3) testifies to not remembering the subject matter;

(4) cannot be present or testify at the trial or hearing because of death or a then-existing infirmity, physical illness, or mental illness; or

(5) is absent from the trial or hearing and the statement's proponent has not been able, by process or other reasonable means, to procure:

---

49. 2 MCCORMICK ON EVIDENCE, *supra* note 4, § 253 at 166-67.

(A)   the declarant's attendance, in the case of a hearsay exception under Rule 804(b)(1) or (6); or

(B)   the declarant's attendance or testimony, in the case of a hearsay exception under Rule 804(b)(2), (3), or (4).

The proponent of the hearsay evidence under FRE 804 must attempt to secure the attendance of the declarant as a witness at trial, and the proponent must show an inability to do so either by subpoena or by other reasonable means. If the declarant cannot be found, the proponent must establish that he or she made a good faith effort to locate the person.[50] The search requirement is less onerous in civil cases, where constitutional confrontation requirements do not apply, than in criminal cases.[51] Ultimately, the trial court has discretion to determine the adequacy of the search.

An even higher standard applies to certain subcategories of evidence under Rule 804. The proponent must also show that he or she could not have deposed the unavailable witness when the proponent seeks admission of a

- statement under belief of impending death under 804(b)(2);
- statement against interest under 804(b)(3); or
- statement of personal or family history under 804(b)(4).

For example, assume Douglas, the husband's business partner, told Wanda that he and her husband have been laundering cash for years (a statement against interest). In order for Wanda to testify to this out-of-court statement, she has to establish that Douglas is now unavailable to testify and that she could not have taken his deposition. For example, Douglas may have left the country or his lawyer may have filed a motion to quash a subpoena for

---

50. Ohio v. Roberts, 448 U.S. 56 (1980).
51. 2 McCormick on Evidence, *supra* note 4, § 253 at 170-71.

a deposition on Fifth Amendment grounds and the motion was granted. Assuming Wanda can establish Douglas's unavailability, the court would permit her to testify to the out-of-court statement by Douglas.

Some courts and legislatures have found children to be unavailable merely by virtue of their minority. The federal rules have no such provision.[52] Some courts have found unavailability based on the emotional trauma the testimony would cause the child.[53]

Exceptions—Prior Testimony

If an unavailable witness testified under oath in an earlier court proceeding and the adverse party had the opportunity to examine the witness, Rule 804(b)(1) allows the earlier testimony as a hearsay exception. The issues in the two proceedings must be similar but need not be identical. The standard for admissibility is whether the issues in the first proceeding were substantially similar to those in the current proceeding and whether the adverse party had a sufficient motive for cross-examination in the first proceeding. If so, the earlier testimony may be offered as an acceptable substitute for the live testimony of the witness. There are four ways of offering this type of earlier testimony:

(1)   A firsthand observer to the earlier testimony may testify from memory as long as the witness can satisfy the court that they can fairly report the substance of the earlier testimony.

(2)   A firsthand observer can use a memorandum or notes that refresh their recollection and allow them to testify to the earlier testimony.

---

52. *See, e.g.,* Kansas Stat. Ann. § 60-459(g)(2) (2009).
53. *E.g.,* State v. Robinson, 153 Ariz. 191, 735 P.2d 801 (Ariz. 1987).

(3) An unavailable witness's notes or memoranda prepared at or shortly after the first hearing may be used as past recollection recorded at the later trial.

(4) Presentation of an official certified transcript of the earlier proceeding.[54]

A certified transcript is certainly the most compelling medium under these circumstances. Without a transcript, the opportunity to present prior testimony may be lost. Good practice demands a record at any evidentiary hearing. Finally, keep in mind that a court can take judicial notice of an earlier proceeding between the parties.[55]

A lawyer can use FRE 804(b)(1) to offer deposition testimony of a witness who has become unavailable for trial. If health problems or other legitimate reasons might prevent witnesses from attending the trial, depose them while they are still available and offer the salient portions of their testimony under 804(b)(1). Consider this rule for potential witnesses who are elderly or infirm, particularly if their testimony could be critical and a reasonable chance exists that they might be unavailable for trial.

Dying Declaration

The second exception under this rule, FRE 804(b)(2), applies to a statement made under the belief of an impending death. This type of statement is commonly known as a "dying declaration." The exception for a dying declaration allows a declarant's out-of-court statement concerning the cause or circumstances of his or her death. In order to use this exception, the declarant must believe death is imminent when he or she makes the statement.

---

54. 2 McCormick on Evidence, *supra* note 4, § 307 at 359-60.
55. See Chapter 8 on judicial notice.

This belief may be shown by the declarant's own statement or by the overall circumstances. The declarant need not actually die—the person must only believe that death was certain and imminent. If the declarant survives, he or she still must be unavailable for the hearing in order for the rule to apply. This rule applies in all civil cases, including family law cases.

Statements against Interest

FRE 804(b)(3) defines a statement against interest as any statement that would harm the declarant's interests. Like all of the exceptions under FRE 804, such a statement is admissible as an exception to the hearsay rule *only* where the declarant is unavailable to testify. A statement is against a declarant's interest

- if the statement is contrary to the declarant's pecuniary or proprietary interest;
- if the statement tends to subject the declarant to civil or criminal liability; or
- if the statement renders invalid a claim by the declarant against another.

For example, a husband's business partner makes a statement to the wife shortly before the divorce. "You know," the partner says, "we have not been accurately disclosing our true income to the IRS for years." After making this statement, but before a deposition or trial, the business partner dies. The wife could testify to the partner's statement under the declaration against interest exception. When the statement was made, it subjected the now-deceased partner to criminal liability for tax evasion and was therefore a declaration against his interest.

The declarant's statement must be objectively reliable. The rule specifically provides that the statement against interest is one that "a reasonable person in the declarant's position would have made only if the person believed it to be true." To be admissible, a statement cannot be a wild exaggeration or made by a mentally ill person suffering from delusions. It must be a statement by a reasonable person consciously compromising herself. Additional evidence is permitted to prove or disprove whether the declarant's statement reflects an intentional statement against interest.[56]

Admissions Distinguished from Declarations against Interest

Do not confuse a declaration against interest with a party admission. *McCormick* succinctly distinguishes the two rules:

> Unlike declarations against interest, admissions of a party opponent are allowed even if they are self-serving at the time they are made. Another difference is that the party making the admission need not be unavailable at trial for the admission to be allowed. Also, the person making the admission need not have had personal knowledge of the fact being admitted, unlike the declaration against interest exception that requires the declarant to be personally aware of the fact alleged. Finally, a party (or the party's agent or representative) must make an admission. A statement against interest can be made by anyone, assuming the requirements of the rule are met.[57]

---

56. *See, e.g.,* State v. Woodman, 125 N.H. 381, 480 A.2d 169 (1984).
57. 2 McCormick on Evidence, *supra* note 4, § 316 at 375 (citing 5 Wigmore, Evidence § 1475 (Chadbourn rev. 1974)).

Statement of Personal or Family History

Rule 804(b)(4) expands the rule laid out in Rule 803 concerning proof of a family relationship. FRE 803 allows a party to prove a family relationship by records (ordinarily hearsay) and reputation testimony. Rule 804(b)(4) goes one step further and allows admission of an actual statement concerning the family relationship. Unlike FRE 803, FRE 804(b)(4) allows testimony concerning the relationship, but, again, only when the declarant is demonstrably unavailable.

McCormick observes, "One of the oldest exceptions to the hearsay rule encompasses statements concerning family history, such as the date and place of birth and death of members of the family and facts about marriage, descent, and relationship."[58] Rule 804(b)(4) specifically allows a witness to testify to an out-of-court statement by a declarant concerning his or her "own birth, adoption, legitimacy, ancestry, marriage, divorce, relationship by blood, adoption, or marriage, or similar facts of personal or family history." The rule permits a witness who has no firsthand knowledge of an event (the declarant's birthday, for example) to testify to an out-of-court statement by another person about the event, ordinarily considered hearsay.

Forfeiture by Wrongdoing

The final exception in FRE 804 is for a statement offered against a party whose improper action caused a witness's absence. Under 804(b)(6), a party may forfeit the right to object to admission of a declarant's out-of-court statement if the party wrongfully caused the declarant to be absent as a witness. Consider the following:

---

58. 2 MCCORMICK ON EVIDENCE, *supra* note 4, § 322 at 396 (footnote omitted).

Norma, a neighbor of the family, regularly saw Wanda, the wife, using cocaine while Wanda's children were present. Norma told Wanda's husband, Harold, about this and he then added Norma to his witness list. One day before the trial, Wanda, pretending to be a paralegal from the office of Harold's lawyer, calls Norma. Wanda advises Norma that the trial was continued and that she would not need to appear. Norma did not appear. If Harold can prove that Wanda was behind Norma's unavailability, Harold's lawyer could seek to elicit from Harold Norma's hearsay statement about Wanda's drug use. However, the more practical solution would be to seek to reopen the proofs to permit Norma to testify later.

This rule prevents a party from benefitting from his or her subversive act. Because of the nature of the improper conduct, courts have liberally construed this rule to allow hearsay statements under these circumstances.[59] The rule requires that the conduct be wrongful and that it actually result in the witness's absence. The trial judge must make these necessary preliminary findings based on a preponderance of evidence.[60] Consistent with the intent to prohibit misconduct, the proof of this conduct may be made by circumstantial evidence. With regard to such proof, "courts have generally taken a generous view."[61]

Hearsay within Hearsay: FRE 805

If a declarant makes an out-of-court statement that reports a statement made to him or her by another person, both of the statements are hearsay. Admission of each statement requires an independent exception. If an exception does not exist for each hearsay statement,

---

59. *See* United States v. Gray, 405 F.3d 227 (4th Cir. 2005), 2 McCormick on Evidence, *supra* note 4, § 253 at 176.

60. United States v. Scott, 284 F.3d 758 (7th Cir. 2002).

61. 2 McCormick on Evidence, *supra* note 4, § 253 at 176 (footnote omitted).

the entire statement is excluded. The committee comments illustrate this principle:

> Thus a hospital record might contain an entry of the patient's age based upon information furnished by his wife. The hospital record would qualify as a regular entry except that the person who furnished the information was not acting in the routine of the business. However her statement independently qualifies as a statement of pedigree (if she is unavailable) or as a statement made for purposes of diagnosis or treatment, and hence each link in the chain falls under sufficient assurances.[62]

Business records often reflect examples of multiple hearsay statements. If the records are kept routinely in the business, the primary record is admissible under the business records exception. As the above example illustrates, if an additional statement within the record incorporates a statement by a person not acting routinely in the business, the entire record is inadmissible. "Double hearsay exists when a business record is prepared by one employee from information supplied by another; [an] outsider's statement must fall within another hearsay exception to be admissible because it does not have the presumption of accuracy that statements made during the regular course of business have."[63]

Impeaching the Out-of-Court Declarant: FRE 806

A party may challenge the credibility of an out-of-court declarant when the declarant's hearsay statement is admitted. Rule 806 treats the out-of-court declarant as though he or she was in court

---

62. FED. R. EVID. 805 Advisory Committee's Note.
63. United States v. Baker, 693 F.2d 183, 188 (D.C. Cir. 1982).

testifying at the hearing. Thus, the judge can weigh the credibility of both the witness who is testifying to the out-of-court statement as well as the declarant whose statement is the basis of the testimony.

The absent declarant may be impeached by any method available for physically present witnesses. The rule applies to any out-of-court statement that is admitted, whether the statement is hearsay under Rules 803 and 804 or nonhearsay admitted under Rule 801. For example, a prior or subsequent inconsistent statement of the declarant could be used to impeach that declarant. This rule eliminates the usual impeachment requirement that the witness be given an opportunity to deny or explain the inconsistency; the declarant is ordinarily not before the court to offer an explanation. But if the adverse party calls that declarant as a witness, the adverse party may cross-examine that witness.

For example, Larry is unavailable to testify. Sally's lawyer offers into evidence the transcript of Larry's deposition in which Larry testified that he observed Fred neglecting his children. Fred's lawyer could offer evidence that Larry and Sally are lovers to show that Larry was biased and therefore his out-of-court statement was not credible.

The Residual Exception: FRE 807

Rule 807 is the catchall exception that allows reliable hearsay evidence when no other exception applies under Rules 803 and 804. FRE 807 employs a balancing test and allows an out-of-court statement if

(a)   the statement has equivalent circumstantial guarantees of trustworthiness;

(b)   it is offered as evidence of a material fact;

(c)   it is more probative on the point for which it is offered than any other evidence that the proponent can obtain through reasonable efforts; and

(d)   admitting it will best serve the purposes of these rules and the interests of justice.

The proponent of the evidence must give the adverse party reasonable advance notice of the intent to rely on the exception, including the substance of the out-of-court statement and the name and address of the declarant.

Courts have considered the following factors in permitting evidence under this rule:

- Whether the declarant had a motivation to speak truthfully or otherwise
- The spontaneity of the statement, including whether it was elicited by leading questions, and generally the time lapse between the event and the statement
- Whether the statement was under oath
- Whether the declarant was subject to cross-examination at the time the statement was made
- Whether the declarant has recanted or reaffirmed the statement
- Whether the statement was recorded and particularly whether it was videotaped
- Whether the declarant's firsthand knowledge is clearly demonstrated[64]

While it seems somewhat counterintuitive, the one factor the court should *not* consider in determining admissibility is the credibility

---

64. 2 McCormick on Evidence, *supra* note 4, § 324 at 405–07 (footnotes omitted).

of the witness testifying to the statement.[65] The reporter is irrelevant to the reliability of the out-of-court statement.

To qualify under the residual exception, the evidence must be "more probative on the point for which it is offered than any other evidence that the proponent can obtain through reasonable efforts." Courts have inconsistently applied this requirement. Some courts have applied a utilitarian approach, admitting hearsay under this rule where the costs of obtaining alternative evidence would be prohibitive. [66] Other courts have taken a qualitative approach to the evidence. These courts have considered the quality of the out-of-court statement against other considerations such as the burden on the witness.[67] According to McCormick, this qualitative approach imposes a "rough 'best-evidence'" standard on the evidence. Unless the out-of-court statement is superior, it cannot be used.[68]

The residual rule allows trustworthy hearsay evidence that otherwise does not qualify under Rules 803 or 804. But, the rule is not limited to the occasions where no exception exists. It also applies where an exception exists but the proponent cannot meet its exact provisions. For example, in *United States v. Wilson*, 249 F. 3d 366, 374–76 & n.5 (5th Cir. 2001), the court allowed foreign banking records under the residual exception when no custodian was available to testify to the appropriate foundation required by Rule 803(6).[69] Consider this rule where strict standards of admission cannot be met but the evidence is nevertheless trustworthy and important for the court to consider. In trial planning, be prepared

---

65. *Id.* at 407.

66. United States v. Simmons, 773 F.2d 1455 (4th Cir. 1985).

67. State v. Ransom, 124 Idaho 703, 864 P.2d 149 (1993) (use of a videotaped interview of an allegedly abused developmentally disabled child is superior to live testimony due to lapse of time and potential trauma to her).

68. 2 McCormick on Evidence, *supra* note 5, ch. 2, § 324 at 409.

69. *See also* United States v. Clarke, 2 F.3d 81, 83–84 (4th Cir. 1993) (a failure to meet standards of other exceptions does not disqualify the residual exception); United States v. Laster, 258 F.3d 525, 530 (6th Cir. 2001).

to argue admissibility under the primary rules (803 and 804), as well as this residual exception.

Rule 807 has frequently been applied in cases involving children, in particular sexual abuse cases in which other exceptions are unavailable. Common factors courts have considered in allowing a child's hearsay statement under the residual exception include

- the spontaneity and consistency of the statement;
- the general proposition that young children do not invent allegations of the type involved;
- the unusualness of explicit sexual knowledge by a young child;
- use of childish terminology to describe sex.[70]

The cases, however, tend to disallow admission of responses to leading questions by interrogators.[71] This rule is a helpful resource for admission of a statement by a child that would not otherwise qualify under a standard exception. From a defensive perspective, be prepared to oppose the admission of this type of hearsay by arguing lack of notice of intent to use the residual exception (if applicable), improper influence on the child's statement at the time it was made, or doubt about the circumstances under which the statement was made.

Expert Testimony—Rule 703

FRE 703 allows an expert to base an opinion on inadmissible statements of facts if experts ordinarily rely on such statements of fact in formulating an opinion. These statements of fact are not admitted for the truth of the matters asserted; rather, they serve as

---

70. 2 McCormick on Evidence, *supra* note 4, § 324 at 411 (footnotes omitted).
71. *Id.*

the basis of the expert's opinion. As a result, the expert's testimony that relies on these out-of-court statements is not hearsay. As a practical matter, potentially inadmissible hearsay evidence can get before the court through an expert's testimony.[72] But this exception to the rule is not absolute. Under Rule 703, the court needs to weigh the probative value against the prejudice of the evidence. In other words, if an expert relies on hearsay statements, even if the reliance is proper, the court still can exclude that portion of the report if it determines that the ultimate effect is more prejudicial than probative. While this provision is probably more meaningful in a jury trial, it nevertheless can serve as a basis to object to inflammatory hearsay statements by experts.

Practice Points

- Determine whether an oral or written statement is hearsay first. If not, there is no need to determine whether it is admissible under an exception.
- Plan in advance for evidentiary problems. You should not discover at the trial that there is a hearsay problem. Formally prepare a proof chart for all of the issues in the case and anticipate evidentiary problems and their solutions well in advance of the trial. Bring case law as authority. Consider various alternative theories of admissibility.
- Consider using an expert for the purpose of getting admission of crucial hearsay evidence that would be otherwise inadmissible.
- Do not forget about Rule 807, the residual hearsay exception, for vital evidence that may otherwise be inadmissible. Reliance on this rule requires advance notice, so plan ahead.

---

72. See Chapter 14 on expert witnesses and the scope of their testimony.

- Learned treatises allow the court access to information from unaffordable or unavailable world-recognized authorities. Consult with your expert about those authorities and lay the proper foundation to use them in conjunction with your expert's testimony.
- Use your expert to qualify a learned treatise in order to cross-examine an adverse expert.
- During discovery, consider use of a request to admit that a treatise you propose to use is a reliable authority.
- When you subpoena business records, send a certification under Rule 902(11) or (12), for the record keeper to execute attesting that the records are authentic and kept in the regular course of business. By doing so, the records can be admitted as an exception to the hearsay rule under Rule 803(6) (business records exception) without any additional foundation.
- Rule 803(17) is an invaluable resource for proving up the value of certain assets without having to hire an expert. Market quotations can be offered to value publicly traded securities. Consider using Rule 803(17) to prove the value of a vehicle using Kelley Blue Book or a similar publication. Also, potentially admissible under this rule is information published about communities or schools that can be used in a custody or relocation proceeding.
- Understand and be able to apply the present sense impression, excited utterance, and existing physical or mental condition exceptions—Rules 803(1), (2), and (3).
- In a typical case, there is no need to depose a friendly witness. But, if a witness is avoiding process or is in ill health and may be unavailable (either legitimately due to health problems or illegitimately by evading a subpoena), consider deposing him or her for the purpose of using the deposition testimony under Rule 804(b)(1).

Judicial Notice and Presumptions | 8

Judicial notice allows a court to consider certain facts without an evidentiary showing by the parties. Judicial notice must be distinguished from the judge's personal knowledge. The rules allow a court to take notice of common knowledge and certain other indisputable facts. Judges may not, in contrast, consider specific information they personally know as evidence. This chapter will also discuss presumptions and burdens of proof, and their interplay in a family law case.

Rules to consider:

Rule 201. Judicial Notice of Adjudicative Facts

(a) Scope. This rule governs judicial notice of an adjudicative fact only, not a legislative fact.
(b) Kinds of Facts That May Be Judicially Noticed. The court may judicially notice a fact that is not subject to reasonable dispute because it:

(1)   is generally known within the trial court's territorial jurisdiction; or

(2)   can be accurately and readily determined from sources whose accuracy cannot reasonably be questioned.

(c)   Taking Notice. The court:

(1)   may take judicial notice on its own; or

(2)   must take judicial notice if a party requests it and the court is supplied with the necessary information.

(d)   Timing. The court may take judicial notice at any stage of the proceeding.

(e)   Opportunity to Be Heard. On timely request, a party is entitled to be heard on the propriety of taking judicial notice and the nature of the fact to be noticed. If the court takes judicial notice before notifying a party, the party, on request, is still entitled to be heard.

(f)   Instructing the Jury. In a civil case, the court must instruct the jury to accept the noticed fact as conclusive. . . .

Rule 301. Presumptions in Civil Actions Generally

In a civil case, unless a federal statute or these rules provide otherwise, the party against whom a presumption is directed has the burden of producing evidence to rebut the presumption. But this rule does not shift the burden of persuasion, which remains on the party who had it originally.

Rule 302. Applying State Law to Presumptions in Civil Cases

In a civil case, state law governs the effect of a presumption regarding a claim or defense for which state law supplies the rule of decision.

Judicial Notice Defined

FRE 201 addresses judicial notice of facts. Judicial notice allows a court to consider certain information without formal evidentiary offerings. The rule applies to adjudicative facts. Adjudicative facts are the facts of the case. An adjudicative fact is one "that is not subject to reasonable dispute because it: (1) is generally known within the trial court's territorial jurisdiction; or (2) can be accurately and readily determined from sources whose accuracy cannot reasonably be questioned." The theory behind this rule is that certain facts are so obvious that the conventional methods of proof are unnecessary. In the words of Bob Dylan, "You don't need a weatherman to know which way the wind blows."[1] *McCormick* clarifies this standard:

> Though this basis for notice is sometimes loosely described as universal knowledge, manifestly this could not be taken literally and the more reflective opinions speak in terms of the knowledge of "most men" or of "what well-informed persons generally know" or "the knowledge that every intelligent person has."[2]

What a judge "knows" and the proper subject matter for judicial notice are two different things. FRE 201 allows judicial notice of generally known information rather than the judge's personal knowledge of a particular fact. For example, in an alimony modification proceeding, the court can take judicial notice of the implosion of the national economy and the general impact it has had on employment. It is not necessary to bring in an economist to testify to employment figures. But, it would be improper for a

---

1. Bob Dylan, "Subterranean Homesick Blues" (Columbia Records, 1965).
2. 2 McCORMICK ON EVIDENCE, § 328 at 434–35 (footnotes omitted) (Kenneth S. Braun, ed., Thomson West 6th ed. 2006).

judge to consider the fact that he or she personally knows that ABC Corporation is hiring because its president told the judge so at a party last week.

This example illustrates the subtle difference between judicial notice and personal judicial knowledge of something. Especially in a small community, it is sometimes hard to distinguish judicial notice from judicial knowledge. The rule is designed to limit the court's notice to indisputable *general* knowledge, including social, economic, scientific, geographic, and political facts. The judge's personal knowledge about particular facts not in evidence is not a proper subject for judicial notice. Where properly used, the doctrine of judicial notice can simplify and shorten a trial. It gives trial judges a tool to streamline potentially burdensome and time-consuming evidence.

A court may take judicial notice of facts at any stage in the proceeding.[3] Either party may request that a court judicially notice a matter or the court may do so on its own motion. FRE 201(d) provides that on the request of a party, the court must take judicial notice if it is supplied with the appropriate information. "Appropriate information" is not defined, and the court itself must determine what that appropriate information must be. The rule allows the parties the opportunity to object to a court taking judicial notice, even after the court does so, if there was no prior opportunity to be heard on the matter.

If you intend to ask a court to take judicial notice of any matter, plan ahead. If you assume that the court will notice a matter and the court refuses, it is too late. Either at a pretrial conference or through a pretrial motion, request a ruling on whether the court will judicially notice a particular fact. If the court refuses, plan to prove up the disputed fact. Better to discover your evidentiary

---

3. *But see* Vulcan Materials Co. v. Bee Constr., 96 Ill. 2d 159, 449 N.E.2d 812 (1983) (the appellate court will not take judicial notice of critical facts not raised in the trial court).

problems well in advance of trial rather than at a time when it is too late to cure it.

In a family law case, examples of appropriate matters for judicial notice can include calendar dates and corresponding days of the week, well-known economic facts, governmental statistical tables, almanac or encyclopedia facts, and the fair earning power of money or invested capital over a period of time.[4] In contrast, it would generally be improper for the court to take judicial notice of the value of a specific item of property. However, the value of farmland per acre may be common knowledge in a small farming community and therefore eligible for judicial notice.[5]

The court can take judicial notice of its own prior acts and records in the same case or in later proceedings involving the same parties. In postdecree litigation, facts adduced in earlier proceedings are sometimes necessary either as a context or baseline for the later litigation. The court can take judicial notice of the facts and findings of the earlier proceeding.[6]

The court must take judicial notice of the applicable law. This includes not only state common law and statutes, but also any applicable federal law. Federal and state tax law impact child support and alimony. A lawyer may use computer software such as FinPlan,[7] or a similar tax calculation program, to calculate income taxes in various income/support scenarios. In order to present these calculations to the court, consider asking the court to take judicial notice of the reliability of the tax program (assuming the program

---

4. *See In re* Marriage of Ryman, 172 Ill. App. 3d 599, 527 N.E.2d 18 (1988).

5. *See In re* Marriage of Holder, 137 Ill. App. 3d 596, 484 N.E.2d 485 (1985) (it was improper for the court to determine value of specific real property using judicial notice).

6. *In re* Brown, 71 Ill. 2d 151, 374 N.E.2d 209 (1978). *See also* 484 F.3d 988 at 994 n.2.

7. FinPlan is a tax-calculating program used to calculate tax implications related to child support and alimony. It is published by Thomson West. *See* M.O. v. J.C.C., 2010 Del. Fam. Ct. LEXIS 59 (2010) (court took judicial notice of tax implications based on FinPlan computation).

is regularly used and acknowledged as reliable by the local legal community) in order to offer into evidence an exhibit with the calculations. If the court refuses to take judicial notice of the reliability of the program or the accuracy of the calculations, you will need to establish the reliability of the program, by having a representative of the publisher testify to the foundation, or you will need an expert for the purpose of calculating the taxes.

Where an expert is unaffordable, ask your opponent for a stipulation concerning the reliability of the software. Typically, where net income is at issue, both parties need the analysis. Where a stipulation is unavailable, consider arguing that the analysis is really a legal argument, applying the tax laws to the facts of the case. Argue that the exhibit is a demonstrative aid to the court summarizing the results when the tax law is applied to your facts. Fortunately, as courts nationwide have come to rely on this technology themselves, they have accepted its reliability for the purposes of evidence.

Presumptions

Rules 301 and 302 address presumptions in civil cases. Rule 301 applies only to federal cases and is largely irrelevant to family lawyers. Rule 302 provides that in individual state cases, the issue of presumptions should be decided under the appropriate state law. These rules are designed to clarify evidentiary burdens for juries, but do apply in bench trials. Presumptions can be confusing. As *McCormick* wryly observes, "One ventures the assertion that presumption is the slipperiest member of legal terms, except its first cousin, burden of proof."[8] Rule 301 defines this slippery concept:

---

8. 2 McCORMICK ON EVIDENCE, *supra* note 2, § 342 at 495.

[T]he party against whom a presumption is directed has the burden of producing evidence to rebut the presumption. But this rule does not shift the burden of persuasion, which remains on the party who had it originally.

FRE 301 distinguishes the obligations of the litigant who has the ultimate burden of proof from the party challenging a particular presumption.

Burden of Proof

The burden of proof, also known as the burden of persuasion, differs depending on the nature of the case. The three basic standards of proof are

(1) proof by a preponderance of the evidence;
(2) proof by clear and convincing evidence; and
(3) proof beyond a reasonable doubt.

The party with the burden of proof must provide sufficient evidence to meet the burden. State court substantive law determines what the burden is in a particular matter. The preponderance and clear and convincing standards apply in civil cases. In planning for a trial, it is vital to know who has the burden of proof and what that burden is. A more stringent burden requires more compelling evidence. If, for example, a parent seeking to restrict visitation must prove child endangerment by *clear and convincing* evidence, the nature of the evidence must be more compelling than under the less onerous *preponderance* of the evidence standard.

Presumption Distinguished from Burden of Proof

A presumption differs from the burden of proof. A presumption is a legal construct that assumes a particular fact is true in the absence of contrary evidence. The burden of proof, in contrast, is the standard of evidence needed to successfully prove a particular issue. If a presumption exists, the party seeking to challenge it is responsible for producing sufficient evidence to overcome it. In the absence of that evidence, the presumption will stand, constructively resolving the issue in favor of the party possessing the presumption.

Consider this example of the relationship between burden of proof and a presumption. In a modification of child support proceeding, Charlene seeks an increase in support. Under her state law, Charlene has the *burden* to prove a change in circumstances in order to modify an earlier support order, and the local statute *presumes* that child support guidelines apply. Peter is the support-paying parent, and he argues that the court should deviate from the guidelines. He argues that support under the guidelines would exceed the reasonable expenses for the child and would be a windfall to Charlene. Peter has the obligation to present evidence to rebut the presumption of applicability of the guidelines. If Peter cannot overcome the presumption, the guidelines apply. Charlene still must sustain her burden of proving a change in circumstances that warrants an increase in support.

This illustration relies on a common presumption used in setting child support: the presumption in favor of support guidelines. There are many examples of presumptions applicable in family court:

- The presumption of paternity of a child born into an intact marriage
- The presumption in favor of the current custodian in a custody modification proceeding

- A presumption that property is marital or community property in some states, or, in others, that property is separate, nonmarital property
- A presumption in some states that a transfer of property between married persons is a gift to the marital or community estate and, in other states, the presumption that such a transfer is not a gift

Presumptions guide family court proceedings daily. Presumptions impact the nature of the proofs and play an important role in the way a lawyer strategically crafts the case.

Presumptions are state specific and can be thought of as a handicap system that shifts the responsibility of advancing a particular argument. "Most presumptions have come into existence primarily because the judges have believed that proof of fact B renders the inference of the existence of fact A so probable that it is sensible and timesaving to assume the truth of fact A until the adversary disproves it."[9] A presumption under Rule 301 is always rebuttable. An irrebuttable presumption, in contrast, is a predetermined conclusive result based on the facts. By its definition, no evidence is sufficient to overcome an irrebuttable presumption.

Practice Points

- Do not wait until trial if you intend to ask the court to take judicial notice of a key piece of evidence. If the court finds that the evidence is too controversial to take notice of, you will be stuck at that point. Ask for a ruling in advance of the trial to determine whether the court will take judicial notice or if additional evidence will be necessary.

---

9. 2 MCCORMICK ON EVIDENCE, *supra* note 2, § 343 at 500-01 (footnote omitted).

- If you first determine during trial that you need to ask the court to take judicial notice of a fact, be prepared with some authority to support the request. Also make sure you provide any necessary information required by FRE 201(d)
- Understand the particular burden imposed by the law concerning the issue being presented. In defending a claim, argue strenuously the import of a higher burden of proof.

Authentication of Writings and Other Tangible Evidence 9

To obtain admission of a tangible thing, including a writing, photograph, recording, or other physical item of evidence, the proponent must first authenticate the item. A document or thing can be authenticated by witness testimony, judicial notice, a party admission, or pretrial order on the request by a party. Some kinds of documents are self-authenticating, rendering further authentication unnecessary. Even if authenticated, an exhibit must still satisfy all other rules of evidence to be admissible: the hearsay rule, the original writing rule, and the rules of relevance.

Rules to consider:

Rule 901. Authenticating or Identifying Evidence

(a) In General. To satisfy the requirement of authenticating or identifying an item of evidence, the proponent must produce evidence sufficient to support a finding that the item is what the proponent claims it is.

(b) Examples. The following are examples only—not a complete list—of evidence that satisfies the requirement:

(1) *Testimony of a Witness with Knowledge.* Testimony that an item is what it is claimed to be.

(2) *Nonexpert Opinion about Handwriting.* A nonexpert's opinion that handwriting is genuine, based on a familiarity with it that was not acquired for the current litigation.

(3) *Comparison by an Expert Witness or the Trier of Fact.* A comparison with an authenticated specimen by an expert witness or the trier of fact.

(4) *Distinctive Characteristics and the Like.* The appearance, contents, substance, internal patterns, or other distinctive characteristics of the item, taken together with all the circumstances.

(5) *Opinion about a Voice.* An opinion identifying a person's voice—whether heard firsthand or through mechanical or electronic transmission or recording—based on hearing the voice at any time under circumstances that connect it with the alleged speaker.

(6) *Evidence about a Telephone Conversation.* For a telephone conversation, evidence that a call was made to the number assigned at the time to:

(A) a particular person, if circumstances, including self-identification, show that the person answering was the one called; or

(B) a particular business, if the call was made to a business and the call related to business reasonably transacted over the telephone.

(7) *Evidence about Public Records.* Evidence that:

(A) a document was recorded or filed in a public office as authorized by law; or

(B)   a purported public record or statement is from the office where items of this kind are kept.

(8)   *Evidence about Ancient Documents or Data Compilations.* For a document or data compilation, evidence that it:

(A)   is in a condition that creates no suspicion about its authenticity;

(B)   was in a place where, if authentic, it would likely be; and

(C)   is at least 20 years old when offered.

(9)   *Evidence about a Process or System.* Evidence describing a process or system and showing that it produces an accurate result.

(10) *Methods Provided by a Statute or Rule.* Any method of authentication or identification allowed by a federal statute or a rule prescribed by the Supreme Court.

Rule 1006. Summaries to Prove Content

The proponent may use a summary, chart, or calculation to prove the content of voluminous writings, recordings, or photographs that cannot be conveniently examined in court. The proponent must make the originals or duplicates available for examination or copying, or both, by other parties at a reasonable time and place. And the court may order the proponent to produce them in court.

Rule 902. Evidence That Is Self-Authenticating

The following items of evidence are self-authenticating; they require no extrinsic evidence of authenticity in order to be admitted:

(1) Domestic Public Documents That Are Sealed and Signed. A
     document that bears:
     (A) a seal purporting to be that of the United States; any
          state, district, commonwealth, territory, or insular pos-
          session of the United States; the former Panama Canal
          Zone; the Trust Territory of the Pacific Islands; a politi-
          cal subdivision of any of these entities; or a department,
          agency, or officer of any entity named above; and
     (B) a signature purporting to be an execution or attestation.
(2) *Domestic Public Documents That Are Not Sealed but Are
     Signed and Certified.* A document that bears no seal if:
     (A) it bears the signature of an officer or employee of an
          entity named in Rule 902(1)(A); and
     (B) another public officer who has a seal and official duties
          within that same entity certifies under seal—or its equiv-
          alent—that the signer has the official capacity and that
          the signature is genuine.
(3) *Foreign Public Documents.* A document that purports to be
     signed or attested by a person who is authorized by a foreign
     country's law to do so. The document must be accompanied
     by a final certification that certifies the genuineness of the
     signature and official position of the signer or attester—or of
     any foreign official whose certificate of genuineness relates to
     the signature or attestation or is in a chain of certificates of
     genuineness relating to the signature or attestation. The certifi-
     cation may be made by a secretary of a United States embassy
     or legation; by a consul general, vice consul, or consular agent
     of the United States; or by a diplomatic or consular official
     of the foreign country assigned or accredited to the United
     States. If all parties have been given a reasonable opportunity
     to investigate the document's authenticity and accuracy, the
     court may, for good cause, either:

(A) order that it be treated as presumptively authentic without final certification; or

(B) allow it to be evidenced by an attested summary with
or without final certification.

(4) *Certified Copies of Public Records.* A copy of an official
record—or a copy of a document that was recorded or filed
in a public office as authorized by law—if the copy is certified as correct by:

(A) the custodian or another person authorized to make the
certification; or

(B) a certificate that complies with Rule 902(1), (2), or (3),
a federal statute, or a rule prescribed by the Supreme
Court.

(5) *Official Publications.* A book, pamphlet, or other publication
purporting to be issued by a public authority.

(6) *Newspapers and Periodicals.* Printed material purporting to
be a newspaper or periodical.

(7) *Trade Inscriptions and the Like.* An inscription, sign, tag, or
label purporting to have been affixed in the course of business and indicating origin, ownership, or control.

(8) *Acknowledged Documents.* A document accompanied by a
certificate of acknowledgment that is lawfully executed by
a notary public or another officer who is authorized to take
acknowledgments.

(9) *Commercial Paper and Related Documents.* Commercial
paper, a signature on it, and related documents, to the extent
allowed by general commercial law.

(10) *Presumptions under a Federal Statute.* A signature, document,
or anything else that a federal statute declares to be presumptively or prima facie genuine or authentic.

(11) *Certified Domestic Records of a Regularly Conducted Activity.* The original or a copy of a domestic record that meets
the requirements of Rule 803(6)(A)–(C), as shown by a

certification of the custodian or another qualified person that complies with a federal statute or a rule prescribed by the Supreme Court. Before the trial or hearing, the proponent must give an adverse party reasonable written notice of the intent to offer the record—and must make the record and certification available for inspection—so that the party has a fair opportunity to challenge them.

(12) *Certified Foreign Records of a Regularly Conducted Activity.* In a civil case, the original or a copy of a foreign record that meets the requirements of Rule 902(11), modified as follows: the certification, rather than complying with a federal statute or Supreme Court rule, must be signed in a manner that, if falsely made, would subject the maker to a criminal penalty in the country where the certification is signed. The proponent must also meet the notice requirements of Rule 902(11).

Rule 903. Subscribing Witness's Testimony

A subscribing witness's testimony is necessary to authenticate a writing only if required by the law of the jurisdiction that governs its validity.

Authentication of Real Evidence

Real evidence is an object or item that is itself relevant and probative, without more. *McCormick* defines this type of evidence as "independent substantive sources of evidence because the trier of fact may draw inferences from the objects themselves about some fact of consequence."[1] A paddle used to strike a child or copies of

---

1. 2 McCORMICK ON EVIDENCE, § 213 at 11 (footnote omitted) (Kenneth S. Braun, ed., Thomson West 6th ed. 2006).

inappropriate adult magazines left out in the living room when the children were present are examples of real evidence.

One way to authenticate real evidence is to call a witness who can testify that the item is what it purports to be. If the item is unique, the witness would authenticate it by describing its unique or individual properties (e.g., "I recognize the paddle . . . it has my husband's fraternity insignia on it and his initials carved into it"). If the object is not readily identifiable or more generic looking, additional testimony will be needed to support the admission. Under this circumstance, the proponent must present testimony supporting a chain of custody. Doing so "will entail testimony that traces the chain of custody of the item from the moment it was found to its appearance in the courtroom, with sufficient completeness to render it reasonably probable that the original item has neither been exchanged or altered."[2] To authenticate nondistinct real evidence the lawyer must assure the judge that the evidence has not been tampered with or otherwise exchanged. Additionally, the proponent must offer supporting testimony establishing that the item is substantially the same as it was when the event with which it is associated occurred.

In a family law case, the proponent does not need to prove chain of custody for real evidence with the same rigor that a criminal prosecution requires. Assume Janet offers into evidence a garden tool that she claims Frank threw at her. A break in the chain of custody does not necessarily render the item inadmissible as long as her lawyer can show that the exhibit is probably the item it purports to be.[3] Also, a change that does not materially affect an exhibit's probative value does not invalidate its authenticity.[4] If the tool was painted green after the incident, the changed condition

2. 2 McCormick on Evidence, *supra* note 1, § 213 at 11.
3. United States v. Howard-Arias, 679 F.2d 363 (4th Cir. 1982).
4. United States v. Skelley, 501 F.2d 447 (7th Cir. 1974).

has no bearing on its authenticity. To avoid an argument, however, advise your client to secure potential real evidence and make sure it remains in the same condition it was in at the time of the event to which it relates.

Authenticating Photographs

In a family law case, photographs can be compelling evidence. A picture of a bruise or black eye always tells the story better than raw testimony. Pictures of prospective homes and neighborhoods can tell the story better than mere testimony in a relocation or custody dispute. Wherever possible, a trial lawyer should try to include images to support a claim.

To authenticate a photograph through witness testimony, a witness must testify that the scene depicted in the photograph accurately depicts the scene personally observed. The witness does not need to be the photographer, nor does the witness need to have been present when the photograph was taken. The witness only needs to testify that he or she is familiar with the object or scene in the photograph and that the photo fairly and accurately depicts the object or scene. The witness should also testify to the basis of his or her familiarity with the depicted object or scene.

Digital photographs pose a unique problem: they are easy to manipulate. Digital imagery redefines the notion of what is an original since no per se original exists. FRE 1001(d) acknowledges this problem by providing that " 'original' means any printout—or other output readable by sight—if it accurately reflects the information. An 'original' of a photograph includes the negative or a print from it."[5] Any printout of a digital photograph is considered

---

5. FRE 1001–1004, which address use of originals, are discussed in detail in Chapter 10.

an original. Proponents authenticate a digital photograph the same way they would a traditional photograph.

If the photograph is successfully authenticated, it may be conditionally admitted as an exhibit, subject to a later challenge by the opponent. Under the Federal Rules of Evidence, the proponent of the photo need not rule out *all possibilities* of tampering or inauthenticity. The proponent also does not need to conclusively prove that the photo is what it claims to be. Only a threshold showing of authenticity is required.[6] If the opposing party claims that the exhibit has been altered, that party would have the burden of proof of that fact. If the opponent later establishes that the exhibit had been altered, the question of its authenticity would go to its weight; the court would disregard it as it has no probative value.

A party seeking to authenticate or to challenge the authenticity of a digital photograph may use metadata from the digital camera to impeach or support authenticity.[7] Each photograph has a digital thumbprint, known as metadata, which can be accessed to confirm authenticity of the image. An opponent must plan a challenge to a digital image before the trial. It is virtually impossible to successfully challenge a photograph on the spot. To challenge a digital image, consider the following:

• Some cell phones and digital cameras have GPS coordinates built into the metadata, which would identify the exact location of the camera when the picture was taken.

---

6. *See* United States v. Hyles, 479 F.3d 958, 968–69 (8th Cir. 2007); United States v. Tin Yat Chin, 371 F.3d 31, 37–38 (2nd Cir. 2004); State v. Thompson, 777 N.W.2d 617 (N.D. 2010).

7. Joe Kashi, "Authenticating Digital Photographs as Evidence: A Practice Approach Using JPEG Metadata," Law Practice Today (June 2006) <http://apps.americanbar.org/lpm/lpt/articles/tch06061.shtml#>

- Metadata identifies the camera the photograph was taken from. If the picture was not from the camera claimed by the proponent, the photograph's authenticity is suspect.
- Metadata includes the date a photograph was taken. If the actual weather that day does not track with the weather in the photograph, authenticity is suspect.
- Often several pictures of the same scene are taken and one is chosen for admission. Review of the companion pictures may provide insights suggesting manipulation, or they may actually be better representations of the particular image being offered.[8]

As the proponent of a digital photograph, be prepared to present foundational testimony concerning the date of the photograph, camera used, possession of the camera, and any other salient facts about the image. If challenging authenticity, hire an expert witness to evaluate the authenticity of the image. During pretrial investigation, use the discovery rules to obtain information for the expert to complete his or her analysis.[9] Seek a court order requiring production of the original digital device for review of its metadata by the expert.

Here is a sample foundation for offering a photograph (whether digital or traditional) into evidence:

- I want to show you what we have marked as Plaintiff's Exhibit Number 12 for identification. Do you recognize this item? (Yes)
- What is it? (It is a photograph)
- Do you recognize this photograph? (Yes)

---

8. The author would like to thank Joe Howie from Howie Consulting, www. HowieConsulting.com, an expert on e-discovery and legal technology, for his valuable contributions to this topic.

9. For a detailed exposition of the science of forensic analysis of digital images, see "Digital Image Authentication from JPEG Headers" by Eric Kee, Micah K. Johnson, and Hany Farid <http://www.cs.dartmouth.edu/farid/publications/tifs11a.pdf>

- When was the photograph taken? (On June 23, 2012)
- If a digital camera was used: What device did you use to take the picture? (my cell phone camera)
- Has anyone other than you had possession of your phone between the date the picture was taken and today? (No)
- What does the photograph depict? (A picture of my arm with bruises)
- Does this photograph accurately depict the bruises on your arm when the photograph was taken? (Yes)

Authenticating Video and Audio Recordings

A video or voice recording can also help support a particular claim or denial. As always, the proposed exhibit must be material and probative of a particular issue in the case. A video of a parent intently engaged with a child may dispel a claim of disinterest. Or a video of a person engaging in strenuous recreational activity may debunk a claim of being too sick to work.

Traditionally, moving pictures or videotapes required foundational questions about the technology and operation of the recording equipment used to create them. Due to the ubiquity of recording devices, this former standard has been relaxed. Today, a party can authenticate an unscripted video in the same manner as a photograph. A witness who observed the recording must testify that the video fairly and accurately reflects the scene depicted. The proponent must explain all collateral noises or images on the video as well. The photographer could be the authenticating witness but does not need to be.

Scripted videos require more foundation. Scripted videos are created specifically for the litigation, to be used as persuasive tools. In addition to the foregoing authentication requirements, the proponent must also provide information about the production: who decided on the scenes filmed, the normalcy of the routine depicted, the general accuracy of the depiction as compared to normal behavior or functioning, and an explanation of the purpose of the scenes depicted. In at least one family law decision, however, a scripted "day in the life" video made for a contested custody case was found to be irrelevant and inadmissible.[10]

Federal wiretapping laws prohibit the audio recording of another person without that person's knowledge or consent.[11] Violation of the act exposes the violator to civil and criminal penalties. An impermissible recording is excluded as evidence.[12] State laws also govern the recording of others without their knowledge and the use of such recordings in a legal proceeding.[13] Admonish your clients about these rules and their implications.[14]

But in some instances, a litigant can properly use a recording as evidence. A voice recording left on an answering machine or cell phone is admissible, assuming it is relevant and properly authenticated. These types of recordings are made with the full knowledge of the person leaving the message. Thus, there is no expectation of privacy and the recording is not subject to the protections of the wiretap laws.

Authenticate a recording in the following way: A witness who made or overheard the recording can identify it as an accurate recording of what was said by the speaker. Alternatively, have the recipient of a voicemail message, for example, testify that the recording accurately reflects what he or she heard on the recording,

---

10. *See* Willis v. Willis, 234 Ill. App. 3d 156, 599 N.E.2d 179 (court denied use of a "day in the life" video produced as a demonstrative aid to illustrate the nature and extent of a parent's involvement).

11. 18 U.S.C. § 2510 et. seq.

12. *Id.*

13. *See, e.g.,* Illinois Statute 720 ILCS 5/14-1 et seq.

14. *See* Shana K. Rahavy, *The Federal Wiretap Act: the Permissible Scope of Eavesdropping in the Family Home,* JOURNAL OF HIGH TECHNOLOGY LAW, 2003. Also see Allan H. Zerman & Cary J. Mogerman, *Wiretapping and Divorce: A Survey and Analysis of the Federal and State Laws Relating to Electronic Eavesdropping and Their Application in Matrimonial Cases,* 12 J. AM. ACAD. MATRIM. LAW 227, 228 (1994).

identifying the date and time the recording was received. Have the witness identify the speaker's voice, the basis of his or her recognition of the voice, and any other contextual references in the recording. FRE 901(b)(5) allows authentication of a voice based on a witness's past experience: "An opinion identifying a person's voice—whether heard firsthand or through mechanical or electronic transmission or recording—based on hearing the voice at any time under circumstances that connect it with the alleged speaker." No chain of custody of the recording is necessary if the witness can identify the recording in this manner.[15]

Authentication of Writings

Authentication of a writing depends on how the proponent intends to use it. It is the context and the intended purpose of the writing that determines the procedure for authentication. If the purpose of offering the writing is to show the reaction by the reader, it will be authenticated differently than a writing offered to prove the content of the communication or the identity of the author. In the former example, the person who found the document (or another witness who was present at the time the writing was discovered and read) would testify that it is the same document found and is in an unchanged condition. The author is irrelevant for the purpose it is being offered.

If the purpose of offering the writing is to prove the content of the communication, the lawyer must present testimony identifying the author. FRE 901(b)(1) provides that a writing can be authenticated by the testimony of a witness with knowledge of its authenticity. Either the author can authenticate the document as

---

15. 2 McCormick on Evidence, *supra* note 1, § 216 at 31.

his or her writing, or another witness with personal knowledge could verify its authenticity.

Authentication by Identification of Handwriting

Rule 901(b)(2) permits authentication of a writing based on a witness's recognition of handwriting on the exhibit. Authentication is satisfied by "a nonexpert's opinion that handwriting is genuine, based on a familiarity with it that was not acquired for the current litigation." Any witness familiar with the handwriting on an exhibit, who can state a basis for this knowledge, could qualify to authenticate the writing.

Assume Mark wrote a letter making a variety of admissions about his hidden sources of income. Jane's lawyer could authenticate the letter by Jane testifying that based on witnessing his handwriting and signature thousands of times during the marriage, she recognized Mark's handwriting and signature on this particular exhibit. In general, the authenticating witness must testify how they acquired the knowledge of the handwriting, but the requirement is "minimal."[16] In fact, the witness need not conclusively identify the handwriting. The witness must only believe that it is the same. The uncertainty goes to the weight, not the admissibility of the evidence.[17]

Authentication of Writings by Other Means

Writings can be authenticated in other ways. The purpose of authentication is to assure the court that the writing is what it purports

---

16. 2 McCORMICK ON EVIDENCE, *supra* note 1, § 223 at 60–61 (footnote omitted).
17. *Id.* at 61–62.

to be. Authorship can be inferred from the surrounding circumstances, and circumstantial evidence can be used. FRE 901(b)(4) provides that the court can evaluate "appearance, contents, substance, internal patterns, or other distinctive characteristics of the item, taken together with all the circumstances."

For example, personalized stationery or letterhead ties the writing to the owner of the stationery, and that connection could serve to authenticate the writing. Evidence of facts known to the writer could also authenticate it. If a letter alludes to a specific incident that the author demonstrably had knowledge of, the letter could be circumstantially authenticated through evidence of the author's knowledge of the incident. A reply to an earlier communication could be a means of authenticating the previous writing as well.

Authentication of Electronic Communications

The Federal Rules of Evidence do not treat electronic writings differently than nonelectronic writings. There are no special rules for electronic versus pen-and-paper writings. Computer-generated documents, including e-mails, and web pages, have become omnipresent in a modern family law practice. Authentication of these materials is accomplished the same as any other writing: the proponent must give the court proof of the source and legitimacy of the digital evidence. Ordinarily the burden of proving authenticity is not high. The proponent only needs to provide some reasonable predicate proof, usually through a witness, confirming that the proposed exhibit is what it purports to be.[18]

---

18. *Lorraine v. Markel* is probably the most influential decision on the topic of electronic evidence, covering the whole spectrum of issues concerning the admission of electronic evidence. All trial lawyers should read that decision as a primer on this topic. Lorraine v. Markel Am. Ins. Co., 241 F.R.D. 534 (D. Md. 2007).

The method of authentication depends on the type of material being offered.

Faxed Documents

A facsimile is a digital communication. To the extent that it is a writing, authenticate a fax as you would any other writing. In addition, provide information concerning the transmittal procedures and other information concerning the unique identity of the document. Here are some foundational topics to cover:

- Information about the machine it was sent or received on
- Information that the machine was in good working order at the time of the transmittal
- When it was faxed or received
- The phone numbers that were entered (if the sender is authenticating)
- Recognition of the printed identifying marks on the document
- Identification of any machine generated receipts or reports and how they are generated
- Confirmation that the exhibit is in the same condition as the time it was faxed

Electronic Mail

Anyone with personal knowledge of an electronic mail message, including the sender or the recipient, can authenticate it. Rule 901(b)(4) permits authentication of a document based on its distinctive characteristics, including its "appearance, contents, substance, internal patterns, or other distinctive characteristics." The headers on an e-mail that include the electronic address of the author are typically enough to authenticate it. Also, establishing foundation via an e-mail thread is an appropriate means of authentication. For example, if the e-mail was a reply to someone, the digital conversation could serve as the basis of authentication:[19]

- Please identify Defendant's Exhibit 17. (It is a copy of an e-mail I sent to Angela)
- When did you send this e-mail? (July 22, 2012)
- What were the circumstances concerning the message? (I was replying to an e-mail she sent me earlier that day)
- Do you recognize her e-mail address? (Yes)
- What is her e-mail address? (Angela@gmail.com)
- On the e-mail header does it reflect where this e-mail was sent? (Yes)
- Where was it sent? (Angela@gmail.com)

FRE 901(b)(3) permits authentication by comparison: a court itself can authenticate an e-mail by comparing it to other e-mails previously admitted.[20] In that event, the proponent could ask the court to take judicial notice of the earlier admitted e-mails and the similarities between those e-mails and the later one. Some courts have permitted authentication of e-mails based on the fact that the party opponent produced the e-mails during discovery.[21] Production of documents in response to a request for production is inherently an admission of the authenticity of the documents produced.[22] A party would be hard pressed to deny that the documents produced were inauthentic. An expert could also authenticate the communica-

---

19. United States v. Siddiqui, 235 F.3d 1318, 1322 (11th Cir. 2000).

20. *See* United States v. Safavian, 644 F. Supp. 2d 1 (2009) (where the court authenticated an e-mail based on the header).

21. Shaghticoke Tribal Nation v. Kempthorne, 587 F. Supp. 2d 389, 397 (D. Conn. 2008); John Paul Mitchell Sys. v. Quality King Distribs., Inc., 106 F. Supp. 2d 462, 472 (S.D.N.Y. 2000).

22. This is a good example of why it is vital to inventory all documents received during discovery. Specifically, Bates stamp everything received, and send a letter confirming everything that was provided if a detailed inventory is not provided from the party producing the records.

tion as well, but in the average family law case sufficient collateral circumstances should make that unnecessary. Use of an expert to authenticate electronic communications is the exception not the rule. Expert involvement is necessary only where a credible claim of fraud is made.

If the sender of the e-mail is the witness who will authenticate it, here are some foundational topics:

- The electronic address placed on the e-mail is that of the claimed recipient
- The purpose of the communication (why it was sent)
- If applicable, verification that the sender received an earlier e-mail and replied to that earlier e-mail
- Verification that the e-mail was actually sent
- Verification that the recipient acknowledged the communication to the sender or took action based on it

Here is an example of a sample inquiry:

- What is this document? (It is a copy of an e-mail I sent to Joe)
- Do you know Joe's e-mail address? (Yes)
- What is it? (Joe@yahoo.com)
- To whom is this e-mail sent? (Joe@yahoo.com)
- Why did you send this e-mail? (I was confirming our plans later in the evening)
- Did you actually send the e-mail to Joe@yahoo.com? (Yes)
- Did Joe ever acknowledge the e-mail to you? (Yes)
- How? (He called me an hour after I sent the e-mail to discuss our plans)

The other common way of authenticating an e-mail is by offering the testimony of the recipient. The recipient would authenticate it by

- acknowledging that he or she received the e-mail;
- identifying the electronic address of the sender as being the address indicated on the e-mail;
- comparing it to earlier e-mails received by the sender;
- identifying any logos or other identifying information on the e-mail;
- observing whether the e-mail received was in reply to one sent earlier by the recipient;
- testimony concerning any conversations with the sender concerning the communication;
- testimony concerning any actions taken by the sender consistent with the communication.

Here is an example of questions for a recipient:

- What is this document? (It is an e-mail I received from Alice)
- What is the e-mail address of the sender? (Alice@trueblue.com)
- Do you recognize any identifying marks on the e-mail? (Yes; I recognize the corporate logo where she works and her phone number is on the e-mail.)
- When did you receive this e-mail? (Thursday night)
- Had you sent her any e-mails earlier in the day on Thursday? (Yes; this was a reply to an e-mail I sent in the afternoon)
- Why did you e-mail Alice in the afternoon? (I was attempting to set up a time to see the kids)
- Did you have a phone call with her after you received this e-mail? (Yes)
- When? (Ten minutes after I received her e-mail I called her and asked her why I couldn't see the kids Sunday. She told me they were busy. . .)

As a further example, assume that the husband sent to his banker an e-mail discussing the future of the family business, that the market is expanding quickly, and that he expects substantially higher earnings in the next year. Assume the wife wants to offer the e-mail into evidence to establish the husband's income as well as the value of the business. A business evaluator, as an expert, can rely on the communication and testify to it, even making it a part of their report.[23] But if no expert used the e-mail, the wife's lawyer could ask the husband to identify the e-mail as the one he sent to the banker. Assuming he identifies it as the one he sent, the authentication rule is satisfied. If he refuses to acknowledge the e-mail as his, the wife could call the banker to testify that he received the e-mail, that he recognized the husband's e-mail address and that the husband was replying to his request for updated projections for the coming year. The wife could also authenticate the e-mail based on its appearance, recognizing it from other similar looking e-mails she received from her husband. She could produce other e-mails she received from the husband and ask the court to compare those e-mails to authenticate the one at issue.

A party opposing admission of an e-mail may claim it was altered or forged. In *United States v. Safavian,* the court held that unsubstantiated claims are insufficient to deny admission:

> The *possibility* of alteration does not and cannot be the basis for excluding e-mails as unidentified or unauthenticated as a matter of course, any more than it can be the rationale for excluding paper documents (and copies of those documents). We live in an age of technology and computer use where e-mail communication now is a normal and frequent fact for the majority of this nation's population, and is of particular importance in the professional world. The defendant is free to raise this issue with the jury and put on evidence that e-mails are capable of being altered before they are passed on. Absent specific evidence showing alteration, however, the

---

23. See Chapter 13 and the use of experts to get documents before a judge.

Court will not exclude any embedded emails because of the mere possibility that it can be done.[24]

All other evidentiary rules apply to e-mails. Even if an e-mail is authenticated, the proponent must be prepared to argue relevance and admissibility of out-of-court statements of fact as not hearsay or covered under an exception to the hearsay rule. When an e-mail is between spouses, it may be admissible as a party admission pursuant to FRE 801(D)(2) if offered by the adverse party.

Text Messages and Other Instant Messages

There is no unique formula to offer a text message into evidence. As one court held,

> Essentially, appellant would have us create a whole new body of law just to deal with e-mails or instant messages. The argument is that e-mails or text messages are inherently unreliable because of their relative anonymity and the fact that while an electronic message can be traced to a particular computer, it can rarely be connected to a specific author with any certainty. Unless the purported author is actually witnessed sending the e-mail, there is always the possibility it is not from whom it claims. As appellant correctly points out, anybody with the right password can gain access to another's e-mail account and send a message ostensibly from that person. However, the same uncertainties exist with traditional written documents. A signature can be forged; a letter can be typed on another's typewriter; distinct letterhead stationery can be copied or stolen. We believe that e-mail messages and similar forms of electronic communication can be properly authenticated within the existing framework of Pa. R.E. 901 and Pennsylvania case law. . . . We see no justification for constructing unique rules of admissibility

---

24. *See* United States v. Safavian, 644 F. Supp. 2d 1 (2009).

of electronic communications such as instant messages; they are to be evaluated on a case-by-case basis as any other document to determine whether or not there has been an adequate foundational showing of their relevance and authenticity. [25]

The proponent must only satisfy the minimal requirement of showing that the document is what it claims to be. It is not the proponent's burden to disprove an unsupported claim of inauthenticity. An unsupported argument that there was no way of knowing who actually sent the text is insufficient to keep it out.[26]

As with e-mails, courts have allowed text messages to be authenticated by circumstantial evidence. A screen name, context, and other surrounding circumstances can be used to authenticate a text message.[27] The Supreme Court of North Dakota addressed this issue at length in *State v. Thompson.*[28] That court reiterated that authenticity is not a demanding burden and not every uncertainty needs to be conclusively addressed prior to admission.[29] In *Thompson,* the state sought to admit a picture of a text from the defendant to the victim in a domestic violence case. The text was authenticated by the victim testifying about the circumstances between the parties on that day, her knowledge of the defendant's phone number, and the label ("FR: Jen") on the text message. The court allowed admission of a picture of the text despite the fact that no testimony was presented about who took the picture and that it was what it purported to be. The court also allowed testimony about other texts, even though reproductions of the texts were not produced.

---

25. *In re* F.P., 878 A.2d 91, 95–96 (Pa. Super. Ct. 2005).
26. State v. Thompson, 777 N.W.2d 617 (N.D. 2010).
27. Massimo v. State, 144 S.W.3d 210 (Tex. App. 2004).
28. 777 N.W.2d 617.
29. *Id.*

In *People v. Chromik,* an Illinois court (relying on *People v. Thompson*) allowed into evidence a transcript of a text message.[30] In *Chromik,* a high school student claiming her teacher sexually molested her showed her principal lewd text messages from the teacher. The principal typed the messages on his computer, printed them, and the student reviewed them for accuracy. The principal wrote the time and date of the text on the transcript, and the victim then signed the transcripts. At the trial, the court permitted use of the transcript, despite the fact that the spell check feature on the principal's computer automatically corrected spelling errors from the original text.

As with e-mails, the sender or recipient of a text can most easily establish its authenticity. If the sender testifies, the foundational testimony to be considered includes

- the context of the message (why it was sent, its purpose, earlier discussions on a topic of controversy, etc.);
- knowledge that the number it was sent to was that of the recipient;
- identification of a photograph of the actual text that was sent;
- the process of taking the photograph (who took the photo, what camera was used, that it was an accurate reproduction of the actual text, etc.);
- subject to the original writing rules (FRE 1001–1004), reproduction of a transcript of the actual text, including the procedures for making it (transcript was prepared based on the actual text, reviewed by the sender, and verified to be an accurate reflection of the actual text);[31]

---

30. People v. Chromik, 408 Ill. App. 3d 1028, 946 N.E.2d 1039 (2011).

31. See discussion of the original writing rules (FED. R. EVID. 1001–1004) in Chapter 9 as a possible obstacle to admissibility.

- testimony regarding any responsive text received or any verbal acknowledgment by the recipient in relation to the earlier text.

Sample questions to have a sender authenticate a text message might include the following:

- What is this document? (It is a picture of a text message I sent to Ann)
- What number was this text sent to? (555-123-4567)
- Whose number is that? (Ann's)
- When did you send this text? (April 11th at 4:07 p.m.)
- Why did you text her? (I needed to know how much medicine to give the kids)
- Did she reply? (No)
- How did you capture the image contained in this exhibit? (My friend Bob took a picture of my message on his phone and printed it out for me)
- Does the picture accurately reflect how the text looked when you sent it? (Yes)

If the recipient of the text testifies, the authentication testimony might include the following topics:

- Recognition of the number, digital signature or name of the person they received the message from
- Basis of their knowledge of the sender's number (that they have had text conversations with this person at that particular phone number in the past)
- The context of the text conversation (earlier texts or discussions on the topic that is the subject of the text)
- If a photo of the text is used, the process of taking the photograph (who took the photo, what camera was used, that it was an accurate reproduction of the actual text, etc.)

- Subject to the original writing rules (FRE 1001–1004), reproduction of a transcript of the actual text, including the procedures for making it (the transcript was prepared based on the actual text, reviewed by the recipient, and verified to be an accurate reflection of the actual text)

Here are some sample questions for a recipient:

- What is this document? (It is a transcript from a text exchange between my husband and me)
- What is a text exchange? (A series of text messages between us; we were arguing)
- When was the exchange? (All during the morning on the first of April)
- What were you arguing about? (He went to a picnic with his girlfriend and the kids)
- Did you ever speak with him about this by phone? (Yes, later that day)
- How did you prepare this transcript? (I typed the various messages back and forth as they were on my phone)
- Is the typed transcript identical to the actual text messages sent on April 1, 2012? (Yes)
- Did you add or alter any of the texts in your transcript? (No)

Chat Room Communications

The easiest way to authenticate a chat room communication is for the sender to identify himself or herself as the participant in the chat. If the participant is unavailable to do so, however, the proponent of the evidence will need to provide circumstantial evidence to authenticate the communication, which may include

- knowing the screen name of the sender of the communication and the basis for that knowledge;

- connecting the content of the chat to admissions or other statements made by the sender;
- showing that the chat occurred during a time that the sender was available to engage in the chat (e.g., that the sender was at home during the period and had a working computer);
- the participant discussing the chat with a third party who could testify to the conversation.

If the proponent seeks to offer a transcript of the chat, he or she will need to ask additional foundation questions to authenticate the transcript, confirming that the transcript is an accurate reproduction, who prepared it, and when it was prepared.

Websites and Social Media

Websites such as Facebook and MySpace allow members to create an online profile in an individual web page from which they can post pictures, videos, and updates about their life. Articles abound about the impact that Facebook and other social media have had on family law proceedings.[32] The potentially lurid information available on Facebook is an ample resource for family lawyers.

The foundational requirements for authenticating a screenshot from Facebook are the same as for a printout from any other website. The proponent of the evidence must offer foundational testimony that the screenshot was actually on the website, that it

---

32. Leanne Italie, *Facebook is Divorce Lawyers' New Best Friend*, NBCNEWS.com, June 28, 2010, <http://www.msnbc.msn.com/id/37986320>; Nadine Brozan, *Divorce Lawyers' New Friend: Social Networks*, N.Y. TIMES, May 15, 2011, at ST17; Stephanie Chen, *Divorce Attorneys Catching Cheaters on Facebook*, CNN.com, June 1, 2010 <http://www.cnn.com/2010/TECH/social.media/06/01/facebook.divorce.lawyers/index.html>

accurately depicts what was on the website, and that the content is attributable to the owner.[33]

Court decisions are mixed concerning authentication of web pages. Several courts have held that the website owner must provide the necessary foundation to authenticate a page from a website.[34] Other courts have held that a printout from a website may be authenticated by a visitor to the website.[35] The more permissive camp allows authentication testimony from a person who viewed and ultimately captured the website image in a printed screenshot. In order to authenticate that image, the witness must testify that that the depiction "accurately reflects the content of the Web site and the image of the page on the computer at which the [screen-shot] was made."[36]

The more liberal court decisions reflect a common sense approach to this issue. After all, the court can access the website at the bench and authenticate the screenshot by judicial notice. Allowing the viewer of the website to authenticate it also conforms to the long-standing policy that favors a lower threshold for authentication.[37] That being said, the question of authentication is dependent on the reason for which the screenshot is offered and on the nature of the website itself. A screenshot from a recognized corporation, such as a bank or credit card company, should cause less concern than

33. Lorraine v. Markel Am. Ins. Co., 241 F.R.D. 534 (D. Md. 2007).

34. *See, e.g.,* United States v. Jackson, 208 F.3d 633, 637 (7th Cir. 2000); Novak v. Tucows, Inc., No. 06-CV-1909, 2007 U.S. Dist. LEXIS 21269, at *5 (E.D.N.Y. March 26, 2007); Costa ex rel Costa v. Keppel Singmarine Dockyard PTE, Ltd., No. CV 01-11015, 2003 U.S. Dist. LEXIS 16295, at *9 n.74 (C.D. Cal. April 25, 2003).

35. *See, e.g.,* United States v. Standring, No. 1:04cv730, 2006 WL 689116, at *3 (S.D. Ohio March 15, 2006); Moose Creek, Inc. v. Abercrombie & Fitch Co., 331 F. Supp. 2d 1214, 1225 n.4 (C.D. Cal. 2004), *aff'd,* 114 Fed. Appx. 921 (9th Cir. 2004) (unpublished opinion); Perfect 10, Inc. v. Cybernet Adventures, Inc., 213 F. Supp. 2d 1146, 1153–54 (C.D. Cal. 2002).

36. Toytrackerz LLC v. Koehler, No. 08-2297-GLR, 2009 WL 2591329, at 6 (D. Kan. Aug. 21, 2009).

37. United States EEOC v. E.I. DuPont de Nemours & Co., 2004 WL 2347559 (E.D. La. 2004).

a personal blog post where a nonowner can more easily manipulate the content.

Some courts, however, are suspicious of the validity of any website postings:

> While some look to the Internet as an innovative vehicle for communication, the Court continues to warily . . . view it largely as one catalyst for rumor, innuendo, and misinformation. . . . Anyone can put anything on the Internet. No web site is monitored for accuracy and nothing contained therein is under oath or even subject to independent verification absent underlying documentation. Moreover the Court holds no illusions that hackers can adulterate the content of any web site from any location at any time.[38]

But, in general, many courts consider information posted on a commercial website reliable. In fact, information obtained from government websites is considered self-authenticated if the proponent can establish that the information is current and complete.[39]

In order to authenticate a screenshot from a website, the witness should provide the following predicate information to lay the foundation for the authenticity of the screenshot:

- Proof that the witness visited the website
- When the website was visited
- Information reflecting that the website was current, as opposed to stale sites not kept current (e.g., postings reflecting current information, dates, etc.)
- How the site was accessed (e.g., "Via the Internet Explorer web browser, I did a Google search for the website and followed

---

38. St. Clair v. Johnny's Oyster & Shrimp, Inc., 76 F. Supp. 2d 773, 774–75 (S.D. Tex. 1999).
39. United States EEOC v. E.I. DuPont de Nemours & Co., *supra* note 37.

the appropriate links"; or if the web address was known, "I entered the web address into the Internet browser and accessed the website directly")

- A description of the website accessed: identifying material on the website including names, addresses, logos, phone numbers, and so on
- Recognition of the website based on past visits
- Proof that the screenshot was printed from the website
- The date and time that the screenshot was captured
- Proof that the screenshot in the printout is exactly the same as what the witness saw on the computer screen
- Proof that the printout has not been altered or otherwise changed from the image on the computer

As noted above, a screenshot from a Facebook page or other social media page is a page within the social media website at large. People may communicate information on their own page, or post to another's page. Any posting is potentially admissible, assuming it is authenticated, legally obtained, and meets the other substantive rules of evidence (hearsay, relevance, etc.).

To authenticate a screenshot from a social media site, the lawyer must elicit foundation testimony that circumstantially confirms the identity of the person who posted on the site. That testimony should include information about the social media site accessed.[40] Here are some sample questions to authenticate a Facebook page:

- Are you familiar with the social media website Facebook? (Yes)

---

40. *See* Levar Griffin v. State, 419 Md. 343, 19 A.3d 415 (2011) ("The potential for abuse and manipulation of a social networking site by someone other than its purported creator and/or user leads to our conclusion that a printout of an image from such a site requires a greater degree of authentication than merely identifying the date of birth of the creator and the visage in a photograph on the site in order to reflect that Ms. Barber was its creator.").

- How are you familiar with it? (I use it daily)
- How long have you been using it? (Five years)
- Describe generally what you do with the application. (I keep up with my friends' comings and goings)
- What is a Facebook friendship? (The website allows you to follow chosen friends)
- How is one created? (You invite someone to be your friend and if the person accepts, you become Facebook friends)
- Is Sally Jones your Facebook friend? (Yes)
- What is a Facebook wall? (That is someone's personal posting area open to friends for posting messages and interacting)
- How do you access someone's wall? (You click on their profile on the website)
- What type of information is found on a Facebook wall? (Birthdays, place of employment, relationship status, where they live, and other personal information)
- Have you ever visited Sally Jones' Facebook wall? (Many times)
- Did you visit her wall recently? (Yes)
- On what date? (Last Tuesday)
- What did you see on her wall? (I saw that she posted a picture of herself kissing my husband)
- Did you print a copy of what you saw? (Yes)
- Here is petitioner's exhibit 12. Can you identify this document? (It is a copy of the picture printed from her Facebook page)
- Is it an exact copy of what you saw on the screen the day you visited Sally's wall? (Yes)
- What date did you print it? (Yesterday)
- What is the handwriting on this exhibit? (My initials with the date it was printed)
- Have there been any changes to this document since the day you printed it? (No)

The witness could also testify to the specific postings to authenticate the exhibit. For example, if Sally references a particular event on her Facebook page, the witness could testify that she saw Sally at that event. Other follow-up questions might inquire about the witness's knowledge about personal information that is typically listed on the site, such as birthday, hometown, and school attended. Finally, pictures on the site could be used to authenticate it as well (pictures of Sally in this particular case).

Even if the pictures are authentic, the proponent may be barred from getting Facebook images admitted into evidence if they were procured improperly. Some Facebook users allow anyone on the Internet to view their pages. Others are more private, however, and require a prior friendship before their information can be accessed. Lawyers are precluded under the Rules of Professional Conduct from creating a phony friendship to gain access to someone's wall.[41] Also, the source of access to information will be raised in cross-examination, and any disreputable behavior may end up inadvertently impeaching your own witness.

Maryland's highest court has strict rules for authenticating social media sites. In *Griffin v. State of Maryland*, the court of appeals observed, "[A]nyone can create a fictitious account and masquerade under another person's name or gain access to another's account."[42] The court observed that a printout from a social media site (MySpace in this case), which is available to all, is a different type of communication than e-mails and instant messages, which are "sent directly from one party to an intended recipient or recipients."[43]

The court held "[t]he potential for abuse and manipulation of a social networking site by someone other than its purported creator

---

41. Steven Seidenberg, *Seduced: For Lawyers, the Appeal of Social Media Is Obvious. It's Also Dangerous*, A.B.A.J., February 1, 2011.

42. Griffin v. State, 419 Md. 343, 352 (2011).

43. *Id.* at 368 n.13.

and/or user leads to our conclusion that a printout of an image from such a site requires a greater degree of authentication."[44] The Maryland Court of Appeals suggested three ways to properly authenticate this type of evidence: (1) ask the purported creator if he or she created the profile and added the post in question; (2) search the computer of the person who allegedly created the profile, examining its hard drive and internal history to determine if it was that person who originated the profile; or (3) obtain information directly from the social networking website itself that establishes who created and posted the relevant information to the profile. The authentication procedure recommended by the Maryland high court is stringent, particularly where the alleged author denies making the post. But where the evidence is indispensable, authentication by one of these methods is prudent.

The same principles discussed above to authenticate a Facebook screenshot would apply to MySpace, LinkedIn, or Twitter. The purpose of authentication is to provide the court sufficient proof to establish that the document is what it purports to be. Questions should focus on the origination, identification, and purity of the exhibit. Ask enough foundational questions to establish the exhibit is "accurately reflecting the content of the [website] and the image of the page on the computer at which the [screenshot] was made."[45]

Computer-Generated Documents

A proponent authenticates documents prepared on a computer, such as word processing documents, like other writings. The person who created the document can authenticate it. FRE 901(b)(9) describes additional proof necessary to authenticate this type of

---

44. *Id.* at 357.
45. 2 McCormick on Evidence, *supra* note 1, § 227 at 74.

document when the authenticating witness is not the creator: "Evidence describing a process or system and showing that it produces an accurate result." For example, if the wife discovers a letter on the family computer that was written by the husband, she would need to establish its authenticity by testifying to the following facts:

- Where she found the letter (what computer)
- Who had access to that computer
- Where on the computer was it found (e.g., in the My Documents folder on the computer)
- The general topic of the writing
- Any identifying information in the letter
- When she found it
- When she printed it
- That the printed copy is identical to the copy she found on the computer
- That it is in the same condition as when she printed it
- That the document offered is the same one that she printed off the computer[46]

A proponent may need to authenticate the accuracy of a spreadsheet prepared with a computer program such as Excel if the accuracy of the computation is questioned. In that event, present testimony concerning

- the hardware used to make the report;
- the version of the software used;
- the experience of the person using the program;
- the process followed for the input of data;

---

46. *See* Stafford v. Stafford, 161 Vt. 580, 641 A.2d 348 (1993) (testimony by a wife that she found a list of husband's extramarital affairs on the family computer was sufficient to authenticate the document).

- the accuracy of the computations.

Again, it is not necessary to foreclose all possibilities that the evidence may have been tampered with. The possibility of alterations goes toward the *weight*, not the *admissibility* of the evidence. Absent specific evidence showing that the document was altered, the court should not exclude it.[47]

Computerized Business Records

Modern businesses rely on computers for virtually all aspects of their operations. While computerized business records are most easily self-authenticated by a certification under Rule 902(11) and (12), they may be authenticated through testimony as well. The basic foundation to authenticate computerized business records includes the following:

(a) The business uses a computer.
(b) The computer is reliable.
(c) The business has developed a procedure for inserting data into the computer.
(d) The procedure has built-in safeguards to ensure accuracy and identify errors.
(e) The business keeps the computer in a good state of repair.
(f) The business had the computer readout certain data.
(g) The witness used the proper procedures to obtain the readout.
(h) The computer was in good working order at the time the witness obtained the readout.
(i) The witness recognizes the exhibit as the readout.

---

47. *See* United States v. Safavian, 644 F. Supp. 2d 1 (2009).

(j)   If the readout contains strange symbols or terms, the wit-
      ness explains the meaning of the symbols or terms for the
      trier of fact.[48]

Once they are properly authenticated, business records (computerized or otherwise) are admissible as a hearsay exception pursuant
to Rule 803(6).

Demonstrative Aids

A demonstrative aid provides the court with another tool to understand the evidence. These aids can be used to illustrate or help
explain a witness's testimony. They can also be used during opening statements or closing arguments. A family law trial provides
numerous opportunities to use a demonstrative aid, including the
following:

- Enlarge the page of an expert's report to highlight the expert's
  testimony.
- Enlarge copies of detailed records that require explanation.
- Enlarge a clause from an agreement that may be in dispute.
- Print a timeline of salient events that can be used to illustrate
  the testimony.
- In an opening statement, use a chart to illustrate how the evi-
  dence will explain a complicated financial tracing issue.
- At closing, use printed pages from the trial transcript or enlarge-
  ments of important exhibits.

---

48. Edward J. Imwinkelried, Evidentiary Foundations § 4.03(2) at 62 (Matthew
Bender & Co., Inc. 7th ed. 2008).

A demonstrative aid is not ordinarily admissible as substantive evidence (although some jurisdictions allow them as such).[49] *McCormick* highlights the difference between demonstrative aids and ordinary evidence:

> [D]emonstrative aids do not have *independent* probative value for determining the substantive issues in the case. They are relevant, again in theory, only because of the assistance they give to the trier in understanding other real, testimonial and documentary evidence.[50]

For the purposes of a complete appellate record, identify and mark the exhibit, offering it as a demonstrative (as opposed to a substantive) exhibit. Often a demonstrative aid is on a large poster board or is shown on a projector. In that event, provide a paper copy for the court record.

To authenticate a demonstrative aid, the proponent must lay a foundation establishing that the "item is a fair and accurate representation of relevant testimony or documentary evidence otherwise admitted in the case."[51] Mark and identify the aid as a demonstrative exhibit, and have the witness testify that the demonstrative aid accurately represents something the witness is describing and that it will assist the court in understanding their testimony.

Summaries

A summary is a type of a demonstrative aid, but the foundational requirements differ from those of other types of demonstrative aids. FRE 1006 provides, "The proponent may use a summary,

---

49. *See, e.g.,* Verizon Directories Corp. v. Yellow Book USA, Inc., 331 F. Supp. 2d 136 (E.D.N.Y. 2004); Joynt v. Barnes, 388 N.E.2d 1298 (Ill. App. Ct. 2nd 1979).
50. 2 McCormick on Evidence, *supra* note 1, § 214 at 14 (footnotes omitted).
51. *Id.* at 15.

chart, or calculation to prove the content of voluminous writings, recordings, or photographs that cannot be conveniently examined in court." In the event a party seeks to offer a summary, the offering party must provide additional testimony to explain how the summary was prepared, and that it accurately reflects the underlying data summarized in the exhibit. If, for example, an accountant were called to provide forensic testimony regarding the number of deposits into the husband's bank account and he or she produced such a summary, the accountant would testify to how the summary was prepared: the procedures for analyzing the data, the records reviewed and included in the report. Once the summary is admitted, the accountant could use it to testify to his or her conclusions based on the summary of the data.

Unlike a demonstrative aid, a party may offer a summary exhibit as substantive evidence, proof of the information contained therein. Though all of the underlying documents do not have to be offered for admission (although they could be), the documents themselves must be admissible. As one court has held, Rule 1006 is not a "back door vehicle for the introduction of evidence which is otherwise inadmissible."[52] The trial court has discretion whether to admit a summary. A summary may be used when the underlying documents are too voluminous to be conveniently examined in court individually. The original documents need not be produced in court, but they must be made available to the other party for inspection and copying prior to the trial. Some courts have imposed an affirmative duty to provide the records, regardless of whether a discovery request was made.[53] Good practice suggests producing any underlying records to the opponent well in advance of the trial in order to avoid a claim of surprise.

---

52. Peat, Inc. v. Vanguard Research, Inc., 378 F.3d 1154, 1160 (11th Cir. 2004).
53. *See, e.g.,* United States v. Modena, 302 F.3d 626 (6th Cir. 2002).

Use a summary where records are voluminous and can easily be distilled into a summary format. Argue that the summary allows the court a focused view of the data and that it will help the court understand the information. In seeking to restrict the admission of a summary, argue that the offering may not be complete or may mislead the court if it is packaged in a way to skew the data in the opponent's favor. Another defense is that the underlying documents were never tendered for examination. Finally, remember that the rule applies to a summary of voluminous documents and so on. A written summary of all of the husband's domestic contributions to repairs of the house, for example, is not properly admitted under this rule.

Public Records or Reports

Rule 901(7) provides the procedure to authenticate public records: "Evidence that: (A) a document was recorded or filed in a public office as authorized by law; or (B) a purported public record or statement is from the office where items of this kind are kept." Authentication of a report from a state or county child support collection agency, used to prove child support payments, would fall under this rule.

The Advisory Committee Comments note that public records under this rule include data stored in computers, and by reasonable inference, data reflected on websites as well. The exhibit is authenticated simply by a witness testifying to its source (e.g., "I printed it off the federal government website."). Alternatively it could be authenticated by admission or stipulation at the pretrial stage of the case.[54]

---

54. Self-authentication of public records under Rule 902 is discussed later in this Chapter. Also, see Rule 803(8), discussed in Chapter 7, which allows statements in public

Ancient Documents

Rule 901(8) assumes the authenticity of documents at least 20 years old. The rule provides that when such a document or data compilation in any form is not suspicious, or is found in a place that it would likely be if it were authentic, this is sufficient to authenticate it. This rule derives from the common law and now applies to digital information as well. The Advisory Committee Notes address the issue of authentication of older digital data:

> Since the importance of appearance diminishes in this situation, the importance of custody or place where found increases correspondingly. This expansion is necessary in view of the widespread use of methods of storing data in forms other than conventional written records.[55]

In order to authenticate computer data that is more than 20 years old as an ancient document, present evidence of the chain of custody of the data and proofs related to the condition of the computer (or other place where the data is stored).[56]

Self-Authentication of Real Evidence

Rule 902 allows certain documents and things to be self-authenticated. No independent testimony is necessary to authenticate. This is a commonsense rule designed to recognize the authenticity of certain inherently reliable documents and things. The rule provides the following types of documents are self-authenticated:

---

records as an exception to the hearsay rule.

55. FED. R. EVID. 901 Advisory Committee's Notes, 56 F.R.D 183, 332.

56. See Rule 803(16), discussed in Chapter 7, which exempts statements in ancient documents from the hearsay rule.

(a) Domestic public documents under seal
(b) Domestic public documents not under seal
(c) Foreign public documents
(d) Certified documents of public records
(e) Official publications
(f) Newspapers and periodicals
(g) Trade inscriptions and the like
(h) Acknowledged documents
(i) Commercial paper and related documents
(j) Presumptions under acts of Congress
(k) Certified domestic records of regularly conducted activity
(l) Certified foreign records of regularly conducted activity

The presumption of authenticity is rebuttable. The opponent of the evidence may challenge its authenticity. The proponent must give prior notice of the intent to rely on this rule, along with prior disclosure of the documents whose admission the proponent will seek. Prior notice gives the opponent an opportunity to challenge the exhibit's authenticity. That a document is self-authenticated does not guarantee its admission. An opposing party can still object that the exhibit contains inadmissible hearsay statements or is inadmissible for other reasons, such as relevance.

Rule 902, subsections (11) and (12), allows for self-authentication of business records where the appropriate certification is provided from the custodian of the records or other qualified person. The certification is designed to conform to the foundation requirements of the hearsay exception for business records. Prior to the adoption of this rule, the proponent had to call the custodian to physically appear in court and testify to the foundation for the admission of records. Under FRE 902, the custodian's appearance is waived if he or she provides a certification that the record sought to be admitted

(a) was made at or near the time of the occurrence of the matters set forth by, or from information transmitted by, a person with knowledge of those matters;
(b) was kept in the course of the regularly conducted activity; and
(c) was made by the regularly conducted activity as a regular practice.

FRE 902 is a shortcut for the admission of business records that would otherwise require cumbersome and expensive testimony to lay the predicate foundation. This rule needs to be read in conjunction with FRE 803(6) (hearsay exception for business records). By relying on the certification process, the self-authenticated records are admissible as a hearsay exception under FRE 803(6).

Necessity of Subscribing Witness

FRE 903 provides that unless the law otherwise requires, a subscribing or attesting witness is not necessary to authenticate a document. At common law, the proponent had to produce an attesting witness to authenticate a sworn statement. Rule 903 abolished the common law doctrine, except where a document *must* be attested to be valid (e.g., a will in certain states).

Practice Points

- Authenticity is just the starting point: a proponent of evidence needs to overcome relevancy, hearsay, and other rules to obtain admission of any exhibit.
- The easiest way to authenticate any potential exhibit is by a stipulation or use of a request to admit the genuineness of documents. Use these procedures wherever possible.

- Know your opponent and the judge. If your opponent is unreasonable, be more scrupulous in proving authenticity. Similarly, if your judge is more formal with evidence, the same rule applies.
- Make sure you discuss authentication with your authenticating witnesses prior to their testimony so they understand their mission and have a context to work from.
- Authenticate documents by asking authentication questions in a deposition. An admission by an opponent in a deposition concerning authenticity will serve to authenticate the exhibit at trial.
- If you suspect that a digital image may have been altered, you will need to start early. In discovery, request the production of any photos, digital or otherwise, that are in the possession of the opponent. Leave plenty of time to hire an expert to investigate the veracity of the image.
- Any time you intend to use a screenshot, make sure to have your client put his or her initials and date of the printing directly on the face of the document. This will help identify and authenticate it.
- If you subpoena documents from a business, prepare a certification and ask the record keeper to sign it, thus meeting your burden of self authentication under Rules 902(11) and (12). Voluntarily give copies of the subpoenaed documents to opposing counsel along with the certification in advance of trial, in order to comply with the rule.
- Proactively provide copies or access to documents that will be the basis of a summary exhibit. By doing so, you will defeat any objections based on surprise and can potentially generate a stipulation concerning the exhibit.

Original Writing Rule and the Rule of Completeness

10

The original writing rule (also known as the best evidence rule) requires the production of an original document if its material terms are at issue. Despite the name of the rule, duplicates are ordinarily allowed in place of the original. Duplicates are disallowed only if there is a genuine issue concerning the duplicate's authenticity. I also discuss the interaction between testimony and production of documents and clarify some common misconceptions about this topic. Finally, I discuss the rule of completeness that provides that when a party offers a writing or recording as an exhibit, the adverse party may require the introduction of any other part of the writing or recording.

Rules to consider:

Rule 1001. Definitions That Apply to This Article

In this article:

(a)   A "writing" consists of letters, words, numbers, or their equivalent set down in any form.
(b)   A "recording" consists of letters, words, numbers, or their equivalent recorded in any manner.
(c)   A "photograph" means a photographic image or its equivalent stored in any form.
(d)   An "original" of a writing or recording means the writing or recording itself or any counterpart intended to have the same effect by the person who executed or issued it. For electronically stored information, "original" means any printout—or other output readable by sight—if it accurately reflects the information. An "original" of a photograph includes the negative or a print from it.
(e)   A "duplicate" means a counterpart produced by a mechanical, photographic, chemical, electronic, or other equivalent process or technique that accurately reproduces the original.

Rule 1002. Requirement of the Original

An original writing, recording, or photograph is required in order to prove its content unless these rules or a federal statute provides otherwise.

Rule 1003. Admissibility of Duplicates

A duplicate is admissible to the same extent as the original unless a genuine question is raised about the original's authenticity or the circumstances make it unfair to admit the duplicate.

Rule 1004. Admissibility of Other Evidence of Content

An original is not required and other evidence of the content of a writing, recording, or photograph is admissible if:

(a) all the originals are lost or destroyed, and not by the proponent acting in bad faith;

(b) an original cannot be obtained by any available judicial process;

(c) the party against whom the original would be offered had control of the original; was at that time put on notice, by pleadings or otherwise, that the original would be a subject of proof at the trial or hearing; and fails to produce it at the trial or hearing; or

(d) the writing, recording, or photograph is not closely related to a controlling issue.

Rule 1005. Copies of Public Records to Prove Content

The proponent may use a copy to prove the content of an official record—or of a document that was recorded or filed in a public office as authorized by law—if these conditions are met: the record or document is otherwise admissible; and the copy is certified as correct in accordance with Rule 902(4) or is testified to be correct by a witness who has compared it with the original. If no such copy can be obtained by reasonable diligence, then the proponent may use other evidence to prove the content.

Rule 1006. Remainder of or Related Writings or Recorded Statements

If a party introduces all or part of a writing or recorded statement, an adverse party may require the introduction, at that time, of any other part—or any other writing or recorded statement—that in fairness ought to be considered at the same time.

Rule 1007. Testimony or Statement of a Party to Prove Content

The proponent may prove the content of a writing, recording, or photograph by the testimony, deposition, or written statement of the party against whom the evidence is offered. The proponent need not account for the original.

Original Writing Rule

The original writing rule, also known as the best evidence rule, requires the use of an original to prove its content, if the content is material to the case. This rule is related to the authenticity rules discussed above. The purpose of the rule is to deny admission to forgeries, altered documents, or other illegitimate evidence. The rule is also designed to make sure that where documents and recordings are central to an issue, the court can consider the exact content firsthand rather than a secondhand recitation of what it contains. A witness paraphrasing from memory or reliance on secondary sources is less reliable when the original is available to examine. This rule, which was formed in the eighteenth century, has become obsolete due to rigorous pretrial discovery requirements in nearly all jurisdictions, allowing examination of questionable evidence before the trial, and to the availability of exact reproductions. The federal rules allow introduction of duplicates into evidence under most circumstances.[1]

Another purpose of the rule is to prevent misleading the trier of fact through the introduction of select parts of a document, without a full disclosure of all of its terms.

While the rule initially addressed only writings, time and technology have expanded the scope of the rule to include photographs, recordings, and computer data. Where the offered exhibit is a physical writing or recording, the original is the writing or recording itself. If multiple "originals" of a document are prepared, any one of them is considered an original. With digital data no original exists in the traditional sense. FRE 1001 addresses this problem; it defines an original photograph as any print generated from the negative and any printout or output from a computer or other similar device (e.g., a digital camera) that is shown to accurately reflect the data. For example, a print of a digital photograph is an original.

FRE 1002 requires production of the original writing, recording, or photograph to prove its contents. The key question is whether the document is offered into evidence to prove its contents. The Advisory Committee Notes provide examples of this principle: "payment may be proved without producing the written receipt, which was given. Earnings may be proved without producing books of account in which they are entered."[2]

But if the writing, photograph, or recording *itself* is the source of a legal controversy, the rule applies. A classic family law example would be in a suit for enforcement of a premarital agreement. A party who seeks to enforce the agreement must produce the original document (or a conforming copy as provided in Rule 1003). Mere

---

1. FED. R. EVID. 1001 and 1003.
2. FED. R. EVID. 1002 Advisory Committee's Notes, 56 F.R.D. 183, 342.

testimony that "we had one" may not suffice.[3] Other examples include a written marital settlement agreement in which the text of the document itself is central to one of the issues, and a claim that a spouse conveyed an interest in property to the other spouse. In each example, the party needs to present the original document, the agreement or deed, or an exact duplicate.

Distinguish the examples above from a recording of past events. A journal that recorded events is not itself independently legally significant: it has captured past events. The rule does not apply to memoranda, journals, or other documents chronicling past events or conversations. One does not need to present a copy of the journal to reference a conversation that was mentioned in the journal.

Rule 1002 does not apply to collateral matters. Collateral matters include matters that are not central to the contested issues in the case. One would not need to produce a recorded deed to establish that the parties owned a house, unless of course, one of them was challenging ownership.

This rule is often misapplied. The rule does not require the production of documentary evidence in lieu of a witness's testimony unless the actual content of the document is the core issue. Testimonial evidence does not automatically become inadmissible if the same proof is available from a document or recording.

For example, assume a family party was videotaped where the wife made several laudatory statements about the husband's parenting. At trial, the husband's lawyer seeks to elicit testimony from him about those statements. The wife's lawyer objects to the testimony based on the nonproduction of the video. The wife's lawyer cites the best evidence rule. The husband's lawyer would argue that even if the admission was recorded, the husband could still testify to the statement without the tangible evidence corroborating it. The issue is not the content of the video, but the fact that the

---

3.   But see Rule 1004(a) that discusses lost documents.

statement was made. On the other hand, if the issue relates to the video itself, the husband will need to produce the video at the trial.

Use of Duplicates

FRE 1003 addresses admissibility of duplicates. A duplicate is defined in FRE 1001(e) as "a counterpart produced by a mechanical, photographic, chemical, electronic, or other equivalent process or technique that accurately reproduces the original." Rule 1003 provides that a duplicate can be used to the same extent as an original unless "a genuine question is raised about the original's authenticity or the circumstances make it unfair to admit the duplicate." Thus, if no material issue exists as to the authenticity of the original (and thus the duplicate), and if no other substantive reason exists to keep it out, the duplicate is admissible without presenting (or accounting for) the original.

If a party raises a legitimate challenge to the authenticity of an exhibit, the offering party must produce the original unless production of the original is excused under FRE 1004, discussed below. For example, where a party credibly argues that a document is fraudulent, the offering party must produce the original. Or if a duplicate is incomplete and the exhibit is challenged, the offering party must produce the original. The challenge to admissibility must be credible and substantial; a speculative claim of inauthenticity does not suffice to bar admission of a duplicate.[4]

The challenge must affect the reliability of the document itself. For example, a court has held that the unexplained collateral handwriting on a duplicate was insufficient to deny its admission into

---

4. 2 McCormick on Evidence, § 236 at 101 (Kenneth S. Braun, ed., Thomson West 6th ed. 2006; People v. Huehn, 53 P.3d 733 (Colo. App. 2002); Equitable Life Assurance Soc'y v. Starr, 489 N.W.2d 857 (Neb. 1992).

evidence.[5] But when in doubt, where possible, make the original available for inspection, if not actual admission. If a party does not produce the original on request, or otherwise conceals it, the court could exclude the duplicate.[6]

Exceptions to the Requirement for Introduction of Original Document

The rules excuse nonproduction of an original under certain circumstances. FRE 1004 provides that the original is not required, and other evidence of the contents of a document is admissible under the following circumstances:

(a) All the originals are lost or destroyed, and not by the proponent acting in bad faith.

(b) An original cannot be obtained by any available judicial process.

(c) The party against whom the original would be offered had control of the original; was at that time put on notice, by pleadings or otherwise, that the original would be a subject of proof at the trial or hearing; and fails to produce it at the trial or hearing.

(d) The writing, recording, or photograph is not closely related to a controlling issue.

This rule only applies where the original is necessary. As discussed above, production of the original is not necessary under

---

5. United States v. Skillman, 922 F.2d 1370 (9th Cir. 1990).
6. McCarthy v. Northwest Mortg. Closing Servs., 1995 WL 146991 (Minn. Ct. App. 1995).

all circumstances. But where it is necessary, the proponent will need to explain the absence of the original to allow substitute evidence.

If the original is lost or destroyed, it obviously cannot be offered into evidence. The relevant inquiry is good faith. How was the document lost? When was it last seen? How hard did the proponent search for the missing document? The burden is on the person who last possessed the document or who destroyed the document to establish a good faith explanation for the loss or destruction of the document.[7] As the New York Court of Appeals observed on this topic, "Indeed, the more important the document to the resolution of the ultimate issue in the case, 'the stricter becomes the requirement of the evidentiary foundation (establishing loss) for the admission of secondary evidence.' "[8] Assuming the trial judge determines no impropriety, the proponent may substitute secondary evidence to prove up the document's contents.

Where the document is in the possession of a third party and the proponent legitimately cannot obtain it, the court may excuse its admission. There must be evidence of a reasonable attempt to retrieve the document. A subpoena *duces tecum* could be used to retrieve the original. If the possessor is beyond the reach of process and will not voluntarily produce the original, this rule permits secondary evidence to prove its contents. *McCormick* summarizes a common sense application of this rule: "before secondary evidence is used, the proponent must show either that he has made reasonable but unavailing efforts to secure the original from its possessor, or circumstances which persuade the court that such efforts, had they been made, would have been fruitless."[9] If a party

---

7.   2 MCCORMICK ON EVIDENCE, *supra* note 4, § 237 at 104; Seiler v. Lucasfilm, Ltd., 808 F.2d 1316 (9th Cir. 1986).

8.   Schozer v. William Penn Life Ins. Co. of N.Y., 644 N.E.2d 1353; N.Y.S. 2d 797 (1994) at page 4 of LEXIS, citing Harmon v. Matthews, 27 NYS2d 656, 663, citing People v. Dolan, 186 NY 4, 13.

9.   2 MCCORMICK ON EVIDENCE, *supra* note 4, § 227 at 105-06.

can establish the other party's fraud or collusion in the nonproduction of a document, the court can bar the other party from putting in secondary evidence to prove its contents.

Where the opponent has the original document, the court may excuse the proponent from producing it. The party seeking to offer the document into evidence must prove that the opponent possesses the original. The proponent must notify the opponent of the intent to offer the original at the trial or hearing and request that the item be produced at the trial or hearing. The notice requirement is not rigorous, and a simple written request will suffice. If the proponent meets the foregoing requirements, he or she can offer secondary evidence to prove the contents of the original if it is not produced.[10]

If the opponent possesses the original, request it. While secondary evidence may be allowed in this circumstance, production of the original is usually advantageous. Notify the opponent at the commencement of the case to preserve originals, both computerized data as well as any important writings, recordings, or other real evidence. Serve formal discovery to produce the original for inspection. If necessary, file a pretrial motion demanding production of the requested original. By diligently attempting to obtain original documents early in the proceeding, the offering party can argue an adverse inference from the destroyed information and request sanctions.[11]

---

10. 2 McCORMICK ON EVIDENCE, *supra* note 4, § 237 at 106 (citing United States v. Shores, 93 Fed. Appx. 868 (6th Cir. 2004)).

11. *See also* Lauren R. Nichols, *Spare the Rod, Spoil the Litigator? The Varying Degrees of Culpability Required for an Adverse Inference Sanction Regarding Spoliation of Electronic Discovery*, 99 KY. L.J. 881 (2011); for an example of a notice to preserve evidence, *see* Discovery Process, *feature*, 30-WTR. Ram. Advoc. 37 (A.B.A., 2008).

Secondary Evidence Defined

As noted above, if an original is unavailable or its absence is excused, the proponent may be permitted to use secondary evidence. What is secondary evidence? *McCormick* lists a number of examples of secondary evidence:

(a) A duplicate (as defined by FRE 1003);

(b) A copy that does not qualify as a duplicate but was made by one who was looking at the original while they copied or a transcript made while the transcriber was listening to a recording;

(c) A copy, however made, which has been compared by a witness with the original and found correct;

(d) Secondhand or immediate copy, i.e. a copy of a firsthand copy;

(e) A summary or restatement of a writing;

(f) Testimonial evidence as to the contents of a writing, recording, or photograph, with memory aided by a previously made memorandum or notes; and

(g) Testimonial evidence from unaided memory.[12]

Secondary evidence is subject to the other rules of evidence (e.g., hearsay, relevance, etc.); the proponent must lay the proper foundation to admit the secondary evidence.

Rule 1004 does not distinguish between the types of secondary evidence. The rule's drafters designed the rule to avoid preferences, disallowing a claim that a party's failure to produce a superior type of secondary evidence (such as a photocopy) is a basis to deny admission to inferior secondary evidence (such as testimony describing the content of the original). The judge cannot draw an adverse inference from the use of one type of secondary evidence

---

12. 2 MCCORMICK ON EVIDENCE, *supra* note 4, § 238 at 109.

versus another. The rule's drafters designed the rule to avoid preferences, disallowing a claim that one's failure to produce a superior type of secondary evidence (such as a photocopy rather than testimony describing the original) is a basis to deny admission to inferior secondary evidence. The secondary evidence must still be reliable, however. A New York case illustrates the general principle concerning the use of this type of evidence:

> No categorical limitations are placed on the type of secondary evidence that are admissible. Nonetheless, the proponent of such derivative proof has the heavy burden of establishing preliminarily to the court's satisfaction, that it is a reliable and accurate portrayal of the original. Thus as a threshold matter, the trial court must be satisfied that the proffered evidence is authentic and correctly reflects the contents of the original before ruling on admissibility.[13]

Once the secondary evidence is admitted, it is subject to challenge only concerning the weight to be given to it. Thus while inferior secondary evidence is admissible, the opposing lawyer can still argue the weight to be given by the court to the evidence.

Collateral Writings

FRE 1004(4) exempts a party from producing an original if "the writing, recording, or photograph is not closely related to a controlling issue." For example, a party may testify that they have an employment agreement with ABC Corporation. If the terms of the employment are not at issue, the rule exempts production of the agreement due to its lack of centrality to the primary issues in the case. By way of another example:

---

13. Schozer v. William Penn Life Ins. Co. of N.Y., *supra* note 8.

- Did you notify your landlord that you intended to move? (Yes)
- How did you notify her? (I sent her a letter in March)
- *Objection:* The original writing rule requires the production of the letter rather than secondary evidence concerning it.
- *Response:* Your honor, this testimony deals with a collateral issue, that is, when she decided to move rather than the ultimate issue of the propriety of her decision to relocate.

Whether a document is collateral or central to the proceeding is not a bright line test. In determining whether a document is collateral, *McCormick* suggests the following three-part balancing test:[14]

(1) The centrality of the document to the principal issues of the litigation
(2) The complexity of the relevant features of the document
(3) The existence of genuine dispute as to its contents

In a divorce case, some documents are central to the litigation. For example, classification of property may hinge on a document, such as a deed showing when an owner took title. In planning, one must always discern, using the balancing test suggested by *McCormick*, whether a document is central to a core issue in the case. But because of the subjectivity of the court's analysis, be cautious about not offering an original. When in doubt, the lawyer should make sure the original (or a conforming copy) is available if necessary.

Public Records

FRE 1005 provides that a party may offer a certified copy of the record or a witness may testify that he or she has compared the

---

14. 2 McCormick on Evidence, *supra* note 4, § 239 at 112.

copy with the original and can testify that the copy is an accurate copy. In family court, a party may seek to offer into evidence a court order or other court document. In contrast to Rule 1004, Rule 1005 creates a preference for either a certified copy of a public record or a witness who has seen the original and can verify the copy.

Use of an Admission to Prove Content of a Writing

FRE 1007 allows a party to prove the contents of a writing, recording, or photograph by an admission of the adverse party. The proponent need not offer the original (or account for its absence) if the adverse party admits to its contents. The rule limits the use of an admission to one made during sworn testimony or in writing. This principle includes a response to a request for admission. A nonsworn oral admission may be admitted where the proponent explains the missing original. In that circumstance, a court may admit secondary evidence (including a nonsworn admission) to prove the contents of the document.[15]

The Rule of Completeness

Closely related to the original writing rule is the rule of completeness. FRE 106 provides that when a party offers a writing or recording as an exhibit, the adverse party may require the introduction of any other part of the writing or recording that "in fairness ought to be considered at the same time." According to the Advisory Committee Notes, the rule is based on two policy

---

15. Dart Industries, Inc., v. Commercial Union Ins. Co., 52 P.3d 79, 85 (Sup. Ct. Cal. 2002).

considerations. First, the rule is intended to avoid confusion by matters taken out of context. Second, the rule recognizes the inadequacy of repair work if the full story is not told until later in the trial. The rule is limited to writings and recorded statements. Per the committee notes, it specifically does not apply to conversations. Assume, for example, a lawyer is examining his client concerning one page of a three-page agreement executed between the client and a third party. Assume the lawyer offers into evidence that individual page of the agreement. The opponent could object under the rule of completeness and require, as a precondition of admission, that the entire agreement be offered rather than a select page.

Practice Points

- If an original writing or photograph is integral to your case and it is in the possession of the opponent, make sure you send a letter by certified mail requesting that the original be preserved intact.
- Tell your client at the beginning of the case to preserve all originals, and if the originals are vital, make sure they are placed in a safe place or take possession yourself.
- Wherever possible, make copies of any potential evidence in case an original is lost or inadvertently destroyed.
- In planning, consider the availability of original evidence. If a missing original may pose an admissibility problem, consider alternative ways to present the same evidence. Find the most persuasive secondary evidence possible.
- Consider using a deposition to get a nonparty witness to admit to the contents of a writing when the original may be missing. Consider a deposition or request for admission to an opposing party to get such an admission. In planning,

it may be important to get an admission early in the case before the witness (or the witness's attorney) understands the issue.

Competency of Witnesses

Before witnesses can testify, the court must determine whether they are qualified to testify in the first place. Child witnesses pose special problems for the court. Assuming a witness is competent, the person ordinarily must testify to his or her sensory experiences rather than opinions. There are exceptions: a lay witness can testify to certain kinds of opinions based on collective facts and/or life experience. I also address use of interpreters and special problems when a judge or lawyer is a witness.

Rules to consider:

Rule 601. Competency to Testify in General

Every person is competent to be a witness unless these rules provide otherwise. But in a civil case, state law governs the witness's competency regarding a claim or defense for which state law supplies the rule of decision.

Rule 104. Preliminary Questions

(a)   *In General.* The court must decide any preliminary question
        about whether a witness is qualified, a privilege exists, or evi-
        dence is admissible. In so deciding, the court is not bound by
        evidence rules, except those on privilege. . . .

Rule 602. Need for Personal Knowledge

A witness may not testify to a matter unless evidence is introduced
sufficient to support a finding that the witness has personal knowledge of the matter. Evidence to prove personal knowledge may, but
need not, consist of the witness's own testimony. This rule is subject to the provisions of Rule 703, relating to opinion testimony
by expert witnesses.

Rule 603. Oath or Affirmation to Testify Truthfully

Before testifying, a witness must give an oath or affirmation to testify truthfully. It must be in a form designed to impress that duty
on the witness's conscience.

Rule 701. Opinion Testimony by Lay Witnesses

If a witness is not testifying as an expert, testimony in the form of
an opinion is limited to one that is:

(a)   rationally based on the witness's perception;
(b)   helpful to clearly understanding the witness's testimony or to
        determining a fact in issue; and

(c)   not based on scientific, technical, or other specialized knowledge within the scope of Rule 702.

Rule 604. Interpreter

An interpreter must be qualified and must give an oath or affirmation to make a true translation.

Rule 605. Judge's Competency as a Witness

The presiding judge may not testify as a witness at the trial. A party need not object to preserve the issue.

Questions of Witness Competency

Distinguished from the substantive content of testimony, Rules 601 and 602 determine whether a witness is qualified to testify at all. Nothing else matters if the witness is ineligible to testify in the first place. Unless a state law specifically excludes the witness or there are certain provable deficiencies in the witness's ability to testify, he or she is eligible to testify. Formerly, strict rules barred the testimony of an interested party. Those rules also barred witnesses based on mental capacity, moral grounds, religious beliefs, or criminal conviction. Today, most of these restrictions have been eliminated and have been replaced with an emphasis on the weight of the testimony.

FRE 104(a) authorizes the trial judge to determine a preliminary question of competency; the judge has the discretion to disallow an incompetent witness. In order to determine competency, the court may conduct a hearing on this limited issue. In such a hearing, the rules of evidence do not apply, except for the rules pertaining to privileges. The trial judge must resolve three questions to determine competency:

- Does the witness understand the duty imposed by the oath to testify truthfully?
- Does the witness have sufficient memory to testify to the matter at issue?
- Does the witness have the ability to communicate what he saw and heard?[1]

Child Witness

Family law cases often involve children and their observations. There are no specific age limitations for a child witness and courts have recognized children as young as four years old as competent witnesses.[2] While the rules do not specifically require a preliminary inquiry for a child witness, case law requires some proof that the child is mature enough to know the difference between the truth and a lie. Professor Lubet describes the procedure for qualifying a child witness:

> In the case of a very young child, for example, the qualifying examination must establish that the witness is capable of distinguishing reality from fantasy, is able to perceive such relationships as time and distance, and appreciates that it is 'wrong to tell a lie.' Following the preliminary examination, the adverse party should be allowed an opportunity to conduct a 'voir dire' which is a preliminary cross-examination limited to a threshold issue such as competence.[3]

---

1. Thomas A. Mauet & Warren D. Wolfson, Trial Evidence 42 (4th ed. 2009).
2. Evans v. State, 28 P.3d 498 (Nev. 2001).
3. Steven Lubet, Modern Trial Advocacy 47 (4th ed. 2009).

The child need not testify perfectly to be qualified as a witness. As one Illinois court has held, "One imperfect response to a question would not invalidate a finding of competency in light of what is indicated by the totality of the responses."[4]

In-Camera Proceedings

Many states' laws allow the court to consider the wishes of a child in a custody case.[5] In order to insulate the child, the judge is authorized to conduct an in-camera interview of the child. This process allows children a voice in their custody or placement.

Where the judge conducts an in-camera interview of a child, the judge need not qualify the child as a competent witness and the rules of evidence do not apply. While some judges allow the attorneys to propose questions, others ask the questions themselves in these hearings. A court reporter should be present to preserve the record of the child's comments. Since these proceedings are jurisdiction specific, consult your state and local rules.[6]

Oath or Affirmation

Before testifying, witnesses must declare either by oath or affirmation that they will testify truthfully under penalty of perjury. FRE 603 provides that the oath shall be "in a form designed to impress that duty on the witness's conscience." The Advisory Committee

---

4.   People v. Dempsey, 242 Ill. App. 3d 568 at 584 (1st Dist. 1993).
5.   Holiday v. Holiday, 247 P.3d 29 (Wyo. 2011).
6.   For more information on use of children's testimony, see Thomas D. Lyon, *Assessing the Competency of Child Witnesses: Best Practice Informed by Psychology and Law*, in A HANDBOOK OF PSYCHOLOGICAL RESEARCH AND FORENSIC PRACTICE 69–85 (Michael E. Lamb et al. eds., Wiley-Blackwell 2nd ed. 2011) *reprinted in* THE SELECTED WORKS OF THOMAS D. LYON (Univ. of So. Cal. Law, July 2011).

Notes explain, "The rule is designed to afford the flexibility required in dealing with religious adults, atheists, conscientious objectors, mental defectives, and children. Affirmation is simply a solemn undertaking to tell the truth; no special verbal formula is required."[7]

Requirement of Firsthand Knowledge of the Witness

Consistent with the goal of securing the most reliable evidence possible, FRE 602 limits witnesses' testimony to matters within their personal knowledge; witnesses can only testify to information they *noticed, observed, and remembered* personally. This burden to prove personal knowledge is minimal, and any questions concerning reliability should go to the weight of the testimony, rather than its admissibility.[8] The Advisory Committee observes the inherent challenges with this rule: "These foundation requirements may, of course, be furnished by the testimony of the witness himself; hence personal knowledge is not an absolute but may consist of what the witness thinks he knows from personal perception."[9] Sensory perception and thus personal knowledge is a slippery concept for the court to determine, and a commonsense approach is necessary—the court's analysis needs to start and end with the reliability of the testimony.

Questions pertaining to sensory observations are within the personal knowledge of the witness. Also questions regarding the witness's perceptions and thoughts qualify:

- What did you see?

---

7.   FED. R. EVID. 603 Advisory Committee's Note.
8.   1 McCORMICK ON EVIDENCE, § 10 at 49 (Kenneth S. Broun, ed., Thomson West 6th ed. 2006).
9.   FED. R. EVID. 603 Advisory Committee's Note, 56 F.R.D. 183, 263.

- What did you hear?
- What did you think about . . . ?
- What do you remember about . . . ?

These questions all qualify under the rule. By contrast, questions about another person's observations, opinions, or thoughts are inappropriate. The answers to these types of questions are deemed unreliable under the rule.

Rule 602 must be considered in conjunction with the hearsay rules. If the source of the knowledge is a statement from another, the proper objection is that the witness did not have firsthand knowledge, rather than hearsay. If, on the other hand, the witness repeats someone else's observations, hearsay is the appropriate objection. It is important to understand this distinction. If witnesses testify that they are aware of something because they "heard about it through the grapevine," they do not have personal knowledge about whatever they are repeating. Their testimony is based on secondhand information rather than their own observations. Such testimony is not based on firsthand knowledge. Hearsay only excludes the actual statements made by an out-of-court declarant. That would not be the case in this example.

Lay Opinion Testimony

McCormick defines an opinion as "an inference, belief or conclusion." FRE 701 allows certain lay opinion testimony.[10] Courts have developed two categories of lay opinion testimony: collective fact opinion (also known as shorthand rendition opinion) and skilled lay observer opinion.

---

10. 1 McCormick on Evidence, *supra* note 8, § 11 at 55. Expert opinions are addressed in Chapter 13.

Collective Fact Opinions

A collective fact opinion is an opinion by a witness who draws a reasonable inference based on personal perceptions. This type of lay opinion testimony derives from a collection of facts too numerous for the witness to articulate. There are a variety of familiar topics suitable for collective fact lay opinion testimony, including "the appearance of persons or things, identity, the manner of conduct, competency of a person, degrees of light or darkness, sound, size, weight, distance, and an endless number of items that cannot be described factually in words apart from inferences."[11] This includes lay opinions about someone else's intoxication. In that instance, the witness must testify to personal observations, past experience observing drunks, and the basis of his or her opinion.[12]

While the rules create a preference for a witness to testify to concrete facts, collective fact opinion testimony can help explain the witness's observation. As such, it is a convenient way to enhance the testimony:

> [T]o the extent reasonably feasible, the witness should attempt to articulate the concrete primary facts. However, when it is impractical for the witness to verbalize all the data supporting an inference, the preference yields; and the witness's inferential testimony is admissible.[13]

For example, assume Sally's lawyer seeks to elicit her opinion that a proposed parenting schedule would benefit the children. John's lawyer objects: the question is soliciting an improper opinion from a lay witness. Sally's lawyer might argue that she is providing a proper lay opinion because she is testifying to a collective fact

---

11. FED. R. EVID. 701 Advisory Committee's Note (citing Asplundh Mfg. Div. v. Benton Harbor Eng'g, 57 F.3d 1190, 1196 (3d Cir. 1995)).
12. *See, e.g.*, People v. Vanzandt, 679 N.E.2d 130 (Ill. App. Ct. 1997).
13. 1 MCCORMICK ON EVIDENCE, *supra* note 8, § 11 at 56 (footnote omitted).

opinion. The facts underlying her conclusions are too numerous to articulate, and her inferences, as the mother of the children, are reliable in this context.

Skilled Lay Observer Opinion

Rule 701 also allows skilled lay observer opinions. This type of opinion testimony is based on recognition of the value of the witness's "educated opinions." Mere guesses do not suffice. The proponent must lay a foundation to establish the basis of the opinions of the layperson. While collective fact opinion focuses on reasonable inferences drawn from multiple bits of data, skilled lay observer opinion is based on the life experience of the witness.

The opinion testimony of a skilled lay observer includes "lay opinions about a person's voice, handwriting style or even their sanity."[14] Witnesses must provide the basis of their knowledge or experience. For example, to identify someone's handwriting, the witness could testify that he or she observed the author's handwriting many times in the past and recognize it as being identical. Courts also allow owners to testify, as skilled laypersons, to their opinion regarding the value of their property. This type of opinion testimony is a convenient way of proving property value without an expert. Owners must testify to the basis of their knowledge, including their familiarity with the marketplace.[15]

Because of its inherent subjectivity, opinion testimony is allowed only where it is reasonable and helpful to the court. FRE 701 limits opinions or inferences to those that are

(a)   rationally based on the witness's perception;

---

14. Edward J. Imwinklried, Evidentiary Foundations, § 9.02[3] at 380 (Matthew Bender & Co. Inc. 7th ed. 2008.

15. Kim v. Mercedes Benz, U.S.A., Inc., 818 N.E.2d 713 (Ill. App. Ct. 2004).

(b) helpful to clearly understanding the witness's testimony or to determining a fact in issue; and

(c) not based on scientific, technical, or other specialized knowledge within the scope of Rule 702.

The opinion must be "rationally based on the witness's perception." A lay witness cannot testify to an inference based on an observation reported by someone else. Some courts have allowed opinion testimony about another's state of mind, based on that person's conduct and general demeanor, when the witness personally observed the other person's behavior.[16] For example, assume Jane witnessed her daughter cry and whine every time she returned from visitation with her father, Bob. The child complained about her father's preoccupation with his girlfriend. Jane might be asked whether the daughter was upset with her father. Bob's lawyer would object: the question solicits an improper opinion. Jane's lawyer would argue that she observed her daughter and knew her moods. From her observation, she could draw certain conclusions that were reasonable and reliable.

Expert Opinion Differentiated

Rule 701(c) is designed, in part, to disallow expert testimony disguised as layperson testimony. If a witness's testimony relies on "scientific, technical, or other specialized knowledge" (defined by FRE 702), the testimony will be treated as expert testimony and subject to the requirements for admission of such testimony. The Advisory Committee stresses that the rules do not distinguish

---

16. *See, e.g.*, United States v. Hoffner, 777 F.2d 1423, 1425 (10th Cir. 1985) ("Courts have been liberal in admitting witnesses' testimony as to another's state of mind"); 1 MCCORMICK ON EVIDENCE, *supra* note 8, § 11 at 58 n.33 (citing Lightfoot v. Union Carbide Corp., 110 F.3d 898, 911 (2d Cir. 1997)).

between expert and lay *witnesses*; rather, the rules distinguish between expert and lay *testimony*. A witness can testify both as an expert and as a lay witness, and the part of the testimony that is based on his or her expertise is subject to the rules pertaining to experts.[17] The Tennessee Supreme Court has analyzed the difference between expert and lay opinions. In *State v. Brown*, 836 S.W. 2d 530, 549 (1992), the court held that lay testimony "results from a process of reasoning familiar in everyday life." In contrast, expert testimony, "results from a process or reasoning which can be mastered only by specialists in the field."

Opinion on the Ultimate Issue

Rule 704(a) provides that "an opinion is not objectionable just because it embraces an ultimate issue." This rule, which applies to expert and lay opinions alike, allows a witness to testify to an opinion about the ultimate issue in the case. This would include, for example, an opinion about what custodial arrangements are in the best interest of a child.

Use of Interpreters

Rule 604 allows the use of an interpreter as a friend of the court. The rule provides that the interpreter must be qualified, and must take an oath or affirmation as any other witness. In day-to-day practice, an interpreter may not be a professional, but rather a friend or relative of the party. While technically the interpreter must be qualified, some courts will allow a lay interpreter in a routine matter, for the sake of expediency and convenience. The

---

17. FED. R. EVID. 701 Advisory Committee's Note.

court should be consulted before the hearing to see if the court will accept a lay interpreter who is related to the witness or party. Many family law litigants do not have the money or resources to hire a professional, and the court will need to decide whether to allow this type of informal arrangement. Tactically, if the court allows a lay interpreter in an important proceeding, consider having someone familiar with the language sit in the hearing to ensure that the opposing interpreter is accurately interpreting and not enhancing or modifying the witness's testimony.

Competency of the Judge or Lawyer as Witness

Rule 605 provides that a judge presiding at a trial may not testify in the trial as a witness. The rule provides that in the event a judge insists on testifying, no objection to the judge's testimony is necessary to preserve the error on appeal. The purpose of this automatic objection is to protect a litigant from having to choose between challenging the judge directly and losing the right to raise the issue in a higher court.

With regard to lawyer witnesses, the ABA Model Rules of Professional Conduct limit a lawyer's ability to testify. Rule 3.7 provides the following:

Lawyer as Witness
(a) A lawyer shall not act as advocate at a trial in which the lawyer is likely to be a necessary witness unless:
   (1) the testimony relates to an uncontested issue;
   (2) the testimony relates to the nature and value of legal services rendered in the case; or
   (3) disqualification of the lawyer would work substantial hardship on the client.

(b) A lawyer may act as advocate in a trial in which another lawyer in the lawyer's firm is likely to be called as a witness unless
precluded from doing so by Rule 1.7 or Rule 1.9.

Each state has its own code of professional responsibility governing
a lawyer's testimony in proceedings where he or she is representing a party. Those rules should be consulted prior to accepting
employment or at the point that the need for the lawyer's testimony becomes apparent.

Practice Points

- Be cautious about having a child testify against another parent. Any short-term tactical gains may be offset by long-term
  emotional problems for the child. We have a special duty as
  family lawyers to protect children.
- If a child witness is necessary, consider asking the court to conduct an in-camera hearing to determine whether the child is
  qualified to testify. Argue against the child testimony—that the
  evidence the child can offer may be marginally helpful to the
  court but it would be outweighed by the trauma to the child.
  Seek an order barring the child witness under the theory that
  the probative value of the evidence is outweighed by the prejudice, particularly when it may be cumulative.
- If a parent insists on improperly involving a child in a proceeding, consider using a guardian ad litem for the child. While a
  guardian's presence in the litigation will not completely insulate the child, it may have a chilling effect on the bad conduct.
  By using a guardian ad litem, the child's opinions and preferences can be revealed to the court without the actual testimony
  of the child.

- Plan ahead. If your client or a witness needs an interpreter, consult with the judge before the trial to determine if a lay interpreter will be allowed by the court.
- If the opponent is using a friend or relative to interpret, consider hiring your own interpreter to sit in the courtroom to point out any inaccuracies or improprieties with the interpreter's rendition of the witness's testimony.
- Make sure your opponent cannot convince a judge that your lay opinion testimony is a disguised expert opinion. When in doubt, disclose the testimony as though it was expert testimony, in order to avoid a motion to bar the lay opinion as disguised expert testimony.
- Prepare your client who will testify to a lay opinion, for example, his or her opinion of value of personal property. If the opinion is based on information received from a third party, such as a Realtor, be prepared to argue why it is not hearsay. Prepare the client to testify to appropriate factors in drawing his or her conclusions (e.g., what homes in the neighborhood have sold for).

Evidentiary Privileges   12

State law primarily governs privileges. The rules of privilege do not focus on relevance and reliability like the other rules; rather, they focus on competing policy concerns regarding the production and disclosure of protected information. In this chapter, I focus on the protection from forced disclosure of information under the following privileges: the Fifth Amendment privilege against self-incrimination, attorney-client privilege, physician-patient privilege, and marital privilege. I address the circumstances in which a party or witness can properly invoke the privilege as well as when they can waive it.

Rules to consider:

Rule 501. Privileges in General

The common law—as interpreted by United States courts in the light of reason and experience—governs a claim of privilege unless any of the following provides otherwise:

- the United States Constitution;
- a federal statute; or
- rules prescribed by the Supreme Court.

But in a civil case, state law governs privilege regarding a claim or defense for which state law supplies the rule of decision.

Rule 502. Attorney-Client Privilege and Work Product; Limitations on Waiver

The following provisions apply, in the circumstances set out, to disclosure of a communication or information covered by the attorney-client privilege or work-product protection.

(a) Disclosure Made in a Federal Proceeding or to a Federal Office or Agency; Scope of a Waiver.
When the disclosure is made in a federal proceeding or to a federal office or agency and waives the attorney-client privilege or work-product protection, the waiver extends to an undisclosed communication or information in a federal or state proceeding only if:
   (1)   the waiver is intentional;
   (2)   the disclosed and undisclosed communications or information concern the same subject matter; and
   (3)   they ought in fairness to be considered together.
(b) Inadvertent Disclosure. When made in a federal proceeding or to a federal office or agency, the disclosure does not operate as a waiver in a federal or state proceeding if:
   (1)   the disclosure is inadvertent;
   (2)   the holder of the privilege or protection took reasonable steps to prevent disclosure; and

(3) the holder promptly took reasonable steps to rectify the error, including (if applicable) following Federal Rule of Civil Procedure 26(b)(5)(B).

(c) Disclosure Made in a State Proceeding. When the disclosure is made in a state proceeding and is not the subject of a state court order concerning waiver, the disclosure does not operate as a waiver in a federal proceeding if the disclosure:

(1) would not be a waiver under this rule if it had been made in a federal proceeding; or

(2) is not a waiver under the law of the state where the disclosure occurred.

(d) Controlling Effect of a Court Order. A federal court may order that the privilege or protection is not waived by disclosure connected with the litigation pending before the court—in which event the disclosure is also not a waiver in any other federal or state proceeding.

(e) Controlling Effect of a Party Agreement. An agreement on the effect of disclosure in a federal proceeding is binding only on the parties to the agreement, unless it is incorporated into a court order.

(f) Controlling Effect of This Rule. Notwithstanding Rules 101 and 1101, this rule applies to state proceedings and to federal court-annexed and federal court-mandated arbitration proceedings, in the circumstances set out in the rule. And notwithstanding Rule 501, this rule applies even if State law provides the rule of decision.

(g) Definitions. In this rule:

(1) "attorney-client privilege" means the protection that applicable law provides for confidential attorney-client communications; and

(2) "work-product protection" means the protection that applicable law provides for tangible material (or its

intangible equivalent) prepared in anticipation of litigation or for trial.

Privileges Distinguished from Other Evidentiary Considerations

While most rules of evidence focus on protecting the integrity of the proceeding by attempting to ensure the reliability of evidence, the law of privilege addresses other policy concerns—protection of relationships deemed more important than the availability of otherwise relevant evidence. Generally, public policy insists that disclosures made between clergy and penitent, lawyer and client, and physician and patient must be protected to encourage full and honest intercourse in these important relationships, without risk of a later revelation. Thus in any proceeding where a privilege properly applies, a party cannot compel a witness or the other party to testify to protected matter despite its relevance or materiality to the proceeding.

As the rules themselves indicate, the law of privilege is primarily based on case law. While privilege rules were initially included in a working draft of the Federal Rules of Evidence, Congress eliminated them, preferring that they evolve in the common law. The only rule that avoided Congress's knife is a general rule, FRE 501, which provides that state law governs privilege. Commonly, attorney-client relationships, doctor (and mental health provider)-patient relationships, and clergy-penitent relationships are privileged relationships. Also certain spousal communications are protected by privilege. Family lawyers also commonly encounter the constitutional privilege against self-incrimination.

State law often prescribes rules concerning when or how a party or witness must assert a privilege.[1] Timing is important. If a party

---

1. *See* Cope v. Cope, 230 Cal. App. 2d 218 (1964).

waives the privilege at the last minute, after opportunity for the opponent to conduct discovery has lapsed, a court may disallow the party's testimony on the subject matter as to which the privilege was asserted and then waived.

Privilege against Self-Incrimination

Under the Fifth and Fourteenth Amendments to the United States Constitution, an individual cannot be forced to give testimony in a civil or administrative proceeding where an answer might expose the witness to future criminal prosecution.[2] The danger of prosecution must be real and appreciable; an irrational or unrealistic concern about future prosecution does not qualify. Courts have, however, sustained the right to remain silent for questions about sexual activity even though adultery or fornication statutes are rarely enforced.[3] The rule applies only to potential criminal prosecution. A witness may not invoke the privilege, for example, if an admission may merely create civil liability or jeopardize rights in a civil case.

A nonparty witness may invoke the privilege.[4] But a witness cannot invoke the privilege for another; it is personal and can only be raised by the person who is at risk of prosecution.[5] However, a lawyer who is authorized to do so may invoke the privilege on behalf of the client.

---

2. U.S. CONST. amend. V, U.S. CONST. amend. IV; McCarthy v. Arndstein, 266 U.S. 34 (1924).

3. 1 McCORMICK ON EVIDENCE, § 120 at 524 n.3 (Kenneth S. Brown, ed., Thomson West 6th ed. 2006) (citing Brown v. Walker, 161 U.S. 591, 608 (1896)); see also Gunn v. Hess, 367 S.E.2d 399 (N.C. Ct. App. 1988); Hollowell v. Hollowell, 369 S.E.2d 451, 453 (Va. Ct. App. 1988).

4. United States v. Echeles, 352 F.2d 892 (7th Cir. 1965).

5. People v. Adams, 669 N.E.2d 1331 (Ill. App. Ct. 1996).

There is no prescribed formula to assert the privilege; witnesses can do so by simply refusing to answer a question that exposes them to criminal prosecution.[6] But for purposes of a clear record, if witnesses intend to invoke their right to remain silent, they should clearly indicate that they are invoking their constitutional right to remain silent under the Fifth and Fourteenth Amendments.

Family lawyers often use contempt proceedings to enforce prior court orders. Generally, if a party is charged with civil contempt and may be incarcerated, the party may not rely on the protections of the Fifth Amendment.[7] In civil contempt, respondents hold the key to their jail cell and can purge the contempt by compliance with the court order. Therefore, the remedy is not penal but coercive, designed to compel compliance with a court order. In contrast, a criminal contempt proceeding is penal in nature, and the constitutional protections would apply.[8] In a civil contempt proceeding, the alleged contemnor can be called to testify and may not rely on the privilege. In contrast, in a criminal contempt proceeding, the alleged contemnor may rely on the constitutional privilege and refuse to testify.

The right to remain silent "protects against any conduct meeting the other requirements that would furnish a link in the chain of evidence usable to prosecute the person."[9] Production of records that are testimonial in nature and contain incriminating assertions may be subject to protection.[10] But the protection is not absolute: "A person may be required to produce specific documents

---

6.   1 MCCORMICK ON EVIDENCE, *supra* note 3, § 119 at 522 & n.8 (citing State v. Lingle, 140 S.W.3d 178 (Mo. Ct. App. 2004)).

7.   *See* 1 MCCORMICK ON EVIDENCE, *supra* note 3, § 122 at 531 n.17 (citing Ex parte Hulsey, 536 So. 2d 75, 76 (Ala. Civ. App. 1988)) *McCormick also* citing *In re* Contemnor Caron, 744 N.E.2d 787, 834 (Ohio Com. Pl. 2000)).

8.   1 MCCORMICK ON EVIDENCE, *supra* note 3, § 122 at 531 n.18 (citing Carter v. Brodrick, 750 P.2d 843, 845 (Alaska App. 1988)).

9.   1 MCCORMICK ON EVIDENCE, *supra* note 3, § 120 at 524.

10.   United States v. Doe, 465 U.S. 605 (1984).

even though they contain incriminating assertions of fact or belief because the creation of those documents was not 'compelled' within the meaning of the privilege."[11] In other words, when a person creates a document that includes incriminating admissions, the government did not force the person to make the admission; he or she did so voluntarily.

The Fifth Amendment protections apply to compulsory assertions rather than documents or records created voluntarily. But at least one court has held that when the production of records is compelled by court order or subpoena, production of those records may be subject to protection.[12] While Fifth Amendment issues are federal, individual state law guides the amendment's application in a state family law case. For example, assume the husband kept a separate set of books reflecting cash transactions not reported to the government. The wife requests copies of the books. The creation of these records was voluntary; arguably, they are not subject to protection of the rule. Distinguish this situation from one where the husband is asked in an interrogatory to list all of the cash income he did not disclose in his tax returns. That type of question seeks to compel disclosure of information that would be subject to the protections of the privilege.

Remedies for Opposing Party Invoking the Fifth Amendment Privilege

In a civil proceeding, the court can draw an adverse inference if a party invokes his or her Fifth Amendment privilege and by doing so disadvantages the other party.[13] If, for example, the wife invokes

---

11. United States v. Hubbell, 530 U.S. 27, 35 (2000).

12. United States v. Doe, *supra* note 10; Fisher v. United States, 96 S.Ct. 1569 (1976); DeMauro v. DeMauro, 142 N.H. 879 (1998).

13. For a treatise on negative inferences, see 81 AM. JUR. 2D WITNESSES § 119 (2012).

her right to remain silent when asked whether she reported all of her income on her income tax returns, the court could properly infer that she did not report all her income.

The court has various other options as well: dismissal of the case, barring evidence, striking pleadings. But, "the objective of the court in fashioning an appropriate response for a particular case should not be to sanction the party who invoked the privilege but rather to provide a remedy for the party disadvantaged by his opponent's reliance upon the privilege."[14] The goal is to prevent prejudice rather than to punish a litigant for exercising their constitutional right.

A Colorado case provides a balancing test for civil trial courts. This test allows a court to weigh various factors to determine an appropriate remedy for a party's nondisclosure:

(a) Whether the defendant has a substantial need for the with-held information
(b) Whether the defendant has alternative means of obtaining the withheld information
(c) Whether the court can fashion a remedy short of dismissal that will prevent unfair and unnecessary prejudice to the defendant[15]

The balancing test is equally applicable to defendants who invoke the privilege. In a family law case, the question is one of fairness to both parties: Is the person who is denied the requested information prejudiced in a meaningful way? Is the person who invokes the privilege doing so in good faith, or have the person's actions throughout the case been obstructionist? Are there other ways the party seeking the information could get it?

---

14. 1 McCormick on Evidence, *supra* note 3, § 136 at 572 (footnote omitted).
15. Steiner v. Minn. Life Ins. Co., 85 P.3d 135 (Colo. 2004).

Waiver of the Privilege

The privilege against self-incrimination is not automatic; the party or witness must raise it or it is lost. A lawyer must determine as early as possible whether his or her client may have engaged in any illegal conduct that may be relevant in the divorce. If so, the lawyer and client will need to make a choice. The lawyer must weigh the advantages of waiving the privilege versus the potential exposure to prosecution from admitting possible crimes. The waiver rule denies a witness the right to protection once the person opens the door by testifying to a particular subject. The witness is not entitled to testify to a topic and then claim privilege when cross-examined about the details. The Supreme Court comments on this absurdity:

> The accused has the choice, after weighing the advantage of the privilege against self-incrimination against the advantage of putting forward his version of the facts and his reliability as a witness, not to testify at all. He cannot reasonably claim that the Fifth Amendment gives him not only this choice but, if he elects to testify, an immunity from cross-examination on the matters he has himself put in dispute. It would make the Fifth Amendment not only a humane safeguard against judicially coerced self-disclosure but a positive invitation to mutilate the truth a party offers to tell.[16]

A party or witness can waive the right to remain silent either intentionally or inadvertently. An inadvertent waiver results when the party fails to invoke the privilege on a timely basis, thus opening the door for follow-up questions by the opponent. If during cross-examination, the opposing lawyer asks a party questions about criminal behavior in a slow and incremental way, the party's lawyer

---

16. Brown v. United States, 356 U.S. 148 (1958), *quoted in* 1 McCormick on Evidence, *supra* note 3, § 129 at 549.

must not be asleep at the switch and figure out after it is too late that the client is getting set up for an admission about criminal conduct. It is possible that if the client testifies to too much prefatory information, the court could construe the earlier testimony as a waiver of the right. The lawyer must also be conscious of this issue when answering a complaint, responding to interrogatories, or defending a client at a deposition. How much do you let your client say before invoking the privilege? There is no clear-cut answer to this question. The lawyer must use judgment and intuition in evaluating these types of issue.

On the flip side, do not forget that a party can argue that an opponent has waived the privilege. Look for any places earlier in the proceeding, either in testimony or discovery, when the opponent may have "opened the door" during his or her testimony or answers. Particularly in a civil proceeding, the privilege is not inviolate, and avenues may be available to deny the opponent the right to use it as a means to avoid the consequences of his or her conduct.

But if a party successfully asserts the privilege, what are the repercussions? What conclusions will the court draw? Does the risk of prosecution outweigh the party's inability to tell his or her story, when the conduct can be described and explained away? If the client claims the privilege, the court may assume the conduct was more nefarious than it was.

Again, there are no clear guidelines; the lawyer needs to evaluate on a case-by-case basis. If a client had an extramarital affair in a state that criminalizes adultery, does it make any sense to claim the Fifth Amendment when asked about the affair? Does the judge really care about the affair? In many cases, probably not, and claiming the privilege would only draw unnecessary attention to the question. Plus, the court can properly draw a negative inference from the refusal to answer in those states that permit negative inferences. A more difficult example involves tax evasion. If the client did not disclose all income from the family business, the person risks prosecution. If your client admits tax evasion, he or she increases the risk of a conviction if the IRS does prosecute. On the other hand, if the sums were small, the lawyer and client may conclude the matter is not likely to be of interest to an already overwhelmed IRS (or may resolve the matter civilly by filing amended returns and paying the taxes and penalties); the risk of making the disclosure may outweigh the negative presumption the judge will give to remaining silent.

Lawyers must use their judgment and common sense in advising a client to either answer the question or remain silent. But remember, once the right is given up, the court will not allow the witness to use it as a shield later in the proceeding to refuse other questions on the same subject. Consider consulting with a criminal attorney who can help provide insight to the risk of prosecution and the potential for jeopardy if the client makes an admission rather than remaining silent.

Attorney-Client Privilege

The attorney-client privilege protects confidential oral and written communications between client and lawyer made during the professional relationship. Such communications are both undiscoverable and not subject to involuntary disclosure at trial. The privilege applies both to the client's communication to the lawyer and to the lawyer's communication to the client that reveals the nature of the client's communications.[17] The privilege applies broadly and is not limited to communications made while a lawsuit is pending.[18] Earlier prefiling communications also qualify. This privilege reflects the importance of clients' need to discuss their

---

17. 1 McCORMICK ON EVIDENCE, *supra* note 3, § 89 at 401 & n.4.
18. 1 McCORMICK ON EVIDENCE, *supra* note 3, § 92 at 416 n.6.

legal issues freely and candidly with their lawyer and vice versa. If, for example, an opposing lawyer seeks to solicit whether the client had a conversation with his or her lawyer on a topic, the proper objection would be "Objection, your honor, the existence of a possible conversation and any details regarding it is privileged." Remember to distinguish the content of a conversation between a client and lawyer and the underlying facts revealed during the conversation. If the client disclosed the same facts to a friend or the spouse, the privilege does not bar the spouse or friend from testifying to the same information.

While it is the client's privilege, the lawyer can assert the privilege on behalf of the client, but only with the client's consent. Also, the court can raise the privilege on its own motion.[19] Only the client can waive the privilege, however.

Professional Relationship Defined

The privilege only applies where there is a professional relationship between the lawyer and the client. The nature of the relationship is defined by its purpose. Privilege extends only to professional relationships. The privilege applies even if the client does not ultimately hire the lawyer, or if the lawyer did not charge for the consultation. In contrast, a general discussion with a friend who happens to be a lawyer may not be covered by the privilege.[20] The witness or party advancing the privilege has the burden of proof to show that the communication was professional in nature (as opposed to social or casual small talk).

---

19. Tingley v. State, 16 Okla. Crim. 639, 184 P. 599 (Okla. Crim. App. 1919).
20. Modern Woodmen v. Watkins, 132 F.2d 352 (5th Cir. 1942); 1 MCCORMICK ON EVIDENCE, *supra* note 3, § 88 at 397 & n.6.

The term *attorney* is construed broadly so that disclosures made to support staff, law clerks, or other lawyers in the same firm are included.[21] Also included are consulting experts, such as an accountant, psychologist, or business evaluator hired as a consulting expert for the purposes of the litigation.[22] A party's communication with a consulting expert must be distinguished from one with an expert retained to provide an opinion at trial. The latter type of communication is not considered privileged, and the opponent may be entitled to full access to the communication both during discovery or at trial.[23]

Production of Documents Containing Privileged Communications

Written communications between the client and the lawyer are also protected. Memos, e-mails, and letters between the lawyer and client all qualify. A question may arise concerning documents given by the client to the lawyer. Can a lawyer, based on the attorney-client privilege, refuse to disclose documents a client entrusts to the lawyer? No, according to *McCormick*: "[I]f a document would be subject to an order of production if it were in the hands of the client it will be equally subject to such an order if it is in the hands of his attorney."[24] Client cannot avoid their discovery obligations by hiding discoverable information in their lawyer's file.

---

21. Thomas A. Mauet & Warren D. Wolfson, Trial Evidence 263 (4th ed. 2009).
22. United States v. Kovel, 296 F. 2d 918 (2d Cir. 1961).
23. *See* Green v. Nygaard, 213 Ariz. 460 (Ariz. Ct. App. 2006).
24. 1 McCormick on Evidence, *supra* note 3, ch. 3, § 89 at 404.

Impact of the Presence of a Third Party on the Privilege

Generally, the presence of a third person vitiates the privilege. Some clients bring a friend or family member to attend an appointment with the lawyer. Does the mere presence of a third party vitiate the privilege? In other words, if the confidential communication is made in the presence of an interested friend or family member, is the communication protected by the privilege? This issue is state specific.[25]

People in the emotional confusion of divorce often rely on family members to help them understand or recall information that a lawyer provides at an initial consultation. In jurisdictions that recognize a waiver based on the presence of third persons, the lawyer must be careful not to inadvertently waive the client's privilege by allowing family members to attend conferences or meetings. But, even where third-party presence voids the privilege, the lawyer can argue that, like an interpreter (whose presence would not invalidate the privilege), the third person's role really is to help a loved one understand their rights at a traumatic time in their life; to help them make informed choices. The mere presence of these "aids" may not preclude the privilege. The communication is still

---

25. *See* TEX. RULES ANN., § 503(a)(5) (2012) ("A communication is 'confidential' if not intended to be disclosed to third persons other than those to whom disclosure is made in furtherance of the rendition of professional legal services to the client or those reasonably necessary for the transmission of communication"). *See* Tracy v. Tracy, 377 Pa. 420, 424 (1954) ("A communication between attorney and client is not privileged if it takes place in the presence of a third person or of the adverse party"). *See* CAL. EVID. CODE § 952 (West 2003) ("Confidential communication between client and lawyer means information transmitted between a client and his or her lawyer . . . by a means which, so far as the client is aware, discloses the information to no third persons other than those who are present to further the interest of the client in the consultation or those to whom disclosure is reasonably necessary for the transmission of the information").

designed to be confidential, and the presence of an interested family member should not alter that fact.[26]

Waiver of Attorney-Client Privilege

As with the Fifth Amendment privilege, a party can waive attorney-client privilege. For example, assume on cross-examination that the wife's lawyer asks the husband a question concerning his failure to deposit his paycheck for a few months and the location of the funds. The husband answers by stating, "As I told my lawyer, the money was used to pay bills." The wife's lawyer would argue that the husband voluntarily waived the privilege by volunteering information about the discussion with the lawyer and that they could ask follow-up questions concerning the lawyer and client discussions. The husband's lawyer could argue that ordinarily waiver must be voluntary and not the basis of a mistake and that the client's reference to the conversation was inadvertent.

A party may also waive the privilege by revealing a confidential communication to someone outside of the client's "circle of confidence." A circle of confidence consists of those close friends and relatives in whom a person regularly confides. A party's disclosures of confidential communications with his or her lawyer to those outside of the circle may avoid the privilege and require disclosure of the details of the conversation. For example, if the client revealed a confidential conversation with his or her lawyer to a casual acquaintance, that act may constitute a waiver of the privilege as to the subject matter of the discussion. At a cocktail party, Sally revealed to Robert, a casual acquaintance, "I told my divorce lawyer that there was no way anyone could discover that we were skimming money. He told me not to be so sure." Subject

---

26. *See* 1 MCCORMICK ON EVIDENCE, *supra* note 3, § 91 at 408–11.

to satisfaction of the other rules of evidence (relevance, hearsay, etc.), Sally's husband may offer her conversation with Robert, arguing that a waiver occurred because Robert was not a part of her circle of confidence. Robert, Sally, or her lawyer could be forced to testify to that particular conversation if the court determined Sally waived her privilege.

Professor Imwinkelreid describes the foundation necessary to establish waiver based on a statement to one outside the client's circle of confidence:

(a)   Where the out-of-court statement was made
(b)   When the statement was made
(c)   To whom the statement was made
(d)   The holder knew the addressee was outside the circle of confidence
(e)   The holder disclosed information to the addressee
(f)   The disclosure was voluntary[27]

Sally might argue in response that she considered Robert a part of that circle of confidence and did not intend to waive her privilege.

Inadvertent Waiver

As a general rule, a waiver must be voluntary and not the result of mistake. Problems sometime occur during the production of voluminous documents. For example, if a party mistakenly releases a confidential communication with counsel during the discovery process, does that error impact the privilege? *McCormick* addresses inadvertent disclosure during the discovery process:

---

27. EDWARD J. IMWINKELRIED, EVIDENTIARY FOUNDATIONS, § 9.02[2] at 299 (Matthew Bender & Co., Inc. 7th ed. 2008).

[W]hile some courts apparently still adhere to a rather strict approach to waiver, others have considered factors such as the excusability of the error, whether prompt attention to remedy the error was made, and whether preservation of the privilege will occasion unfairness to the opponent. The costs of attempting to avoid waiver under a strict rule would argue strongly for modification along these lines, and it is believed that the decisions are tending in this direction.[28]

Congress adopted FRE 502 in 2008 to respond to this problem. Disclosure does not waive the privilege if the disclosure was inadvertent. Congress designed the rule to "limit the consequences of inadvertent disclosure, thereby relieving litigants of the burden that a single mistake during the discovery process can cost them the protection of a privilege."[29] The rule protects litigants from the daunting task of reviewing every document exchanged in discovery, where an inadvertent omission may result in the loss of the privilege. Try to avoid the problem in the first place. To the extent practical, the lawyer should review all discovery documents before releasing them to make sure they contain no protected material.

Intercepted Correspondence and Privilege

During divorce proceedings, parties may continue to live together and may snoop through each other's private correspondence. A lawyer may send detailed letters to the marital home that the spouse intercepts. Some clients leave strategic information from their lawyer lying on the kitchen table. Parties also communicate

---

28. 1 McCormick on Evidence, *supra* note 3, § 93 at 419-20 (footnotes omitted).

29. Report of Senate Committee on the Judiciary Senate Comm. On Judiciary, Fed. Rules of Evidence, S. Rep. No 264, 110th Cong., 2d Sess. (2008); 2008 U.S. Code Cong. & Ad. New (1305–07), cited in Rules Book West.

electronically with their lawyers and do not change their e-mail passwords, thus allowing their spouse access to their communications with their lawyers.

If a party improperly intercepts an e-mail or letter, that party may not use the correspondence, arguing waiver of privilege by virtue of their possession of the correspondence.[30] But what about the letter left on the kitchen table or an e-mail sent to a "family" e-mail address or left open on the screen? The proponent would argue that the other party waived privilege because the communication was left open in the house and no attempts were made to keep it private; by failing to do so, the party made the correspondence admissible. The opponent of the evidence would argue that the party's actions were not intentional, and the failure to protect the communication was inadvertent, that is, the party did not intentionally waive the privilege.

Avoid this problem by prevention. Advise clients to hide their mail, or, better yet, have correspondence sent to a post office box or a relative's home for safekeeping. Also, advise clients to change the passwords on their e-mail accounts or obtain a new e-mail account. Remind them not to leave legal communications on their computer screen.

Disclosures in Fee Petition

When a party asserts a claim for fees from their spouse, they ordinarily must provide an itemized basis for the claim, including a summary of the services rendered. The fee award proceeding may require production of invoices with confidential communications. These disclosures in pleadings and testimony present another potential waiver issue. The use of an itemized time and billing statement

---

30. *See, e.g.,* State v. Schmidt, 474 So. 2d 899 (Fla. Dist. Ct. App. 1985).

does not ordinarily waive the privilege; a time entry referencing a conference between the client and the lawyer would not destroy the privilege.[31] If the mere act of itemizing and memorializing time for the purposes of a fee hearing invalidates the privilege, it would emasculate legislative intent to provide for fee allocation hearings in divorce cases.[32]

More problematic are details referenced in descriptions of services on an invoice, for example, a time entry that discusses trial strategy or specific research that may disclose a particular legal theory. If that confidential information is included in time entries, redact the specific entries in order to preserve the strategy or confidential information. But when possible, avoid any time postings that may later affect the client. Instead of referencing the specific subject matter that was discussed, post a generic "Conference with client" time entry and then prepare an internal memo summarizing the nature of the conference. Likewise with trial strategy—do not reveal any more information than necessary in the time entry. If confidential information does end up in the time entry, another option would be to redact the details of the time entry before filing the fee petition.

---

31. *See, e.g.,* Lane v. Sharp Packaging Sys., Inc. 640 N.W.2d 788, 804–805 (Wis. 2002), 750 ILCS 503(j)(3) (filing a petition for contribution of fees in a divorce action does not waive the attorney-client privilege between the petitioning party and their lawyer).

32. *See, e.g.,* 750 Ill. Comp. Stat. Ann. 5/503(j)(3) (LexisNexis 2011). ("The filing of a petition for contribution shall not be deemed to constitute a waiver of the attorney-client privilege between the petitioning party and current or former counsel; and such a waiver shall not constitute a prerequisite to a hearing for contribution. If either party's presentation on contribution, however, includes evidence within the scope of the attorney-client privilege, the disclosure or disclosures shall be narrowly construed and shall not be deemed by the court to constitute a general waiver of the privilege as to matters beyond the scope of the presentation.")

Matters to Which the Attorney-Client Privilege Does Not Apply

Attorney-client privilege does not apply where the lawyer and the client themselves become adversaries. For example, if the client sues the lawyer for malpractice or files an ethical grievance, any otherwise privileged communications are no longer privileged. The lawyer can testify to client confidences in defense of the claim. Additionally, if the lawyer sues the client for outstanding fees, the lawyer may testify to the substance of client communications. Consult your local ethical rules to determine the limits on disclosure of these confidences.[33]

Privilege does not generally extend to the mere fact that a party had a consultation with a lawyer (as distinguished from the substance of the discussion during the consultation). Also, information such as the client's identity, payment of any fees, terms of employment, or other nonspecific information is not protected by the privilege. The rule is not absolute. The trend favors extending the privilege to client identity and fee arrangements if the consultation itself tends to reveal the nature of the communication.[34] For example, assume the husband is attempting to prove when the marriage started to break down. He may offer a copy of a check evidencing a consult the wife had with the attorney several years earlier. The wife would argue that the consult itself disclosed confidential information in this instance. The fact that she engaged in a consult revealed the nature of the conversation and that the disclosure violated the privilege. The husband would argue that the physical act of meeting with an attorney was not protected and that no confidential communication would be disclosed by evidence of such a meeting.

---

33. Model Rules of Professional Conduct Rule 1.6 (2010).
34. 1 McCormick on Evidence, *supra* note 3, § 90 at 407.

The privilege does not extend to discussions with the lawyer concerning future fraudulent or illegal activity. If, for example, the client consults with his or her lawyer about future illegal activity, the privilege does not apply. This is distinguished from a client's disclosure of a past crime to get advice about the implications of the crime. If a client discloses a scheme to defraud his or her spouse in their divorce case, the client is not entitled to use the privilege as a shield. In theory, the lawyer could be compelled to testify to the content of the communication. Ethically, the lawyer must attempt to dissuade the client from this type of conduct and must not join as a conspirator.

While not evidentiary, the rules of professional responsibility speak to the issue of lawyers maintaining client confidences as well. The ABA Model Rules of Professional Conduct govern the disclosure of client confidences under these circumstances. Rule 1.6 provides in pertinent part,

> A lawyer may reveal information relating to the representation of a client to the extent the lawyer reasonably believes necessary:
>> to prevent reasonably certain death or substantial bodily harm;
>> to prevent the client from committing a crime or fraud that is reasonably certain to result in substantial injury to the financial interests or property of another and in furtherance of which the client has used or is using the lawyer's services.

Forewarn clients about your ethical duties and admonish them immediately if they disclose a scheme to commit a fraud on their spouse or engage in any illegal activity that involves use of your services. And when in doubt, consider withdrawing from the case in order to avoid any complicity or ethical repercussions.

Work-Product Doctrine

Distinct from the attorney-client privilege, the work-product doctrine protects materials prepared by the attorney while representing
the client. Also protected are the "mental impressions, conclusions,
opinions and legal theories of an attorney."[35] Unlike the attorney-client privilege, this privilege attaches only when litigation is
anticipated or has actually commenced. It is not necessary that a
suit actually be pending when the materials are created.

The work-product doctrine is broader than the attorney-client
privilege and is easier to invade than the attorney-client privilege.
The Supreme Court created protection for attorney work product
in the case of *Hickman v. Taylor,* 329 U.S. 495 (1947). There the
court held materials prepared by an attorney in preparation for trial
were not discoverable. The Supreme Court codified this privilege
as Rule 26(b) of the Federal Rules of Civil Procedure: "Ordinarily,
a party may not discover documents and tangible things that are
prepared in anticipation of litigation or for trial by or for another
party or its representative (including the other party's attorney, con-
sultant, surety, indemnitor, insurer, or agent)." This rule applies to
discovery of work product as distinguished from its admissibility.
Initially the work-product doctrine only applied as a discovery limi-
tation but it ultimately evolved into an evidentiary privilege that a
party may assert at a trial or hearing to prevent an opposing party
from obtaining protected materials for admission into evidence.

The prohibition is not absolute. If the party seeking the protected
materials establishes a substantial need for information contained
in the work product and proves an inability to otherwise obtain
the information without substantial hardship, the party may be

---

35. Fed R. Civ. P. 26 (b)(3) *quoted in* 1 McCormick on Evidence, *supra* note 3, §
96 at 439.

entitled to these materials. The party seeking these materials can overcome the privilege by a "compelling showing of need."[36]

Discovery of mental impressions, personal notes, or trial strategy of the lawyer is subject to a more stringent burden than discovery of other types of work product.[37] The prohibition on discovery of the opposing lawyer's mental impressions, conclusions, opinions, or legal theories is near absolute. However, the problem is definitional; distinguishing an opinion or theory from ordinary work product is often difficult.[38]

The work product privilege does not exclude all of the fruits of a lawyer's investigation. For example, it does not exclude the identities of potential witnesses or persons having information, including discoverable documents, that may be relevant to the case. Work product is material that is *derivative* rather than *primary*. Primary material is historically connected to the case, evidence that is preexisting or independent of the litigation itself. Primary materials are not work product and are thus both discoverable and available as evidence. Derivative materials, on the other hand, are those secondary materials that derive from the attorney's "effort and imagination."[39] For example, tax returns are preexisting and independent. Thus, they are subject to production during the discovery process and may be admissible at trial. As a demonstrative aid, lawyers or their staff may compile a summary of the tax return data in a spreadsheet. This summary is derivative and need not be produced in discovery (unless of course the lawyer intends to offer it as a summary exhibit). Again, this is a qualified privilege, and a showing of hardship could cause a judge to compel

---

36. IMWINKELRIED, *supra* note 27, § 706(1) at 308.

37. *See, e.g.,* Waste Management Inc. v. International Surplus Lines Ins. Co., 144 Ill. 2d 178, 579 N.E.2d 322 (1991) (requiring a showing of compelling need and "impossibility" of getting the information elsewhere).

38. IMWINKELRIED, *supra* note 27, § 7.06[2] at 314.

39. *Id.*

production. More difficult would be a worksheet the lawyer prepared summarizing the tax data along with his or her impressions for preparation for cross-examination. The opposing party would have a more challenging burden seeking production of the lawyer's notes of his or her impressions, and one cannot conceive of any reasonable example of hardship sufficient to convince a judge to force their production.

In contested custody cases, clients sometimes prepare a journal or other personal memoranda to keep track of the other parent's comings and goings. This document would ordinarily be discoverable (and should always be sought from the opposing party). But where the journal is kept at the behest of the lawyer, the lawyer may argue that it is the lawyer's work product and therefore not discoverable and excluded from admission at trial.[40] Therefore it is important to memorialize a request that the client keep such a journal as an aid to the attorney in preparing the case. By doing so, the information may be protected from disclosure.[41]

Distinguish this situation from a journal the client kept prior to meeting with the attorney, or an ordinary calendar kept for daily comings and goings. A party would be hard-pressed to support an argument that a journal started two years before meeting the lawyer was the lawyer's work product. Also, be aware that if the journal is used as an exhibit or relied on as a past recollection recorded, the opponent can seek to bar its use at trial if the calendar was not produced during the discovery process based on the work-product doctrine. A party cannot hide behind the doctrine during discovery and then disregard it if he or she wants to use the work product as an exhibit.

---

40. *See, e.g.,* Roe v. Roe, 253 N.J. Super. 418, 601 A.2d 1201 (N.J. Super. Ct. App. Div. 1992) (holding that a diary that the attorney advised the wife to keep about specific events occurring between herself and her husband was considered work product of the lawyer and thus not discoverable).

41. *See* FED. R. CIV. P. 26(b)(1).

Physician-Patient Privilege

Certain communications between physicians and their patients are confidential. The physician-patient privilege bars disclosure of confidential communications between a patient and his or her doctor. The historical rationale for this privilege is that patients must be able to confide personal and potentially embarrassing details about their health to receive proper treatment. This privilege, while not originally recognized in the common law, has been codified in most of the states. The privilege has been extended to mental health professionals and their patients. Even those states that do not recognize the physician-patient privilege protect communications between mental health providers and patients.[42] The United States Supreme Court recognized the mental health privilege in *Jaffee v. Redmond*, 518 U.S. 1 (1996), expanding the privilege beyond psychiatrists and psychologists to licensed clinical social workers.

Patient Privacy and HIPAA

Federal law and regulations protect patient health information in judicial proceedings. The Health Insurance Portability and Accountability Act of 1996 (HIPAA) protects patient privacy, while recognizing that disclosure is sometimes necessary in a judicial proceeding.[43] HIPAA applies to any healthcare provider, including physicians, health insurance companies, pharmacies, laboratories, and life insurance companies. Prior to HIPAA, pharmacy records could easily be subpoenaed. Post-HIPAA, access to this information

---

42. 1 McCormick on Evidence, *supra* note 3, § 98 at 450 n.11 (noting that Alabama, Maryland, Massachusetts, South Carolina, Tennessee, and West Virginia, while providing no statutory protection for doctor-patient communications, protect communications related to mental health).

43. 45 C.F.R. § 164.512 (2003).

has become significantly more complicated. HIPAA rules protect all medical records and other individually identifiable health information. *Health information* is defined as any information that "relates to the past, present, or future physical or mental health or condition of an individual."[44]

A party may obtain medical records of another person by a patient release that complies with the HIPAA regulations. Ordinarily, a health-care provider may not disclose patient information without the patient's consent. The healthcare provider must procure a release from the patient before releasing the information to a third party. The format of the release greatly restricts use of the information by anyone. But once obtained, the HIPAA rules themselves do not limit the admissibility of these records as evidence. 45 C.F.R. §164.512(e) governs the use of records in connection with a judicial proceeding.

A party may also obtain information from a subpoena or court order that satisfies HIPAA regulations. Lawyers who seek such information pursuant to a subpoena must provide assurances to the healthcare provider that they have made reasonable efforts to notify the patient of the request, or that they have made reasonable efforts to secure a qualified protective order.

It is important to distinguish rights under the HIPAA regulations and the disclosure of medical information under state statutes or common law. HIPAA may allow release of information, but that information may still be privileged and nondiscoverable. States may have their own rules regarding the disclosure or discoverability of medical records and a party must comply with both. And obtaining the physical or mental health records of the opponent is only the first step—their ultimate admission is another. Some states, such as Illinois, provide procedures for the court to review records in-camera to determine the propriety of their release to the

---

44. 42 U.S.C. § 1320d(4)(B).

opponent. In the absence of any specific prohibitions, the records may be admissible subject to all of the other rules of evidence (e.g., hearsay, authentication).

Waiver of Physician-Patient Privilege

Like the attorney-client privilege, the physician-patient privilege belongs to the patient, who can waive it. Parties may waive the privilege expressly by offering their medical records into evidence, or implicitly by disclosing the information during the course of the proceeding or by putting their mental or physical health in issue. A party cannot use his or her privilege as a shield and a sword: "a patient voluntarily placing his or her physical or mental condition in issue in a judicial proceeding waives the privilege with respect to information relative to that condition."[45] This concept is statutory and in some jurisdictions, placing one's mental or physical health condition before the court does not result in an automatic waiver of the privilege.[46]

In a child custody case, both parents' mental and physical health is a factor the court is to consider in determining the best interest of the children. Individual state law governs whether the statutory directive to consider a party's physical or mental health opens the door to discovery of this information, since the statute places the matter "at issue." In Illinois, for example, one cannot evade the privilege based solely on the fact that the statute places one's mental or physical health at issue in a custody case.[47] Consult your local case law to determine the limits of waiver under these circumstances.

---

45. 1 McCormick on Evidence, *supra* note 3, § 103 at 464.
46. *See* Koch v. Koch, 961 So.2d 1134 (Fla. Dist. Ct. App.)(2007) (acknowledging an alcohol problem is not enough to put mental health at issue, so privilege of privacy is not waived). *See* 1 McCormick on Evidence, *supra* note 3, § 103 at 465–66.
47. *See, e.g., In re* Marriage of Lombaer, 200 Ill. App. 3d 712 (1990).

The physician-patient privilege applies to children. However, an appropriate adult must decide whether to waive a child's privilege. The law is mixed. In some jurisdictions, either parent can waive the privilege.[48] Still other jurisdictions may appoint a guardian ad litem to address the release of this information.[49] A child's health (both physical and mental) may be relevant in custody litigation. Other circumstances warranting the release of this information might include a parent's claim that he or she cannot work because of the child's health problems. Finances are impacted by a child's health needs. Know the rules in your jurisdiction. Be able to support a claim for the propriety of a release of the child's health records by appropriate statutory and case law.

In a family law case, litigants may claim that physical problems preclude them from working. Such a claim may open the door for the opponent to obtain a litigant's medical records either for review or as a resource for an independent medical evaluation. In the event harmful information is in the records, counsel needs to consider the repercussions of the release of the information. Plan in advance. For example, assume the wife claims she cannot work because of persistent health problems. If she repeatedly visited the doctor, and the doctor wrote in the records that he suspects her claims are fantastical and that she has some psychological problems, the release of those records may impact her claim for custody. The lesson is this: There are many moving parts in family law litigation and they must be considered together. Issues bleed into each other and a lawyer

---

48. *See in re* Marriage of Kerman, 253 Ill. App. 3d 492, 624 N.E.2d 870 (Ill. App. Ct. 1993).

49. Attorney ad litem for D.K. v. Parents of D.K., 780 So. 2d 301 (Fla. Dist. Ct. App. 2001) (in a custody dispute, parents are not authorized to release a minor's psychotherapy records; an attorney ad litem was necessary to assert the child's claims of privilege and speak for the child). *See also* In re Berg, 152 N.H. 658 (N.H. 2005); *see also* Nagle v. Hooks, 296 Md. 123 (1983).

must always look at the big picture before undertaking a plan of attack.

Marital Privileges

There are two types of marital privileges. The first protects a spouse from being forced to testify against his or her spouse in a proceeding. This privilege has been disfavored by most jurisdictions and would rarely, if ever, apply in a divorce.[50] The second marital privilege protects interspousal communications. This marital privilege prevents disclosure in a legal proceeding of confidential communications between spouses. The key here is the nature of the communication—it applies only to a communication intended as confidential at the time the communication was made. Assume a husband told his wife that he was intentionally suppressing his income to pay less child support to his first wife. If the first wife subpoenaed the second wife to testify to this conversation, the husband could argue it was protected by the privilege. The communication was made in confidence to his second wife. Wife number one would argue that the privilege should not apply to the husband's disclosure of fraudulent behavior, such as what was occurring here.[51]

The interspousal communications privilege is recognized in all jurisdictions. The holder varies by jurisdiction. In some jurisdictions the holder of the privilege is the spouse who made the statement, and in others, either spouse involved in the confidential

---

50. *See* ARIZ. REV. STAT. ANN. § 12-2232(A)(1)(2012). ("A husband or wife ... without the consent of the other, shall not be examined as to any communications made by one to the other during the marriage, except: 1. In an action for divorce or a civil action by one against the other.")

51. United States v. Marashi, 913 F.2d 724, 731 ("Thus we join our sister circuits in holding that the marital communications privilege does not apply to statements made in furtherance of joint criminal activity.")

conversation can assert the privilege. The holder can waive the privilege.

Practice Points

- Learn your local rules concerning attorney-client privilege. Knowledge of these rules is important from an evidentiary as well as ethical perspective.
- Tell your clients to change their e-mail address and provide a secure, never-before-used password for any communication they have with you. By failing to change their password, clients may inadvertently allow a snoopy spouse to spy on their conversations with you.
- Probe your clients to determine the necessity of invoking the Fifth Amendment right to remain silent as to a subject. By evaluating the issue in advance, you can have the time to develop a thoughtful game plan. If hearing about it for the first time at a deposition or hearing, a visceral snap judgment may create problems down the road.
- If clients want to bring a friend or relative to an appointment, advise them of the possibility of losing the attorney-client privilege.
- Scrupulously review all discovery documents before releasing them, making sure you made no inadvertent disclosures that imperil the attorney-client privilege.
- In order to protect client journals under the work-product rule, advise clients in writing at the beginning of the case to write down their notes about relevant occurrences or their observations in order to assist you in trial preparation. By doing so a court may rule the journal is the lawyer's work product and is not discoverable. To further strengthen the work-product

argument, prepare a form journal with your logo on it and give it to clients to use for their thoughts.
- To get health records admitted, make sure you comply with both HIPAA regulations as well as state law. Be wary of placing your clients' mental or physical health at issue due to unintended consequences or surprise disclosures.

Expert Witnesses | 13

Experts are pervasive in many aspects of family law litigation. The proponent of an expert's testimony must show the propriety of the subject matter of the expert's report and testimony, the qualifications of the expert, the reliability of the theory being used, and the factual bases of the expert's opinion. In this chapter, I explore these topics.

Rules to consider:

Rule 702. Testimony by Expert Witnesses

A witness who is qualified as an expert by knowledge, skill, experience, training, or education may testify in the form of an opinion or otherwise if:

(a) the expert's scientific, technical, or other specialized knowledge will help the trier of fact to understand the evidence or to determine a fact in issue;

(b) the testimony is based on sufficient facts or data;

(c) the testimony is the product of reliable principles and methods; and

(d) the expert has reliably applied the principles and methods to the facts of the case.

Rule 703. Bases of an Expert's Opinion Testimony

An expert may base an opinion on facts or data in the case that the expert has been made aware of or personally observed. If experts in the particular field would reasonably rely on those kinds of facts or data in forming an opinion on the subject, they need not be admissible for the opinion to be admitted. But if the facts or data would otherwise be inadmissible, the proponent of the opinion may disclose them to the jury only if their probative value in helping the jury evaluate the opinion substantially outweighs their prejudicial effect.

Rule 704. Opinion on an Ultimate Issue

(a) In General—Not Automatically Objectionable. An opinion is not objectionable just because it embraces an ultimate issue.

(b) Exception. In a criminal case, an expert witness must not state an opinion about whether the defendant did or did not have a mental state or condition that constitutes an element of the crime charged or of a defense. Those matters are for the trier of fact alone.

Rule 705. Disclosing the Facts or Data Underlying an Expert's Opinion

Unless the court orders otherwise, an expert may state an opinion—and give the reasons for it—without first testifying to the underlying facts or data. But the expert may be required to disclose those facts or data on cross-examination.

Rule 706. Court-Appointed Expert Witnesses

(a) Appointment Process. On a party's motion or on its own, the court may order the parties to show cause why expert witnesses should not be appointed and may ask the parties to submit nominations. The court may appoint any expert that the parties agree on and any of its own choosing. But the court may only appoint someone who consents to act.

(b) Expert's Role. The court must inform the expert of the expert's duties. The court may do so in writing and have a copy filed with the clerk or may do so orally at a conference in which the parties have an opportunity to participate. The expert:

   (1) must advise the parties of any findings the expert makes;
   (2) may be deposed by any party;
   (3) may be called to testify by the court or any party; and
   (4) may be cross-examined by any party, including the party that called the expert.

(c) Compensation. The expert is entitled to a reasonable compensation, as set by the court. The compensation is payable as follows:

   (1) in a criminal case or in a civil case involving just compensation under the Fifth Amendment, from any funds that are provided by law; and
   (2) in any other civil case, by the parties in the proportion and at the time that the court directs—and the compensation is then charged like other costs.

(d) Disclosing the Appointment to the Jury. The court may authorize disclosure to the jury that the court appointed the expert.

(e) Parties' Choice of Their Own Experts. This rule does not limit a party in calling its own experts.

Use of Experts in Family Law Litigation

Experts play a significant role in family law litigation. Lawyers use experts in custody litigation, to value businesses and other assets, to determine the employability of a party, and to provide forensic assistance in tracing or finding assets. Many statutes allow family court judges to appoint their own experts, particularly in custody cases.[1] As a litigation resource, the expert's importance cannot be overlooked. A thorough understanding of how to use experts is vital in family law advocacy.

Subject Matter of Expert Testimony

In order to use expert testimony, the proponent must establish that the subject matter of the testimony relates to some specialized knowledge, and that the expert possesses sufficient skill to reliably testify. The subject matter of the testimony must be appropriate for this particular witness and beyond the knowledge of a layperson. Specifically, FRE 702 provides that an expert may testify if "the expert's scientific, technical, or other specialized knowledge will help the trier of fact to understand the evidence or to determine a fact in issue." The expert's testimony is not limited to scientific or technical matters; an expert may be called on for a variety of purposes. If the expert has any specialized knowledge that will assist the trial court, the court may consider it. An expert can render an opinion concerning any relevant topic as long as it assists the judge.

---

1.   *See, e.g.*, La. Rev. Stat. Ann. § 2801(b)(3) (allowing the court to appoint an expert to assist it in dividing marital property).

Liberal trends regarding opinion testimony do not extend to opinions concerning law. With the exception of foreign law, the Federal Rules of Evidence prohibit expert opinion about the law. The judge is the ultimate authority on the law, rendering an opinion as to the law by an expert witness irrelevant. Some commentators have criticized this rule, especially as law becomes more complex.[2] Family law is becoming increasingly federalized (e.g., bankruptcy law, federal tax law, Hague Conventions). Allowing an expert to testify to these complex areas of law, which essentially become species of fact in light of their complexity, is sensible and can be helpful to the trial court.

The Role of the Expert

The expert's role is not limited to rendering an opinion. The Advisory Committee's comments on FRE 702 describe the job description more expansively: "an expert on the stand may give a dissertation or exposition of scientific or other principles relevant to the case, leaving the trier of fact to apply them to the facts."[3] For example, in a divorce case involving a family farm, a farmer who has substantial experience in farming could provide expert testimony on how farmers generate income from farming. Or, in a child relocation case a psychologist could give an exposition on clinical studies that relate to uprooting adolescents from their home. The creative use of experts can assist the court in making an informed decision.

---

2.   *See, e.g., The Impropriety of Expert Witness Testimony on the Law,* 40 U. KAN. L. REV. 325 (1992); 1 McCORMICK ON EVIDENCE, § 12 at 63 n.19 (Kenneth S. Broun, ed., Thomson West 6th ed. 2006) (citing Erhardt, *The Conflict Concerning Expert Witness and Legal Conclusions,* 92 W. VA. L. REV. 645 (1990)).

3.   FED. R. EVID. 702 Advisory Committee's Note, 56 F.R.D. 183, 282.

The Expert's Assignment

The scope of the expert's assignment is often described in syllogistic terms. The general theory or principle underlying the expert's report is called the major premise. The minor premise is the case-specific information that the expert relies on. When the facts of the case are applied to the theory, it results in the expert's ultimate conclusion. The starting point is to determine whether the major premise is reliable under FRE 702.

Reliability of Scientific Expert Testimony

The first case to explore the reliability of scientific evidence was *Frye v. United States.*[4] In *Frye,* the U.S. Court of Appeals for the D.C. Circuit articulated a standard for admission of scientific testimony: whether the proposed theory is generally accepted in the scientific community.[5] The *Frye* standard relied on consensus in the scientific community as a yardstick to measure the reliability of scientific evidence. Only those methodologies considered reliable by the general scientific community were acceptable. In the 1970s, the *Frye* standard came under attack. Critics complained that *Frye* precluded cutting-edge scientific evidence that was too new to be recognized by the scientific community at large. This criticism culminated in FRE 702, which rejects *Frye*'s "general acceptance" theory in favor of a general reliability standard.

In *Daubert v. Merrell Dow Pharmaceuticals, Inc.,*[6] the Supreme Court held that while *Frye*'s general acceptance theory was valuable, the trial court must inquire further. The Court held that the

---

4.   Frye v. United States, 293 Fed. 1013 (D.C. Cir. 1923).
5.   1 McCormick on Evidence, *supra* note 2, § 203 at 827.
6.   Daubert v. Merrell Dow Pharmaceuticals, Inc., 509 U.S. 579 (1993).

federal rules' "reliability test" supplanted *Frye*'s general acceptance standard.[7] The Court described the new standard: the proponent of scientific evidence must first establish that the expert's technique is scientifically reliable by establishing that the expert's hypothesis is empirically valid. To evaluate the validity of the hypothesis, the trial judge should consider the following:

- Whether the proposition is testable and has been tested;
- Whether the proposition has been subjected to peer review and publication;
- Whether the methodology has a known error rate;
- Whether there are standards for using the methodology; and
- Whether the methodology is generally accepted.[8]

In order to gauge the reliability of potential expert testimony, the court actually conducts a preliminary hearing. At that hearing the parties present evidence concerning the validity of the expert's hypothesis. Other experts may be called to support or refute the theories to be relied on in the case before the court. If the court determines that the expert's major premise is unreliable, the expert's testimony is inadmissible. If not, the court will allow the expert to testify, subject to any other challenges regarding the reliability of the expert's conclusions. For example, the expert's application of the scientifically reliable technique may have been flawed, or the expert may have drawn incorrect conclusions from the data.

---

7. *Id.* at 589–90.
8. 1 MCCORMICK ON EVIDENCE, *supra* note 2, § 13 at 73 (citing Daubert v. Merrell Dow Pharmaceuticals, Inc., *supra* note 6).

Reliability of Nonscientific Expert Testimony

An expert's testimony need not be based on scientific calculations. A business valuation, for example, involves an expert with specialized knowledge, but the expertise is not scientific in nature. The Supreme Court responded to this issue in *Kumho Tire Co. v. Carmichael*.[9] In *Kumho,* the Court held that while the *Daubert* factors remain valid for scientific evidence, nonscientific testimony must be scrutinized differently. The trial judge may consider any pertinent *Daubert* factors and disregard those that are inapplicable. FRE 702, in its present form, codifies the *Kumho* decision by granting the trial judge discretion to determine whether "the expert has reliably applied the principles and methods to the facts of the case."[10]

Using Expert Testimony

In order to qualify as admissible, the expert's testimony must be fundamentally reliable and applicable to the facts of the case. *McCormick* observes three preliminary questions that a court must answer prior to admitting an expert report and testimony:

(1) What is the specific theory or technique that the expert will testify about?

(2) Which type of use is the expert putting the theory or technique to?

(3) How can the proponent validate the type of use of the expert's specific theory or technique?[11]

---

9.   Kumho Tire Co., Ltd. v. Carmichael, 526 U.S. 137 (1999).

10. FED. R. EVID. 702.

11. 1 MCCORMICK ON EVIDENCE, *supra* note 2, § 13 at 75–80.

First, the trial judge must consider the specific theory the expert relied on, rather than the general reliability of the expert's discipline. The focus must be a narrow one. For example, assume a custody evaluator relied on an untested assessment that he or she created, which determines a preferred parent by monitoring a child's eye movement when a series of pictures of each parent is presented to the child. The expert's reliance on the untested assessment may invalidate the testimony, even though psychological testimony generally is considered reliable in custody cases.

Be cognizant that the custody expert may use a novel theory, or a controversial testing procedure, as part of a custody evaluation. For example, is it proper for an expert to rely on the controversial "parental alienation syndrome" as a basis to recommend an award of custody?[12] Are the custody evaluator's testing procedures properly validated and reliable?[13] While it is beyond the scope of this book to address the propriety of particular theories or tests, lawyers need to recognize that these controversies do exist and there are opportunities to challenge an expert who relies on questionable theories or procedures. Scrupulously review expert reports in child custody cases to determine the propriety and reliability of all tests administered. Many times psychologists will rely on faulty or unreliable tests and that reliance may subject the entire report to disqualification.

Assuming the testimony is valid, what exactly is the expert's role in the particular case? Is the expert offered solely to testify to his or her observations? Or does the opposing party seek to have the expert go further and actually draw an inference from the observations? For example, a forensic accountant might testify to the specific transactions that he or she observed going through years

---

12. *In re* Marriage of Bates, 212 Ill. 2d 489 (2004).
13. *See* Dave Medoff, *The Scientific Basis of Psychological Testing: Considerations Following Daubert, Kumho, and Joiner*, 41 Fam. Ct. Rev. 199 (2003).

of bank statements. Or the accountant might go further and render an opinion that, based on his or her review of the data, hundreds of thousands of dollars are missing. The trial judge needs to evaluate how the expert's testimony is being used in the particular case.

Finally, the trial judge must determine whether the expert is properly applying the facts to the theory in the particular case. If the expert accountant drew a conclusion based on the evidence, the proponent will need to establish that the process (or techniques used) to draw the conclusion is reliable, and that the expert properly applied his or her evaluative process to the facts of the case.

Some states continue to use the *Frye* test (substantial acceptance) to evaluate controversial expert evidence.[14] Other states rely on the Federal Rules of Evidence that descend from the *Daubert* and *Kumho* cases, requiring a balancing test of various factors to determine reliability of the testimony.[15] It is important to know what standard your jurisdiction uses and apply that standard to seek admission of or to challenge admissibility of an expert's testimony as to a particular subject matter. The lawyer can bring a pretrial motion to bar an expert's testimony if it is based on junk science, a controversial theory, or an otherwise improper foundation.

Qualifying the Expert

Before experts may testify, they must be qualified. To qualify a witness as an expert, the lawyer should ask questions to determine the expert's qualifications. Common information to elicit when qualifying the expert includes the following:

- The witness has acquired degrees from educational institutions.

---

14. Illinois, for example, continues to rely on the *Frye* test.
15. 90 A.L.R. 5th 453 (2001).

- The witness has had other specialized training in this field of expertise.
- The witness is licensed to practice in the field.
- The witness has practiced in the field for a substantial period of time.
- The witness has taught in the field.
- The witness has published in the field.
- The witness belongs to professional organizations in the field.
- The witness has previously testified as an expert on this subject.[16]

Procedurally, the proponent must first establish that the expert has appropriate qualifications to reliably testify. After laying the foundation for the expert's qualifications, the expert is tendered to the court: *"May it please the court, I tender Joe Smith to the court as an expert in business valuation."* The adverse party has the right at that point to conduct a preliminary examination of the witness and ask the expert questions about his or her credentials. This process is known as the voir dire of the witness. The opponent can examine the expert regarding his or her credentials or qualifications, challenging the person's expertise. Voir dire questions could cover the following topics:

- Lack of education of the expert
- Deficient training
- Lack of skill in implementing any objective testing
- Testimony does not involve specialized knowledge
- Lack of adequate information (e.g., meets only one party and intends to render an opinion regarding placement of a child)

---

16. Edward J. Imwinkelreid, Evidentiary Foundations § 9.03[2] at 383 (Matthew Bender & Co., Inc. 7th ed. 2008.

- Reliance on improper facts, test procedures, or legal principles
  (e.g., the expert intends to offer an opinion about custody based
  on the tender years doctrine when the law disallows the court
  from considering the doctrine)

If the judge deems the expert unqualified, the testimony and report
are barred. Alternatively, the court could require more foundational
questions prior to qualifying the expert, or the judge may qualify
the expert and the direct examination may proceed. The opposing party may cross-examine the expert at the conclusion of the
direct examination on any and all of the topics addressed during
voir dire and direct testimony.

The Factual Basis of the Expert's Testimony

Ordinarily the expert is retained to render an opinion, but not
always. As noted above, the expert could testify to research or
other data and leave it to the trial court to apply the research to
the facts of the case.[17] Either way, the expert will need to testify to
the basis of his or her testimony, referred to as the minor premise
of the report. What did the expert consider? What information did
the expert review as part of his or her investigation in this particular case? FRE 703 controls the nature of this testimony:

> An expert may base an opinion on facts or data in the case that the
> expert has been made aware of or personally observed. If experts in
> the particular field would reasonably rely on those kinds of facts or
> data in forming an opinion on the subject, they need not be admis-
> sible for the opinion to be admitted.[18]

---

17. FED. R. EVID. 702.
18. FED. R. EVID. 703.

There are three factual sources for the expert's opinion.[19] The first source is facts the expert personally knows. The foundation for this type of testimony consists of

(a)   where the expert witness observed the fact;
(b)   when the witness observed the fact;
(c)   who was present;
(d)   how the witness observed the fact;
(e)   a description of the fact(s) observed.

Examples include a custody evaluator's interviews and a business valuator's site visit where the valuator observed the operations of the business.

The second factual basis for the expert's opinions is hearsay statements from third parties. FRE 703 specifically allows an expert to rely on hearsay "[i]f experts in the particular field would reasonably rely on those kinds of facts or data in forming an opinion on the subject." However, the states are split concerning an expert's reliance on hearsay or other inadmissible evidence in reaching his or her conclusions.[20] The trial judge maintains the discretion to determine whether the expert's reliance on the hearsay information was reasonable under the circumstances. Deference to the specialty's use of this information is the general rule. If the court ultimately believes the expert's reliance on hearsay was improper, the court can disregard the expert's opinion.[21]

To lay the foundation for an expert's testimony that is based, in part, on hearsay the examiner must elicit

---

19. IMWINKELRIED, *supra* note 16, ch. 9, § 9.04[4][b] at 390–91.
20. *See* M.E.D. v. J.P.M., 3 Va. App. 391, 400, n. 10 (1986). ("The expert's reliance upon hearsay is a matter affecting the weight to be given to his conclusions.") *See also* Linn v. Fossum, 946 So. 2d 1032 (Fla. 2007) ("An expert is not permitted to testify on direct examination that the expert relied on consultations with colleagues or other experts in reaching his or her opinion").
21. IMWINKELRIED, *supra* note 16, ch. 9, § 9.03[4][c][3] at 392.

(a)   the source of the third party report;
(b)   the content or tenor of the report;
(c)   whether it is customary within the specialty to consider that
       type of report.

Examples of this type of information include statements made by
a third party to a custody evaluator concerning a parent's fitness
and a statement made to a business evaluator by a company comptroller concerning the business's fiscal health.

Consider using an expert to get otherwise inadmissible hearsay
information before the court. For example, in a relocation case,
the parent who wants to move may want to offer evidence about
prospective schools or other information about the new location.
This information may be considered hearsay and inadmissible.[22]
Consider using an educational expert who could testify to this data
in reaching an opinion concerning the relative merits of school
districts. Or a psychologist, retained to opine concerning the children's best interest, could review and testify to this information.

The final factual basis of the expert's opinion is assumed facts.
Under some circumstances, the expert does not personally conduct an investigation but may nevertheless testify and render an
opinion based on assumed facts. Assumed facts are presented in a
hypothetical question. The expert may testify based on the assumed
facts in the hypothetical question. Parties may use a hypothetical
question on direct examination of their expert as well as on cross-
examination of the opposing expert. The questioner may ask the
opposing expert a question based on certain alternative facts the
questioner wants the expert to assume. For example, "Mr. Jones,
assuming the capital expenditure adjustment was $40,000 instead

22. Although, one could argue that the materials are not hearsay: they show the delib-
erative process (state of mind) of the moving parent and are not being offered for the truth
of the matter asserted.

of the $20,000 figure you relied on, all things being equal, how would that affect the value of the business?" This format is more typical of cross-examination, but it could be equally applicable during a direct examination, to perhaps highlight various differences between the assumptions or opinions of the dueling experts.

The Expert's Opinion

To recap, the proponent of an expert's testimony must lay a foundation for the following:

- The propriety of the subject matter of the report and testimony
- The qualifications of the expert
- The reliability of the theory being used (major premise)
- The factual bases of the expert's opinion (minor premise)

Assuming the foregoing elements of proof are met, the expert will be qualified to render his or her opinion. Traditionally, many jurisdictions required experts to cloak their opinion as being based on "a reasonable degree of certainty."[23] The Federal Rules of Evidence do not require the opinion to be based on this "reasonable degree of certainty" language. Consult your state law to determine the proper foundational language for eliciting the opinion of an expert.

FRE 704 allows expert testimony concerning the ultimate issue. For example, experts may testify to the best interest of the children and recommend a particular custodial arrangement. FRE 705 provides that experts may give their opinion on direct examination without providing all of the underlying facts or data relied on in reaching the conclusion. The rule essentially shifts the burden to

---

23. Avery v. State Farm Mut. Auto Ins. Co., 216 Ill. 2d 100 (2005); Gardini v. Moyer, 61 Ohio St. 3d 479 (1991).

the cross-examiner to elicit any facts the expert relied on. The rule avoids the necessity of a lengthy recitation of information prior to the expert rendering an opinion. In practice, however, it is rarely effective for an expert to disclose facts for the first time during an adverse examination. The facts should be revealed during direct examination to create a more persuasive presentation. While the rule does not require it, common sense dictates that experts *must* explain their opinions for maximum impact.

From a practical perspective, Rule 705 allows a lawyer examining an expert witness to start with the expert's opinion, rather than concluding with it. In other words, experts can give their opinion at the beginning of their testimony and continue elaborating on their major and minor premises. The lawyer will have to decide whether it is more persuasive to have an expert testify in a pyramid fashion (starting with the ultimate opinion and working downward) or using an inverted pyramid system (walking the expert through the process prior to revealing his or her ultimate opinion). Either way is proper; how to proceed is determined by the strategic preference of the lawyer. The important thing to remember is to make sure the opinion, whether at the beginning or the end, is reasonable and strongly supported by the facts and the expert's methodology.

Admission of the Expert's Report

With regard to admission of the expert's report, if the proponent offers the report into evidence at the beginning of the testimony, the opposing lawyer may object to the expert's testimony as being cumulative since the report itself is already in evidence. On the flip side, if the expert testifies first and the report is offered at the conclusion of the testimony, there may be an objection based on the fact that the expert has already testified and the report itself is cumulative. Neither of these objections is particularly persuasive.

FRE 403 does not preclude all cumulative evidence, only "need-lessly . . . cumulative evidence." In a bench trial, the lawyer can argue that the court should liberally admit relevant evidence and that nothing in the rules precludes an expert from both submitting a report and testifying to its highlights.

The lawyer must make the tactical choice of whether to offer the report and then examine the expert, or let the expert testify first and offer the report at the conclusion of the testimony. I typically opt for the former, getting the report in right away and then walking the expert through it to elaborate on some of the important sections. By having the report in front of the judge, it provides a context for the expert's testimony. Some lawyers prefer to offer the report at the conclusion of the testimony. They argue that by allowing the expert to testify before submitting the report, the judge listens more intently and is not distracted by the document in front of him or her. Neither method is per se right or wrong, and all law-yers will need to determine which procedure works best for them.

In order to lay a foundation for admission of the written report, consider some the following topics:

- What was the expert retained to do? (The assignment)
- Who prepared the report? (The expert himself or herself, the staff, or a team approach)
- Does the report contain all of the expert's findings and conclusions?
- Does the report truly and accurately reflect the expert's analy-sis in this case?
- Is the report based on theories or tests generally accepted in the expert's field?
- What is the nature of the data relied on in preparing the report? (Firsthand observations, reference materials, staff number crunching, test results, etc.)

Here is a sample foundation for admission of a business valuation report:

- Mrs. Lincoln, what was the scope of your employment in this case? (I was hired to determine the fair market value of Harold White's interest in ABC Services, Inc.)
- I'm showing you what I've marked as Plaintiff's Exhibit 14. What is this? (A report I prepared in connection with my valuation of ABC Services, Inc.)
- Generally, what information is contained in this report? (My analysis of the fair market value of ABC Services, Inc.)
- Who prepared this report? (I did, with the assistance of Marlene Jones, a staff member at my firm)
- What information did you rely on in preparing this report and in reaching your ultimate conclusions? (I reviewed five years of financial statements, interviewed the owner and CFO, reviewed comparable business data, reviewed industry data and a number of other pertinent material)
- Did you review this report before tendering it to the court here today? (Yes)
- Does this report accurately state your analysis and conclusions concerning the fair market value of ABC Services, Inc.? (Yes)

Court-Appointed Experts

Most jurisdictions allow a trial court to seek its own independent evaluation of the best interests of children.[24] Some states allow a trial judge to appoint his or her own financial expert to serve as a friend of the court. FRE 706 codifies the rules pertaining to court-appointed experts. This rule authorizes a trial judge to appoint his

---

24. *See, e.g.,* 750 ILCS 5/604(b); see also *Mental Health Evaluations in Child Custody Disputes,* 43 FAM. CT. REV. 187 (2005).

or her own expert, either one agreed on by the parties or one chosen by the judge. Compensation and other terms are specified in the rule. Ordinarily, neither party is prohibited from hiring their own expert. However, the Advisory Committee Notes state, "The ever-present possibility that the judge may appoint an expert in a given case must inevitably exert a sobering effect on the expert witness of a party and upon the person utilizing his service."[25]

Assuming the court does appoint his or her own expert, that expert would typically prepare a report and tender it to both parties for review. Depending on the rules of the jurisdiction, the report may be automatically admissible as the court's exhibit, subject to either party calling the expert for cross-examination. From a tactical perspective, remember this is the court's hand-picked witness. The lawyer must behave accordingly and treat the court's witness with proper respect. Also, local rules or procedure may limit either lawyer's ability to contact or discuss information with the court's expert. Do not violate any rules or protocols that will taint the report or aggravate the judge.

Direct Examination of the Expert

Direct examination of an expert should be clear, concise, and cover all of the important fundamentals of the expert's analysis and conclusions. An effective direct examination should allow the expert to reveal his or her mission, expertise, analysis, and conclusions. Chronologically, an effective direct should start with the assignment. While obvious, it is important that the court understand exactly what the expert was retained to do. Next, tell the story:

• Who did the expert talk to?

---

25. FED. R. EVID. 706 Advisory Committee's Notes, 56 F.R.D. 183, 286.

- What information did the expert review and rely on?
- What methodologies did the expert employ in reaching his or her conclusions?
- What tests did the expert administer?
- Are the expert's methods or tests generally accepted in his or her professional field?
- Describe in detail the expert's analysis.
- Did the expert rely on any learned treatises or other published data?
- Describe why the expert chose a particular method, test, or approach.
- If appropriate, have the expert explain why he or she made certain subjective assumptions and provide support for those assumptions.

The expert should also be prepared to critique the opposing expert's report. Have your expert challenge certain key assumptions or describe any flaws in the opposing expert's analysis. After building up the credibility of your expert and hopefully impugning the credibility of the opposing expert, end with the ultimate opinion of the expert. The aforesaid formula does not apply in all cases, but it gives a general outline for lawyers to consider when preparing the direct examination of their expert.

Cross-Examination of the Expert

There are no specific rules that pertain to cross-examination of an expert versus a nonexpert, but the nature of the task is different. While the scope of cross-examination is typically within the discretion of the trial judge, most courts permit wide latitude in testing an expert's reasoning and opinions. Here are a few broad subjects to consider:

- Bias of the expert—how frequently the expert works for the other attorney, for example
- Earlier published articles or other reports by the expert that contradict his or her testimony in this case
- How the nonexistence of one of the expert's assumed facts might change his or her opinion
- Whether the expert's opinion would change if a factual assumption that he or she relied on was untrue
- Choice of tests or methodologies relied on
- Limitations on the expert's knowledge or experience
- Challenge to the expert's knowledge of things he or she should know (e.g., request that the business valuator recite the factors of Revenue Ruling 59–60, the cornerstone of business valuation)

Also, remember FRE 803: a learned treatise may be used in cross-examination of an expert.[26]

Practice Points

- Choose your expert wisely. Stay away from hired guns. Experts who overtly advocate are ineffective. They are usually easy to impeach and not particularly helpful in the long run.
- If your expert uses any controversial testing methods, be prepared to support them in the event of a challenge. Consult a second expert if necessary for support. Conversely, if the opposing expert uses a specious method, consider a pretrial challenge to the report.

---

26. See Chapter 7 on learned treatises as an exception to the hearsay rule.

- Use your expert to help you prepare the cross of the opposing expert. The expert will be able to help you find the weak spots in the analysis or report.
- Thoroughly prepare your expert in advance of the trial. The person may be an expert in business evaluation but may not be comfortable testifying. Explain to your expert the mechanics of the objections, how to act with the opposing counsel, and how to behave generally.
- Use your expert to lay the foundation for any learned treatises that you will use to cross examine the opposing expert (see FRE 803(18)).

Examination of Witnesses | 14

I have thus far focused on the substantive rules of evidence; those rules addressing the reliability and admissibility of evidence. Now I will concentrate on the procedural rules of testimony. Procedural rules govern the propriety of the process, including the manner of asking questions.

Rules to consider:

Rule 607. Who May Impeach a Witness

Any party, including the party that called the witness, may attack the witness's credibility.

Rule 608. A Witness's Character for Truthfulness or Untruthfulness

(a) Reputation or Opinion Evidence. A witness's credibility may be attacked or supported by testimony about the witness's reputation for having a character for truthfulness or untruthfulness, or by testimony in the form of an opinion about that character. But evidence of truthful character is admissible only after the witness's character for truthfulness has been attacked.

(b)   Specific Instances of Conduct. Except for a criminal conviction under Rule 609, extrinsic evidence is not admissible to prove specific instances of a witness's conduct in order to attack or support the witness's character for truthfulness. But the court may, on cross-examination, allow them to be inquired into if they are probative of the character for truthfulness or untruthfulness of:

(1)   the witness; or

(2)   another witness whose character the witness being cross-examined has testified about. By testifying on another matter, a witness does not waive any privilege against self-incrimination for testimony that relates only to the witness's character for truthfulness.

Rule 609. Impeachment by Evidence of a Criminal Conviction

(a)   In General. The following rules apply to attacking a witness's character for truthfulness by evidence of a criminal conviction:

(1)   for a crime that, in the convicting jurisdiction, was punishable by death or by imprisonment for more than one year, the evidence:

(A)   must be admitted, subject to Rule 403, in a civil case or in a criminal case in which the witness is not a defendant; and

(B)   must be admitted in a criminal case in which the witness is a defendant, if the probative value of the evidence outweighs its prejudicial effect to that defendant; and

(2) for any crime regardless of the punishment, the evidence must be admitted if the court can readily determine that establishing the elements of the crime required proving—or the witness's admitting—a dishonest act or false statement.

(b) Limit on Using the Evidence after 10 Years. This subdivision (b) applies if more than 10 years have passed since the witness's conviction or release from confinement for it, whichever is later. Evidence of the conviction is admissible only if:

(1) its probative value, supported by specific facts and circumstances, substantially outweighs its prejudicial effect; and

(2) the proponent gives an adverse party reasonable written notice of the intent to use it so that the party has a fair opportunity to contest its use.

(c) Effect of a Pardon, Annulment, or Certificate of Rehabilitation. Evidence of a conviction is not admissible if:

(1) the conviction has been the subject of a pardon, annulment, certificate of rehabilitation, or other equivalent procedure based on a finding that the person has been rehabilitated, and the person has not been convicted of a later crime punishable by death or by imprisonment for more than one year; or

(2) the conviction has been the subject of a pardon, annulment, or other equivalent procedure based on a finding of innocence.

(d) Juvenile Adjudications. Evidence of a juvenile adjudication is admissible under this rule only if:

(1) it is offered in a criminal case;

(2) the adjudication was of a witness other than the defendant;

(3) an adult's conviction for that offense would be admissible to attack the adult's credibility; and

> (4) admitting the evidence is necessary to fairly determine guilt or innocence.

(e) Pendency of an Appeal. A conviction that satisfies this rule is admissible even if an appeal is pending. Evidence of the pendency is also admissible.

Rule 610. Religious Beliefs or Opinions

Evidence of a witness's religious beliefs or opinions is not admissible to attack or support the witness's credibility.

Rule 611. Mode and Order of Examining Witnesses and Presenting Evidence

(a) Control by the Court; Purposes. The court should exercise reasonable control over the mode and order of examining witnesses and presenting evidence so as to:
> (1) make those procedures effective for determining the truth;
> (2) avoid wasting time; and
> (3) protect witnesses from harassment or undue embarrassment.

(b) Scope of Cross-Examination. Cross-examination should not go beyond the subject matter of the direct examination and matters affecting the witness's credibility. The court may allow inquiry into additional matters as if on direct examination.

(c) Leading Questions. Leading questions should not be used on direct examination except as necessary to develop the witness's testimony. Ordinarily, the court should allow leading questions:
> (1) on cross-examination; and

(2)   when a party calls a hostile witness, an adverse party, or a witness identified with an adverse party.

Rule 612. Writing Used to Refresh a Witness's Memory

(a)   Scope. This rule gives an adverse party certain options when a witness uses a writing to refresh memory:

(1)   while testifying; or

(2)   before testifying, if the court decides that justice requires the party to have those options.

(b)   Adverse Party's Options; Deleting Unrelated Matter. Unless 18 U.S.C. § 3500 provides otherwise in a criminal case, an adverse party is entitled to have the writing produced at the hearing, to inspect it, to cross-examine the witness about it, and to introduce in evidence any portion that relates to the witness's testimony. If the producing party claims that the writing includes unrelated matter, the court must examine the writing in camera, delete any unrelated portion, and order that the rest be delivered to the adverse party. Any portion deleted over objection must be preserved for the record.

(c)   Failure to Produce or Deliver the Writing. If a writing is not produced or is not delivered as ordered, the court may issue any appropriate order. But if the prosecution does not comply in a criminal case, the court must strike the witness's testimony or—if justice so requires—declare a mistrial.

Rule 613. Witness's Prior Statement

(a)   Showing or Disclosing the Statement during Examination. When examining a witness about the witness's prior statement, a party need not show it or disclose its contents to the witness. But the party must, on request, show it or disclose its contents to an adverse party's attorney.

(b) Extrinsic Evidence of a Prior Inconsistent Statement. Extrinsic evidence of a witness's prior inconsistent statement is admissible only if the witness is given an opportunity to explain or deny the statement and an adverse party is given an opportunity to examine the witness about it, or if justice so requires. This subdivision (b) does not apply to an opposing party's statement under Rule 801(d)(2).

Rule 614. Court's Calling or Examining a Witness

(a) Calling. The court may call a witness on its own or at a party's request. Each party is entitled to cross-examine the witness.

(b) Examining. The court may examine a witness regardless of who calls the witness.

(c) Objections. A party may object to the court's calling or examining a witness either at that time or at the next opportunity when the jury is not present.

Rule 615. Excluding Witnesses

At a party's request, the court must order witnesses excluded so that they cannot hear other witnesses' testimony. Or the court may do so on its own. But this rule does not authorize excluding:

(a) a party who is a natural person;

(b) an officer or employee of a party that is not a natural person, after being designated as the party's representative by its attorney;

(c) a person whose presence a party shows to be essential to presenting the party's claim or defense; or

(d) a person authorized by statute to be present.

Direct Examination

Direct examination is the name for the examination of a party's own witness. A party can conduct a direct examination of a friendly witness, that is, a witness who is cooperative, or an adverse witness, that is, an adverse party or a witness who is identified with the adverse party and who may be less than cooperative. The rules provide that ordinarily on direct examination, the examiner cannot lead the witness. Leading a witness involves suggesting an answer in the question (e.g., "Isn't it true that you always gave the children their bath at night?"). When the witness is deemed hostile, however, leading questions are proper.

Form of Direct Examination

Ordinarily, during direct examination, the examiner asks questions to elicit information. The goal of a direct examination, as with all parts of a trial, is to accumulate evidence for the fact finder to consider or alternatively to lay foundations for documentary or real evidence. An effective direct examination must be structured to persuasively communicate that information. The examination should be phrased as a series of short questions: "Who did you arrive with?" "When did you get there?" "Please explain why you did that." The system advocated by the National Institute for Trial Advocacy suggests framing questions on direct examination to start with the following words or phrases:

- Who?
- What?
- Where?
- When?
- How?
- Which?
- Why?

- Please explain . . .

By consciously relying on these buzzwords, the examiner can avoid falling into the habit of leading the witness. Questions should be precise and be designed to elicit one fact per question. Stay away from compound or ambiguous questions to avoid objections and to maintain good rhythm and a cogent examination. Effective direct examination focuses on the witness telling the story, rather than the lawyer telling the story via leading questions.

As a general rule, even if the opponent does not object to leading questions on direct, it is a bad idea to ask them. Other than for preliminary matters, examining a friendly witness in this fashion is counterproductive. Testimony by the witness in his or her own words is superior to testimony by the lawyer through leading questions. Obviously, there may be times that the witness breaks down or is too nervous to respond. In such cases, one may need to ask leading questions, at least initially, to prompt the witness. But as a general rule, good trial lawyers do not lead nonhostile witnesses on important testimony.

There are two types of direct examination questions: open-ended questions, which invite a free form narrative response, and tighter questions designed to obtain definite answers. Both have advantages and disadvantages. Specific questions elicit more focused answers but narrative answers are more human and usually more interesting. Ask focused questions with unfocused clients who tend to ramble even when they are not nervous. Some courts preclude questions calling for a narrative response. But, some courts actually prefer narrative testimony of expert witnesses.[1] No per se rule prohibits questions soliciting a narrative response, and they are technically proper. As always, it is up to the court to determine a question's propriety in a given context.

---

1.   STEVEN LUBET, MODERN TRIAL ADVOCACY 49 (4th ed. 2009).

Leading Questions

FRE 611(c) allows leading questions on cross-examination or when examining an adverse or hostile witness in one's own case. The rule disallows leading questions on direct examination, except for preliminary or inconsequential background questions: "Ordinarily, the court should allow leading questions: (1) on cross-examination; and (2) when a party calls a hostile witness, an adverse party, or a witness identified with an adverse party." A leading question is defined as one that suggests the desired answer by its phrasing. "Your husband never put the kids to bed, isn't that right Mrs. Jones," is an obvious example of a leading question. There are less obvious examples ("Didn't you stop drinking at some point?"). Crafting clear non-leading questions is a challenge for any examiner.

Leading questions are deceptive: "Does your husband work late frequently?" This question may or may not be leading, depending on the judge. Some might argue the context suggests the answer; late nights are regular. Others might indicate otherwise.

Foundation for Testimony

The word *foundation* is a bit confusing. It is used frequently in the discussion of evidence and can mean different things in different contexts. For example, in authentication of exhibits, the word *foundation* means the predicate proof of the trustworthiness of the exhibit; that the thing offered is what it purports to be. When referring to the examination of witnesses, the foundation means the preliminary questions establishing the reliability of the testimonial evidence by showing that the witness can properly testify to the matters to be covered in the questions to follow. Generally speaking, foundational questions allow a court and the opposing party to determine if the information to be elicited by the question is relevant, reliable, and otherwise admissible.

The nature of the foundation will differ based on the nature of the testimony. Regardless of the type of evidence, there must be a threshold showing that the evidence is fair and reliable and that it properly comports with the rules. Foundation questions are not themselves subject to the rules of evidence, except those rules pertaining to privilege.[2] This means that when laying a foundation for testimony or an exhibit, an examiner may ask the witness a question that falls outside of the rules of evidence, for example, soliciting hearsay testimony. This point is important to remember; if a hearsay objection is made, for example, while you are establishing a foundation, point out that foundations are not subject to the general rules of evidence under Rule 104(a).

In addition to establishing the basis of a witness's testimony or supporting the admission of exhibits, foundational testimony provides a context for the court. This contextual framework allows the court sufficient background information to determine the reliability of the testimony and also better understand it. For example, the foundational testimony for a conversation might include the following questions:

- Mrs. Jones, did you have a conversation with your husband about the children's failing grades?
- When did you have the conversation?
- Where did the conversation take place?
- Who was present during the conversation?
- Who initiated the conversation?
- What was the general subject matter discussed during the conversation?
- What did he say to you and what was your response?

---

2.   FED. R. EVID. 104(a).

Ultimately, the foundation assures the court that the evidence, whether documentary or testimonial, is fair, reliable, credible, and accurate.[3]

Refreshing Recollection

No matter how well prepared, witnesses forget things on the stand—even basic facts such as their date of birth or marriage. If the forgotten fact is important to the case, the failure of memory can pose a serious problem. Trial procedure and the rules of evidence have evolved to provide remedies for the absent-minded witness.

Here is the procedure to refresh a witness's recollection:

- When did you first discover the affair? (I can't remember)
- Is your memory exhausted concerning this question? (Yes)
- Is there anything that would help refresh you recollection? (Yes)
- What? (If I was to review the love letter that I found)
- Sir, I'm showing what has been marked as Plaintiff's Exhibit 9 for identification. Please review this document, place it face down in front of you, and tell the court whether you now remember the date you first discovered the affair. (I now remember)
- When was that? (February 14, 2010)

Anything can be used to refresh the witness's memory: a photograph, an object, a recording, a diary, a document, anything that can be used to stimulate recall. And the item used to refresh the witness's recollection need not be admitted into evidence. Again

---

3. The Appendix has a summary of common evidentiary foundations necessary for the admission of records and testimonial facts.

the purpose here is to stimulate the witness's memory, not to offer the refreshing item as substantive evidence. Also, a lawyer can ask a leading question to refresh a witness's memory.[4] Specifically, the lawyer could ask the witness, "Would your diary refresh your recollection on this subject?" If the opponent objects based on leading, argue that anything, including leading questions, is permissible to refresh the witness's recollection and also that the question is foundational and thus not subject to the rules of evidence.

A document is the most common way to allow witnesses to refresh their recollection. FRE 612 requires that if a party relies on a writing to refresh the recollection of the witness, the writing must be provided to the opponent, who can attempt to offer it as an exhibit, to the extent that it is relevant. After handing the witness the refreshing item, give the witness an opportunity to silently review it. Then ask the witness whether his or her recollection has been refreshed. If the answer is yes, remove the document and continue with the examination. The witness can only review the refreshing materials; the witness cannot just read the contents of a document into the record.[5]

While this procedure applies to any witness, it is most frequently used with your own client in a family law case, where the parties are usually the primary witnesses. If the client still cannot remember the necessary fact after reviewing the object or document, ask the witness if there is anything else that would refresh his or her recollection. If not, consider offering the document used to attempt to refresh the witness's recollection as a recollection recorded (see discussion of FRE 803(5) in Chapter 6). If all else fails, ask for a recess, calm your jittery client down, and then hopefully the client will remember and be able to testify after the break.[6]

---

4.   LUBET, *supra* note 1.
5.   While a witness can read from a document that has been admitted into evidence (see below), here we are focused on testimony based on recall.
6.   Judges frequently admonish the witness not to discuss the testimony during the

Before the trial, advise the witness of the protocol if he or she forgets something on the stand. Give the client a context. Advise the client to answer affirmatively if asked whether his or her memory is exhausted and that by doing so, the witness can then review materials to help remind him or her of the answer. Have materials handy that might be needed to remedy a memory lapse. If appropriate, prepare notes for the witness to review in the event of a memory lapse. Recognize, however, that if the lawyer uses the notes to refresh the witness's recollection, FRE 612 authorizes the opponent to review (and offer them into evidence), even if they are a work product.

The procedure for refreshing recollection is the same, whether done during direct or cross-examination. Refreshing a hostile or adverse witness requires more finesse, though. It is possible that the witness will deny that the intended refreshing information helped him or her recall the answer, in which case the examiner will need to have a Plan B to get in the desired information. But judges are not stupid, and when a witness refuses to accept the obvious, that fact alone usually helps positively advance the theory of the case.

Use of Nonadmitted Documents

Offer an exhibit as soon as it can be authenticated. Prior to an exhibit's admission, a witness may read pertinent portions of an exhibit to provide a foundational context for its admission; but the witness may not read portions of the exhibit into the record.[7] The text of a yet-to-be admitted document is an out-of-court statement,

---

break. There appears to be no authority that disallows a lawyer from speaking with a client about his or her testimony though. The lawyer should respectfully request permission to discuss the testimony under the theory that the client always has a right to consult with his or her lawyer during the proceeding.

7.   Lianos v. Andreuci, 48 A.2d 343 (R.I. 1947).

and the lawyer must properly authenticate the document and present a valid hearsay exception before the document can be admitted and relied on as a reference. Once admitted, subject to other substantive rules, such as relevance, a witness can read portions of the text out loud and the witness can use it to illustrate his or her testimony. An opposing counsel may object, claiming the document speaks for itself and reading from it is improper. The actual objection would be a relevance objection based on the testimony being cumulative of the writing already in evidence. The response to the objection is that under Rule 403, the rule only bars "needless" cumulative evidence. Here the testimony helps explain or elaborate on the writing.

Cross-Examination Generally

Cross-examination has been described as a right rather than a privilege.[8] Our adversarial system is premised on legal rivals being given a full and fair opportunity to challenge the completeness and accuracy of the opponent's evidence. A witness who offers evidence is subject to cross-examination, and if the witness refuses to answer questions on cross, the court can strike his or her direct testimony.[9] Unlike direct examination, a witness can be cross-examined with leading questions. Cross-examination by well-crafted leading questions allows the examiner to control the witness and force the witness to agree with factual statements the examiner wants the court to hear.

---

8. Resurrection Gold Mining Co. v. Fortune Gold Mining Co., 129 Fed. 668 (8th Cir. 1904).

9. *See, e.g.,* Williams v. Borg, 139 F.3d 737 (9th Cir. 1998).

Scope of Cross-Examination

FRE 611(B) limits the scope of cross-examination to those topics covered during direct examination: "Cross-examination should not go beyond the subject matter of the direct examination and matters affecting the witness's credibility. The court may allow inquiry into additional matters as if on direct examination." Scope should be interpreted broadly to include topics and any inferences and deductions arising from the questions asked on direct.[10]

Courts have discretion to interpret scope expansively, but there are limitations on the judge's discretion. A scope objection complains that the cross-examiner has asked the witness a question about a subject not addressed in direct examination. If a third party witness testifies on direct solely about Alice's income or financial dealings, questions about her parenting skills are beyond the scope of direct, and opposing counsel can object on that ground. As always, planning is essential. If you want to examine a witness on a topic that will not likely be explored with the witness during the opponent's direct examination, call the witness in your case to expand the inquiry.

Request to Examine a Witness for Voir Dire

There may be instances where the lawyer wants to affirmatively challenge the opponent's evidence before its admission. With the court's permission, an opponent may ask the witness questions to determine the propriety of the evidence before it is offered. For example, under the original writing rule, one must first establish

---

10. 1 McCormick on Evidence, § 21 at 116-17 (Kenneth S. Brown, ed., Thomson West, 6th ed. 2006.

that a writing is an original.[11] Voir dire on the question of original-ity may be appropriate before the document is admitted. Subject to the judge's consent, the opponent could seek to conduct a mini-cross-examination of the witness concerning that issue prior to the court ruling on the admissibility of the writing.

The party wishing to conduct such an examination asks the court for an opportunity to voir dire the witness: "Your honor, I object on the ground that the tendered document is not an origi-nal writing, and I would request an opportunity to voir dire the witness in support of this objection." Since the examination is in the nature of a mini-cross-examination, the examiner may ask leading questions.[12]

This procedure could also be used to challenge an expert's cre-dentials or questionable foundational evidence. Tactically the lawyer must choose when to invoke this procedure. Remember that most judges must balance allowing arguments over admission of evi-dence and the clock, and a procedure such as this slows things down. Use a voir dire when there is a good chance of success in challenging the foundation for the evidence and when the evidence is important. Do not use the procedure for less important evidence that will likely get admitted anyway.

Impeachment of Witnesses

Impeachment occurs when a witness's general credibility is chal-lenged or when the witness's truthfulness is challenged based on a prior inconsistent statement. FRE 607 provides, "Any party, includ-ing the party that called the witness, may attack the witness's

---

11. See Chapter 10 on the original writing rule.
12. *See* FRE 611(c).

credibility." This rule supplanted the common law rule that disallowed a party from impeaching his or her own witness.

McCormick categorizes the rules of evidence related to witness credibility:

- Rules related to attempts to bolster a witness's credibility before it has even been challenged
- Rules related to techniques to attack or challenge the credibility of an opposing witness
- Rules concerning the methods of rehabilitating a witness whose credibility has been successfully challenged[13]

With regard to the first category, FRE 608(a)(2) denies a party the opportunity to bolster the witness's credibility before the other party has made a challenge to it. For example, on direct examination a lawyer may not ask the witness, "Do you always tell the truth?" After the credibility of a party's witness is actually challenged, that party may, on redirect examination, elicit testimony from the witness to rebut the charge of dishonesty.

The second category involves a challenge to an adverse witness's credibility. There are various ways to accomplish this. Most common is to call attention to a witness's self-contradiction through use of the witness's prior inconsistent statement. Another way of attacking the witness is to challenge his or her credibility based on emotional considerations, such as bias, self-interest, or alliance with the opposing party. Also, a party may challenge the credibility of a witness based on the witness's character. Finally, an examiner may confront the witness with external evidence such as the testimony of another person who contradicts facts testified to by the witness. Much of cross-examination is spent showing that the

---

13. 1 MCCORMICK ON EVIDENCE, *supra* note 10, § 33 at 146-49.

witness is not a reliable source of information, through the process of impeachment.

Impeachment with Prior Inconsistent Statement

When a witness has made a prior statement that is inconsistent with his or her testimony in court, a cross-examiner may challenge the witness's credibility based on the inconsistency. When done properly, this technique is dramatic and effective. A prior inconsistent statement can demonstrate that a witness has changed his or her story and therefore allow the lawyer to ask the court to question the witness's accuracy or honesty. This form of impeachment does not depend on the truth of either statement; it is the inconsistency that is important. When the witness is not a party and the statement is unsworn, the earlier statement is only admissible to prove the inconsistency and not as substantive proof of a particular proposition.[14] However, if the witness's prior inconsistent statement is a sworn statement, it is admissible as substantive evidence of its truth under FRE 801. Moreover, if a party made the prior statement, it is also admissible for its truth.[15]

If counsel seeks to impeach a witness based on a prior inconsistent statement, the trial judge must first determine if the earlier statement is indeed inconsistent. The general view is that "any material variance between the testimony and the previous statement suffices."[16]

Traditionally, there are three steps to impeach a witness with a prior inconsistent statement: (1) recommit, (2) validate, and (3) confront.[17] The first step, recommitting the witness, involves locking the witness into the earlier testimony. Recommitment is most simply

---

14. The earlier statement is not offered for the truth of the matter but rather for the fact of the inconsistency. *See* Chapter 6 on hearsay.

15. See Chapter 6 on admissions.

16. 1 McCORMICK ON EVIDENCE, *supra* note 10, § 34 at 151 (footnote omitted).

17. LUBET, *supra* note 1, at 145.

done by the cross-examiner restating the witness's trial testimony (e.g., "Sir, in your direct examination, you testified that you never had an account at the First National Bank, correct?"). The rules do not require that the examiner restate the direct testimony verbatim as long as it generally accurately reflects the testimony. "The purpose of recommitment is only to focus attention on the inconsistency between the courtroom testimony and the prior statement. It is therefore possible to recommit the witness to the content of the current testimony without repeating it word for word."[18] But for the evasive witness, a verbatim transcript of the earlier testimony can be helpful.

Once the examiner recommits the witness to his or her prior testimony, the examiner needs to validate the earlier inconsistency. Validation involves the witness's acknowledgment that he or she actually made the prior statement. Here are traditional examples of validation of deposition testimony:

- Sir, you remember appearing at my office last March where we conducted your deposition, correct?
- Your attorney and I were present along with your wife and the court reporter, correct?
- Before we started, the court reporter placed you under oath, right?
- And you swore that you would answer all of my questions truthfully, correct?
- I asked a number of questions and you answered my questions, true?
- After your deposition, you read and signed the transcript, correct? (Alternative: At the conclusion of your deposition, you waived the right to read and sign the deposition transcript?)

---

18. *Id.* at 148.

FRE 613(a) alters the common law requirement that a cross-examiner show the actual prior statement to the witness at the time of impeachment. But on request, the statement must be shown to the opposing counsel. If the witness denies the earlier out-of-court statement, then it must be produced to prove up the impeachment. Therefore, the examiner must have a copy of the statement or transcript of testimony available. This deviation from the common law expedites the process. Assume the witness testifies that he or she never had any accounts other than at the Acme Bank. The lawyer may ask, "Sir, at your deposition you told me that you did have an account at ABC Bank, correct?" If the witness answers yes, the impeachment is concluded. If the witness denies making the statement, ask the prefatory questions about the witness's attendance at a deposition and then hand the witness a copy of the transcript and ask him or her to read along with you as you read the witness's testimony from the deposition. The proper question asks the witness whether you, as the examiner, read the transcript correctly, rather than whether the witness actually answered the question in the fashion he or she did. The latter question practically begs for the witness to equivocate: "I didn't understand the question," or "I was confused that day," for example. It is unlikely the witness reading along with you will challenge the accuracy of your reading. If the witness acknowledges the accuracy of your reading, that is it. No additional commentary (e.g., "Were you lying then or are you lying now?") is necessary or appropriate. The impeachment based on a prior inconsistent statement is complete.

This same procedure applies if the witness made the prior inconsistent statement in a document, an interrogatory answer, or some other writing. Ask the witness to acknowledge making the prior statement. If the witness does so, the impeachment is complete; if the witness denies making the statement, the lawyer may use external evidence to prove that the witness made the statement. If the witness denies the earlier statement, show the witness the document.

Ask the witness to silently read it while you read the statement out loud. Ask the witness if you read the statement accurately. If the witness agrees, the impeachment is complete. If the statement is an interrogatory, signed under oath, you can admit the document as a sworn statement under FRE 801. If the witness again denies making the statement, authenticate the external exhibit under FRE 901 and offer it to prove the inconsistency.

Impeachment through Other Witnesses

A party can use a third party witness to impeach another witness. This form of impeachment is restricted. According to *McCormick*, the general rule pertaining to impeachment with third parties is that "[y]ou cannot contradict as to collateral matters."[19] For example, Mrs. Jones's failure to return a library book 20 years ago is arguably collateral to her honesty in a divorce case today; therefore, testimony from a third party to establish her failure to return the book is inappropriate. In this context, the question of what is collateral boils down to its probative value to prove a fact in issue. While the rules themselves are silent and do not categorically bar extrinsic evidence to impeach, the trial court may limit the proof when its probative value is outweighed by other considerations.

FRE 613(b) allows one to examine a witness concerning a prior inconsistency of another witness, without first asking the impeached witness about the inconsistency. For example, assume Mr. Smith seeks to impeach Mrs. Smith concerning a statement she made to a third person that is inconsistent with her trial testimony. Mr. Smith's lawyer need not first ask Mrs. Smith about the discrepancy during her cross-examination. Rather, his lawyer could call the impeaching witness to testify to the inconsistent statement. In general, though, the party who called the impeached witness must later be given an opportunity to explain or deny the purported

---

19. 1 McCormick on Evidence, *supra* note 10, § 36 at 156.

inconsistent statement. That party must also be given the opportunity to examine the nonparty witness concerning the alleged inconsistency.

Despite the rule's permissiveness, good trial technique and fair play warrant raising the issue with the witness at the time of his or her testimony. *McCormick* argues, "[A] strong case can be constructed that . . . [courts] should require under Rules 403 and 611 that the traditional foundation be laid on cross examination before the introduction of extrinsic evidence or prior statements admissible solely to impeach unless the interests of justice require otherwise."[20] In other words, the impeached witness should first be confronted with the third party statement before it is offered to impeach them.

Impeachment Based on Bias

Bias, either positive or negative, may be used to impeach a witness's credibility. While the rules do not specifically reference this type of impeachment, case law recognizes it.[21] Some common examples of bias include a family relationship, a sexual relationship, friendship, a business relationship, shared membership in a club or organization, or any other conduct or affiliation that creates a special bond with a party. Negative bias can be shown by hostility toward a party or expressed antipathy toward the party by words or conduct. In no event, however, can a witness be impeached based on religious beliefs or opinions.[22]

While the rules are silent concerning the foundation for bias impeachment, the majority of common law decisions require a foundation prior to the introduction of evidence of bias. And good practice requires a context for the impeachment to be effective.

---

20. *Id.*
21. United States v. Abel, 469 U.S. 45 (1984).
22. Fed. R. Evid. 601, *see also* United States v. Weinland, No. 2:11-70-DCR, 2012 WL 1902153, at *1 (Ky. E.D. 2012).

When challenging a witness based on bias, ask questions about the facts or statements showing the bias:

- You have played bridge with Mrs. Jones for ten years, correct?
- You have been in a reading group with her for the last five years, correct?
- Your children play together weekly, correct?

If the witness admits to these facts, the impeachment is complete. As with prior inconsistent statement impeachment, no further editorializing is necessary or proper. During closing argument, the lawyer can argue that the witness was biased and the court should discount the witness's testimony.

As always, the trial judge has discretion to control the examination. In the above example, in addition to examining a witness about the extent of his or her relationship to the party, a lawyer may try to call other mutual friends to confirm the long-standing friendship. If the witness admits to the facts of the relationship, the mission is accomplished; it is unnecessary to bring in other friends to further hammer the point home. This is a waste of time and cumulative. On the other hand, if the witness is evasive and denies the long-standing relationship, another witness may be necessary to prove the relationship to the extent that the court does not consider it collateral.

Impeachment Based on Character Traits

While the general rule prohibits character evidence to show a witness may have acted consistent with a particular character trait, it is permissible to offer evidence of a witness's character for truth to support or impugn his or her credibility. If a witness has previously engaged in deceptive or dishonest behavior, such conduct may be probative of the witness's honesty and may therefore be admissible to impeach the individual's testimony.

Generally there are three types of character impeachment:

(1) Evidence of character based on conduct
(2) Evidence of a conviction of a crime
(3) Reputation evidence[23]

FRE 608(b) allows inquiry into acts that reflect negatively on the witness's truthfulness. While some courts allow evidence of moral misconduct, the consensus and the federal rules themselves see no connection between moral conduct and a witness's propensity to lie or tell the truth. The Federal Rules of Evidence disallow evidence of "moral behavior" to impeach a witness.[24] As always, the rules of examination are subject to the discretion of the trial judge, and this is explicitly provided for by FRE 608(b).

So when should a lawyer consider the use of character evidence to impeach a witness? *McCormick* suggests some considerations:

(a) Whether the witness's testimony is crucial or unimportant
(b) The relevancy of the act of misconduct to truthfulness
(c) The nearness or remoteness of the misconduct to the time of trial
(d) Whether the matter inquired into is likely to lead to time-consuming, distracting explanations on cross-examination or reexamination
(e) Whether there will be unfair humiliation of the witness and undue prejudice to the party who called the witness

"Of course, a good faith basis in fact for the inquiry is always required."[25]

---

23. Remember that anticipatory evidence to bolster a witness's credibility is inadmissible under FRE 608(a)(2).
24. 1 McCORMICK ON EVIDENCE, *supra* note 10, § 41 at 179-80.
25. *Id.* at 181 (footnote omitted).

For example, in a divorce between Robert and Jane, assume Robert wants to impeach Jane's credibility based on her dishonest character. What can he do? He cannot offer evidence of her promiscuity, as that fact has no relation to her honesty. He cannot show that she was a bad housekeeper. Again, this fact is unrelated to her honesty. He probably would not be allowed to show a petty infraction, such as stealing ketchup packets from restaurants. If, on the other hand, Jane's employer admonished her for unethical behavior at work, questions about that conduct might be allowed. But what if Jane denies the admonishment? FRE 608(b) generally disallows extrinsic proof of the reprimand. The lawyer probably could not call the employer to prove up the admonishment. The rules generally discourage a long detour with a witness to prove bad acts for the purpose of impeachment.

There is an exception to the prohibition on the use of extrinsic evidence of bad acts to impeach a witness for dishonesty. Where the witness is competent to authenticate the extrinsic evidence and actually does so, the lawyer may use it to impeach the witness. In the example above, the lawyer could show Jane the letter admonishing her and ask her to acknowledge its authenticity and that she received it. If she denies its authenticity, the subject is closed and the impeachment failed. If she acknowledges the letter's authenticity, the cross-examiner could offer it *only* to show her bad character (and not substantively) and the impeachment is complete.

Impeachment Based on a Conviction of a Crime

The second way to use character evidence for impeachment is to present proof of conviction of a crime. FRE 609 allows proof of a criminal conviction to impeach a witness. Impeachment for criminal conviction highlights the witness' lack of credibility. FRE 609(a)(1) provides that conviction of a crime that carried a punishment of death or imprisonment in excess of one year may be used for impeachment, if the court finds its probative value exceeds its prejudicial effect. Under FRE 609(a)(2) any conviction for a crime involving dishonesty or untruthfulness, regardless of the sentence, may be admitted for the purposes of impeachment. The rule is limited to convictions less than 10 years old. The case law defines crimes of dishonesty as those "which involve some element of deceit, untruthfulness or falsification bearing on the accused's propensity to testify truthfully."[26]

The procedure to impeach a witness with a prior conviction is the following:

- Sir, is it true that you were convicted of the crime of forgery? (If the witness replies in the affirmative, the impeachment is concluded. But assume the witness here denies the conviction.)
- Sir, I am showing you Defendant's Exhibit 14 for identification, which is a certified copy of your conviction for forgery. Let me ask you again. Isn't true that you were convicted of the crime of forgery on March 11, 2012? (Yes)

Traditionally, a certified copy of the conviction was necessary even if the witness admitted the conviction. But the rules of most jurisdictions now permit the admission alone to satisfy the requirements for impeachment. [27]

Reputation Impeachment

The final form of character impeachment is through reputation evidence. The Federal Rules of Evidence permit, as a form of impeachment, a witness to offer an opinion of another witness's reputation. FRE 608 generally provides that a party may attack the credibility of a witness using reputation evidence. The majority of

---

26. 1 McCormick on Evidence, *supra* note 10, § 42 at 189 (quoting S.E.C. v. Sargent, 229 F.3d 68 (1st Cir. 2000)).

27. 1 McCormick on Evidence, *supra* note 10, § 42 at 194.

courts limit the admissibility of reputation testimony to an opinion about a witness's honesty, although some courts have permitted reputation testimony about other character traits of the challenged witness.[28] And it is important to remember that the purpose of this type of evidence is not to challenge the witness's specific trial testimony; rather, it is more broadly an attack on their propensity for truthfulness.

Reputation testimony must be based on the personal knowledge and perceptions of the witness about reputation. Testimony about specific events supporting the claim of untruthfulness is inadmissible. FRE 608(b) provides, "Except for a criminal conviction under Rule 609, extrinsic evidence is not admissible to prove specific instances of a witness's conduct in order to attack or support the witness's character for truthfulness."

Timing is also important. The salient period is the present, when the witness's propensity for truthfulness is relevant. The impeachee's truthfulness 10 years ago is marginally relevant to his or her credibility today. According to *McCormick*, most courts recognize this fact and have responded to

(1) . . . permit the reputation witness to testify about the impeachee's 'present' reputation as of the time of the trial, and (2) to accept testimony about reputation as of any time before trial that the judge in his discretion finds is not too remote. This practice should be followed under Federal Rules of Evidence 608(a). A witness's opinion permitted by the federal rule ought to have a similar temporal relation to the trial.[29]

---

28. 1 McCORMICK ON EVIDENCE, *supra* note 10, § 47 at 202.
29. *Id.* at 203–04.

The proponent of the reputation evidence must show that the witness is acquainted with the impeachee and has sufficient knowledge to testify concerning their reputation for truthfulness:

- Do you know John Jones? (Yes)
- How do you know him? (I work with him)
- Are you aware of his reputation for truthfulness at work? (Yes)
- And what is that reputation? (He is considered a cheat and a liar)

Specific examples of conduct that show why the witness has a reputation as a cheat are inadmissible. The rule only permits evidence of reputation generally.

Rehabilitating the Impeached Witness

The rules allow a party whose witness has been impeached to rebut the evidence supporting the attack on the witness's credibility. This process is known as rehabilitation of the witness. A party may not rehabilitate the witness unless the witness's credibility is first attacked; proactive rehabilitation or anticipatory bolstering is disallowed. When a witness is attacked based on his or her credibility, the party who called the witness may offer counter evidence to bolster the witness's credibility.

The two most common rehabilitative methods are (1) introduction of supportive evidence of good character of the witness attacked and (2) proof of the witness's consistent statements.[30] If a witness is attacked based on a prior inconsistent statement, the witness should be allowed the opportunity to explain the reason for the inconsistency. If a witness is challenged based on his or her character, the proponent of the witness should be able to present other reputation or opinion evidence concerning their truthfulness.

---

30. 1 MCCORMICK ON EVIDENCE, *supra* note 10, § 47 at 221.

The rehabilitation must directly address the facts supporting the attack. A generalized statement that does not correspond to the attack is inadmissible: "The wall, attacked at one point, may not be fortified at another distinct point."[31] Thus, offering a prior consistent statement by the witness attacked based on the witness's reputation for dishonesty would be improper and objectionable. On the other hand, while the rehabilitation must respond to the direct attack, a court may allow rebuttal evidence of the witness's reputation for truthfulness to counterattack a prior inconsistent statement.[32]

While specific instances of conduct may not be used to attack a witness's credibility using reputation impeachment, FRE 608(b) does allow specific instances of good conduct to rehabilitate the witness once he or she is impeached by reputation evidence. The specific examples of conduct must be probative of "the character for truthfulness or untruthfulness of (1) the witness; or (2) another witness whose character the witness being cross-examined has testified about."

In summary, to rehabilitate an impeached witness, present evidence to neutralize the attack. If the witness is challenged based on a prior inconsistent statement, rehabilitate the witness either by having the witness explain the inconsistency, offer a prior consistent statement to bolster the witness's testimony, or provide reputation evidence concerning his or her truthfulness. If the witness is challenged based on bias, offer rebuttal evidence disputing the bias (e.g., have the witness explain that he or she may like Mrs. Jones but certainly would not lie for her). If the witness is impeached based on reputation, offer counter reputation evidence showing that

---

31. *Id.*
32. 1 McCORMICK ON EVIDENCE, *supra* note 10, § 47 at 223 n.18 ("the preferable approach under the Fed. R. Evid., is to place this matter in the discretion of the judge who can consider the circumstances under which each inconsistent statement was made").

others consider the witness truthful, including specific instances of conduct dispelling any claims of dishonesty.

Scope of Redirect and Re-Cross Examination

McCormick defines the scope of redirect examination and examinations thereafter as being subject to the "rule of first opportunity."[33] The examiner should prove as much as possible during their first opportunity, rather than tactically deferring proofs until a later examination. Under FRE 611, the court has discretion to determine the propriety of questions in redirect and thereafter, but as a general rule, the proofs on redirect (or re-cross) should be limited in scope to those matters raised in the preceding examination. Redirect examination should focus on three primary areas of inquiry:

(1) Redirect examination is proper when it explains, avoids, qualifies, or develops matters raised during the cross-examination.
(2) The redirect examination can bring out other parts of statements, recordings, events, or transactions if the cross-examiner has brought out parts of them (thus opening the door).
(3) Where the witness has been impeached during cross-examination, the redirect examination may bring out matters that will reduce the impact of the impeachment.[34]

Court Witnesses

FRE 614 permits judges to call and question their own witnesses. A court expert or guardian ad litem ordinarily testifies as the court's

33. 1 McCormick on Evidence, *supra* note 10, § 32 at 142.
34. Thomas A. Mauet & Warren D. Wolfson, Trial Evidence 414 (4th ed. 2009).

witness.[35] Either party may examine the court's witness. The rules pertaining to cross-examination apply, allowing the examining lawyer to ask leading questions.

Judicial Questioning of Witnesses

The judge has the right to examine a witness called by either party. If either party has omitted certain facts or the court needs clarification of a witness's testimony, the court can ask its own questions of the witness. Both parties should be able to ask questions based on questions asked by the court. While the rules are silent, proper protocol suggests that the judge, as the ultimate authority in the courtroom, should avoid leading questions that may tend to influence the witness. Either litigant may object to the judge's questions. As in all cases, one needs to make a complete record in the event of an appeal. Accordingly register the appropriate objections to preserve the record for a later appeal.

Exclusion of Witnesses

FRE 615 authorizes the court to exclude a witness from the courtroom so the witness cannot hear the testimony of another witness. The purpose of the rule is to ensure a witness does not modify his or her testimony to be consistent with an earlier witness's testimony. Either party can move to exclude witnesses or the court can do so on its own motion. The court has no discretion to deny a motion to exclude nonparty witnesses, unless an exception applies. The parties to the lawsuit may not be excluded.

---

35. *See* FED. R. EVID. 706 (allowing the court to retain its own experts, as its own witnesses).

The rule also exempts from exclusion, with permission of the court, "a person whose presence a party shows to be essential to presenting the party's claim or defense." For example, a party could request that the expert be allowed to observe the other expert's testimony in order to help the lawyer formulate his or her cross of the opposing expert. Some courts allow a guardian ad litem to observe even though he or she will also be testifying. A strong argument can be made for allowing all experts, whose opinions may be influenced by trial testimony, an opportunity to hear the other witnesses testify.[36] For example, a party may be able to argue that the judge will benefit by allowing the custody evaluator the opportunity to observe the other witnesses who will testify at trial. An argument against allowing the expert witness to observe the whole trial and then use the observations to formulate his or her testimony includes preventing the opposing party from discovering the new opinions based on the testimony, in advance of the trial. It will be up to the individual trial judge to decide.

Rule 615 does not address discussions with witnesses. However, the rule implicitly authorizes a judge to limit disclosure of evidence to witnesses who have not yet testified. Thus while the rules do not expressly provide, it follows that the judge is authorized to order a witness, the parties, or their lawyers not to discuss the evidence with future nonparty witnesses.

Practice Points

- Use discretion with your objections; do not object to leading foundational questions unless they are truly improper and you can cite a good faith reason to the court.

---

36. 1 McCormick on Evidence, *supra* note 10, § 50 at 242.

- Be careful not to open the door unintentionally with questions of your witnesses. In other words, do not inadvertently open a subject of inquiry that could damage your client and that would otherwise be objectionable.
- Avoid leading questions during direct examination even if your opponent does not object.
- Prepare your clients in advance for the protocols for refreshing recollection if they forget something: "If I ask you if your memory is exhausted, say *yes*!"
- If there is important testimony that you need from the opposing party, call the person as an adverse witness. If you wait until the person testifies, you may be boxed in by a scope objection on cross-examination.
- Depositions are valuable resources. Abstract the transcripts to provide an index or summary of the testimony as a trial aid for the purpose of impeaching trial testimony.
- In an appropriate case, ask the court to permit your expert to sit in during the other expert's testimony to help you prepare the opposing expert's cross. The opposing expert would then be permitted to sit in during your expert's testimony for rebuttal purposes.

Tendering Exhibits, Objections, and Offers of Proof

15

This chapter focuses on the procedures for admission of exhibits and proper objections to the admission of both exhibits and testimonial evidence. I also discuss how to preserve the record for appeal. The Federal Rules of Evidence were primarily designed to protect lay jurors from drawing improper conclusions from the evidence. A judge is not subject to the same confusion. Nevertheless, while somewhat relaxed, the rules of evidence still apply in bench trials. While appellate courts rarely reverse trial court rulings concerning the propriety of evidence, the lawyer must know how to preserve any errors.[1] In order to preserve the record for the appeal, the lawyer must make appropriate objections and offers of proof.

---

1.   1 McCormick on Evidence, §60 at 299 (Kenneth S. Broun, ed., Thomson West, 6th ed. 2006).

Rule to consider:

Rule 103. Rulings on Evidence

(a) Preserving a Claim of Error. A party may claim error in a ruling to admit or exclude evidence only if the error affects a substantial right of the party and:

   (1) if the ruling admits evidence, a party, on the record:
       (A) timely objects or moves to strike; and
       (B) states the specific ground, unless it was apparent from the context; or

   (2) if the ruling excludes evidence, a party informs the court of its substance by an offer of proof, unless the substance was apparent from the context.

(b) Not Needing to Renew an Objection or Offer of Proof. Once the court rules definitively on the record—either before or at trial—a party need not renew an objection or offer of proof to preserve a claim of error for appeal.

(c) Court's Statement about the Ruling; Directing an Offer of Proof. The court may make any statement about the character or form of the evidence, the objection made, and the ruling. The court may direct that an offer of proof be made in question-and-answer form.

(d) Preventing the Jury from Hearing Inadmissible Evidence. To the extent practicable, the court must conduct a jury trial so that inadmissible evidence is not suggested to the jury by any means.

(e) Taking Notice of Plain Error. A court may take notice of a plain error affecting a substantial right, even if the claim of error was not properly preserved.

Procedure for Admission of Exhibits

The proper procedure for offering an exhibit into evidence is outlined below. Assume that Tom and Sally are divorcing. Sally wrote Tom a letter admitting an infidelity. If Tom wants to offer the letter, his lawyer would do the following:

- Have the proposed exhibit marked for identification.
- After marking the exhibit, show it to the opposing counsel (or give them a copy of the exhibit).
- Seek leave of court to approach the witness.
- Have the witness lay the appropriate foundation by their testimony. Here, ask Tom questions in order to identify and authenticate the exhibit (e.g., Who wrote this document? Do you recognize the handwriting? When did you receive it? How was it delivered to you? What were the surrounding circumstances?).
- Tender the exhibit to the judge stating, "Plaintiff offers the letter from Sally to Tom that has been marked as Plaintiff's Exhibit 12 for identification into evidence as Plaintiff's Exhibit 12."

Admission of Documents on Cross-Examination

The traditional view was that a party could not offer an exhibit into evidence during cross-examination. But, according to Imwinkelried, that view is incorrect. "If the exhibit relates to a matter raised on direct examination, 'new exhibits properly may be introduced during cross-examination.'"[2] Consistent with this notion, FRE 611 grants the court broad discretion concerning the order of proofs

---

2. EDWARD J. IMWINKELREID, EVIDENTIARY FOUNDATIONS § 1.04[2] at 7 (citing J. TANFORD, THE TRIAL PROCESS: LAW, TACTICS AND ETHICS 289–90 (3d ed., LexisNexis 2002)).

and the admission of exhibits. But beware—if a party rests their case, the court may disallow the presentation of new evidence during the opponent's case. In that event, file a motion to reopen the proofs, citing appropriate support for the relief.

Objections to Exhibits

Prior to the court's ruling on admission of a document, Sally's lawyer may object to its admission and the court then rules on its admission. With an exhibit, the basis for the objection may be substantive (hearsay, relevance, original writing), or it may be procedural (improper authentication, rule of completeness). In either event, counsel needs to object at the time the exhibit is offered. Once a party objects, the lawyers argue admissibility and the court rules, either admitting the exhibit outright, conditionally admitting the exhibit subject to later foundational proof, or denying admission of the exhibit. In some cases, the court may reserve ruling on admission, pending a review of legal authority or other information to be provided at a later time.

Objections Generally

There are two forms of objection, specific and general. The manner of making an objection differs with individual judges but generally the lawyer raises the objection by stating, "I object" and then identifying the basis for the objection. In a more formal setting, the objecting lawyer would stand and state the objection. The lawyer should clearly state the basis, whether it is to the form of the question, a substantive reason (hearsay, e.g.), an improper response to a question, or any other proper legal ground.

An objection that cites a specific reason is a specific objection. Specific objections should be short and precise. Avoid the speaking objection, which is a wordy argument. Similarly, the examining lawyer should avoid an extended argument defending admissibility. If, for example, the objection is based on relevancy, the lawyer should not go into detail about why the proposed evidence is irrelevant, unless, of course, the court solicits an explanation.

Speaking objections pose special problems for lawyers because they are often a way for advocates to coach their witness by suggesting the appropriate answer. If this occurs, politely interrupt, asking the court permission to intervene and pose an objection to improper coaching. While the damage may already be done, perhaps the court will give the testimony less weight and the lawyer may be reined in.

In contrast to a specific objection, a general objection is an objection without a stated basis. The objecting lawyer states "objection" and nothing more. The rules do not require a specific objection, and the court may properly grant a general objection. Sometimes the court may grant the objection for a completely different reason than the objector intended. General objections pose potential problems, though. The record on appeal becomes muddled if the lawyer does not clearly state a specific basis for the objection. In fact, many decisions have automatically denied relief based on the general nature of the objection.[3]

FRE 103(a)(1) provides, "A party may claim error in a ruling to admit or exclude evidence only if the error affects a substantial right of the party and: (1) if the ruling admits evidence, a party, on the record: (A) timely objects or moves to strike; and (B) states the specific ground, unless it was apparent from the context." Good

---

3. *See* LaPrade v. LaPrade, 784 S.W.2d 490, 491–92 (Tex. 1990) (holding that an objection was not specific enough to preserve an error for appeal; therefore, the error was not preserved and the point of error was overruled).

practice and the policy of the Federal Rules of Evidence require the use of specific objections. As a general rule, be prepared to identify the basic problem succinctly and clearly, citing proper authority to support the objection. By doing so, the lawyer preserves the record on appeal, and there are no questions in the event an appellate court later reviews the matter.

Objections may be made to any claimed impropriety, either substantively or procedurally. A substantive objection, for example, would apply to the admission of the exhibit or testimony; that it violated some substantive rule of evidence such as relevance, hearsay, privilege, or the original writing rule. A procedural objection applies both to the process, letting a witness testify out of order, for example, and to the form of the question asked to the witness. Questions must be framed properly or an objection is available to bar the evidence. While not specified in the Federal Rules of Evidence, here are common form objections to improper questions asked on direct examination:

(a) *Asked and answered.* If a witness has been asked a question and answers it, the opposing party may object if the examiner asks the same question a second time.

(b) *Assumes facts not in evidence.* A question that contains a fact not yet in evidence is objectionable. For example, "How did your child react after his mother slapped him?" would be improper unless preliminarily evidence supports the claim that the mother slapped him.

(c) *Compound question.* A question that contains two separate questions is improper. The witness cannot properly answer a question formulated this way.

(d) *Vague question.* A vague question is one that is confusing, unintelligible, or makes no sense.

(e) *Misstates the facts.* Related to the rule barring a question that assumes facts not in evidence, this rule bars a question that misstates the facts already in evidence. For example, if earlier unrebutted evidence reveals that the husband's income was $50,000 for the past three years, a question that asks how the family accumulated so much debt in light of the husband's *six-figure* salary is improper and objectionable.

(f) *Narrative.* A question that calls for a narrative answer may be objectionable.[4]

(g) *Nonresponsive answer.* If a witness answers a question nonresponsively, in most courts, only the examining lawyer may object. If an examiner asks a witness if he or she has been employed in the last six months, it would be nonresponsive for the witness to answer, "I have been sick." Here, the objection is to the answer rather than the question.

(h) *Volunteered.* If a witness "volunteers" testimony that is substantively improper (hearsay, conclusions, lack of foundation, etc.), the adverse party may object on this ground and seek to strike the improper testimony.

(i) *Speculation.* A question that invites the witness to speculate or guess is improper. A witness may not testify to information outside of his or her personal knowledge (FRE 602). "Do you think there are jobs available for your husband in his chosen field?" is speculative, unless the examiner can first lay an adequate foundation concerning the witness's knowledge of the marketplace.

Objections on Cross-Examination

While judges typically allow some latitude to a cross-examiner who is confronting a hostile or adverse witness, there are limitations.

---

4.   As noted above, there is no specific prohibition in the rules against narrative questions. However, in the court's role as gatekeeper of the evidence, certain judges may consider such a question improper. *See* STEVEN LUBET, MODERN TRIAL ADVOCACY 49 (4th ed. 2009).

FRE 611(a) charges the trial judge with the responsibility to "(1) make those procedures effective for determining the truth; (2) avoid wasting time; and (3) protect witnesses from harassment or undue embarrassment." While inherently confrontational, a judge may constrain a cross-examination under this rule if it becomes unreasonably hostile or argumentative. Here is a sampling of objections frequently raised in cross-examination:

(a) *Scope.* If the cross-examiner goes beyond the topics raised on direct, the appropriate objection would be "Beyond the scope."

(b) *Argumentative.* An argumentative question is one that is not designed to have a question answered, but rather to advance a particular argument of the examiner. It is designed to force the witness to agree with the examiner's inferences. "Do you really expect the judge to believe you are fit to have custody?" is an example of an argumentative question.

(c) *Badgering.* Badgering occurs when an examiner is beating up the witness. For example, if a witness indicates he or she does not know an answer to a question and the examiner unreasonably persists in asking for an answer, this is badgering.

(d) *Denying the witness the chance to respond.* Sometimes a poorly stated, nonleading question results in an answer that the examiner dislikes or did not intend. If such a question is asked and the witness starts responding, the examiner is not entitled to cut off the witness; the witness must be permitted to answer the question. An examiner can make an objection to a nonresponsive answer if the witness does not respond to the question asked. Also, a narrative objection can be raised if a witness goes on beyond the question and starts to ramble.[5]

---

5. One can avoid many of these headaches by asking good questions and using good witness control techniques. LARRY POZNER AND ROGER DODD, CROSS EXAMINATION:

(e) *Misleading question.* A misleading question is one that denies the witness a fair opportunity to affirm or deny a fact. Most frequently, these questions assume facts not in evidence. (e.g., "Mr. Jones, when did you stop wearing your wife's underwear?") An examiner may object to a question that assumes facts not in evidence on cross-examination just as they can on direct examination.

(f) *Vague question.* A vague question is one that is confusing or unintelligible. Such a question is objectionable on cross as it is on direct. If the fundamental question is unsound, it will elicit an unreliable answer.

Protecting Your Witnesses

To the extent possible, use these objections to protect your client and your witnesses from a bullying examiner or an examiner who is trying to trick the witness. Prepare the client in advance on how not to react improperly to provocation. Explain to the witness that if he or she gets into a fight with the opposing lawyer while on the stand, the witness will likely lose. Explain that courts dislike evasive answers and that you will have a right to clarify the witness's testimony on redirect examination.

Responding to Objections

Judges differ in their preferences concerning responses to objections. Some judges do not want a response until they solicit it. Others are more informal and allow a brief response with reasons. Regardless, prior to the trial or hearing, learn the preferences of the court and be in compliance. Assuming a response is permissible, when an

---

SCIENCE & TECHNIQUES (2d ed., The Miche Company 2004).

objection is made either to the admission of an exhibit or testimony, the examining lawyer may argue the admissibility of the evidence: *"Your honor, this is not hearsay because it is a party admission."* Sometimes a judge may sustain a general objection without a clear indication of the basis for the objection. If the court summarily sustains an objection or grants a general objection, the offering party may request the basis of the ruling: "Your honor, may I request the basis for the court's ruling?" This can clarify the ruling for the record (and make the judge accountable). Also, sometimes lawyers object based on an inadequate foundation. Sometimes inexperienced lawyers flail around trying to figure out how their foundation is inadequate. If you are uncertain where your foundation is lacking, you can ask either the court or opposing counsel the specific basis for the claim that the foundation is lacking.[6]

Timing of Objections

An objection must be made on a timely basis; a failure to do so can result in the waiver of any claim of error on appeal. The objection must be made as soon as its basis is known. When an improper question is asked, or a question that calls for an improper answer, the objection should be made before the witness answers the question. Trial lawyers need to be on their toes during witness examinations. Prejudicial and improper evidence sometimes gets into the record due to the lawyer being distracted or furiously trying to keep notes. Admonish your client prior to trial how important it is for you to concentrate and not to distract you by speaking to you during the witness testimony. Encourage your client to write notes that you can review at a convenient time. Listen to the testimony rather than trying to record it verbatim in your

---

6.   U.S. v. Dwyer, 539 F. 2d 924 (2d Cir. 1976).

notes. Notes should be triggers for your memory not a handwritten transcript. Listening is probably the most important of all the trial skills.

Sometimes a proper question will be asked, but the witness may answer it improperly or may give inadmissible testimony. In that event, make an oral motion to strike the improper answer. Generally a motion to strike should be used any time a question is improperly answered, even if it is discovered later in the trial. A motion to strike is important because it preserves the record for the purpose of an appeal.

As a general rule, be conscious of your record for the purposes of appeal. All cases should be tried *both* to the trial court as well as the court of review. A timely, specific objection helps clarify the record and is usually required to successfully challenge an evidentiary ruling in the appellate court. When a lawyer objects to a question and the court overrules the objection, allowing the testimony to proceed, there may be further questions on the same objectionable subject matter. In some courts the error is automatically preserved without continued objections.[7] However the lawyer should object to the further objectionable questions to preserve the error.

Alternatively, the lawyer can ask for a continuing objection to the line of questions instead of laboriously objecting to each follow-up question. In the event the court grants a continuing objection, the lawyer should later indicate for the record when the continuing objection ceases.

---

7. 1 McCormick on Evidence, *supra* note 1, § 52 at 263–65.

Objections during Opening Statement or Closing Argument

Objections can be made during both the opening statement and the closing argument. The opening is designed to be a summary of anticipated facts, not an unabashed argument. Argument is improper and objectionable. A well-placed objection may stop the conduct. Other possible objections include the lawyer expressing a personal opinion or presenting facts that have been excluded by a pretrial order.

Closing argument, on the other hand, is designed to be argumentative. Possible objections during closing include recitation of facts not in the record and misstating the evidence. As with the opening, the lawyer's personal opinions are objectionable. Also, an ad hominem attack on the character of the opponent is objectionable. Objections during closing should be rare and should be limited to outrageous conduct.

Offers of Proof

When the judge denies the admission of evidence, the lawyer may request to make an offer of proof, also called a proffer. If evidence is excluded, FRE 103(a)(2) requires that the substance of the excluded evidence be provided for the record. An offer of proof is the mechanism to do this. Without the offer, the appellate court would have no way to determine the propriety of the evidentiary ruling, unless it was obvious from the entire context of the questioning. An offer of proof also gives the trial court the opportunity to reconsider its ruling after it hears the previously excluded evidence.

The Federal Rules of Evidence do not prescribe the proper way to provide the offer of proof. One method is a narrative from the lawyer. The narrative should concisely summarize the excluded evidence without embellishment or argument. In some jurisdictions, the witness testifies to the excluded evidence. In that event, the record should reflect when the offer of proof starts and concludes so as not to confuse it with later evidence that is not part of the offer. If the court denies admission of an exhibit, seek to have the court admit it, not as a substantive exhibit, but only as an offer of proof for the reviewing court. By doing so, the appellate court could review the excluded exhibit to determine error.

Plain Error Rule; Harmless Error Rule

FRE 103(d) is the plain error rule: "A court may take notice of a plain error affecting a substantial right, even if the claim of error was not properly preserved." This rule is a failsafe mechanism that allows an appellate court to correct an obvious error even if it was not preserved properly. The error must affect a substantial right or result in a gross injustice if not corrected. An appellate court can reverse, despite the lack of objection, based on the plain error doctrine, when a trial judge admits a key piece of evidence that was very prejudicial and obviously improper. The plain error rule is a procedure to correct trial court errors if they are grievous and obvious.

By contrast, appellate courts often cite the harmless error rule as a basis to affirm a case despite error. Under the harmless error rule, a trial court error may be overlooked if it was harmless or inconsequential. Many evidentiary rulings in family law cases are considered harmless error.

Practice Points

- Know your judge's preferences for objections prior to trial. Some judges only want responses on request, and others will permit immediate argument.
- Make specific, rather than general, objections wherever possible. Specific objections lead to a cleaner record for appeal and allow the trial judge to make an intelligent decision instead of having to guess at the basis for the objection.
- Timely objections need not be made contemporaneously. The rule requires that they be made at the point that the error becomes apparent. This may come later in the trial, for example, where later proofs show the impropriety of earlier evidence. The lawyer can then object to the earlier evidence along with a motion to strike it from the record.
- If your opponent objects to admissibility based on an inadequate foundation for the testimony or exhibit, and the court sustains the objection, ask the court for the specific basis for the ruling.
- Do not forget to move to strike evidence, admitted improperly, if it slips in before the objection can be made.
- Make an offer of proof if the judge sustains an objection to your evidence.

Procedures for Streamlining Admission of Evidence

16

The less time spent on evidentiary issues, the shorter the trial. Any procedure that can streamline the presentation of evidence should be considered. Thoughtful analysis of ways to shorten trial time is an ethical duty; we all have an obligation to our clients to be well-organized case managers as well as courtroom advocates. The following are some procedures to consider for streamlining trials.

Requests to Admit Facts and Genuineness of Documents

Most jurisdictions have a mechanism to request that a fact be admitted or a document acknowledged as authentic prior to trial. Use this procedure wherever possible to save valuable trial time authenticating exhibits or arguing their admission. Rules of discovery generally sanction unreasonable denial of the genuineness of documents if the requesting party then incurs expenses proving authenticity. A request for admission of facts can dispose of multiple routine facts, saving substantial foundational testimony. This is a highly effective procedure for the authentication and admission of evidence.

Pretrial Motion in Limine

Either the proponent or the opponent of a disputed piece of evidence can file a pretrial motion seeking a ruling concerning the admissibility or inadmissibility of a particular piece of evidence. This procedure can save valuable trial time. For example, if witnesses disclosed in discovery appear to be cumulative on a given point, a motion in limine may result in an order restricting the number of witnesses or limiting their testimony. Or if certain information was not disclosed in discovery on a timely basis, a motion to bar the evidence at trial may be more effective than challenging the evidence when the witness is already on the witness stand. At that point the court may be less inclined to deny admission of the testimony inasmuch as the witness is already there.

The proponent of the evidence could use this procedure as well. If there is questionable evidence, the lawyer may seek to have its admissibility ruled on in advance to save the cost of bringing in witnesses whose testimony may be barred.[1] Also, pretrial rulings allow the opportunity for a more detailed written offer of proof, as opposed to having to do it on the fly at the trial. Strongly consider using a pretrial motion to determine anticipated claims of privilege.

Stipulations

Where possible, lawyers should sit down before the trial to try to work out any issues concerning admissibility of each other's proposed exhibits. By doing this, lawyers can save valuable trial

---

1. Although in some instances, courts may deem the ruling advisory in nature and deny a party a ruling. Consult your local case law and rules.

time. Parties can stipulate to authenticity of exhibits, foundations, and the scheduling of witnesses. Parties can offer all exhibits at the beginning of the trial, with admissibility stipulated, also saving time. Consider a stipulated exhibit binder, given to the judge at the beginning of the case, with copies of all stipulated exhibits. This procedure allows the judge an easy reference during the trial. Also, consider a stipulation only to authenticity that preserves the opponents right to challenge the exhibit on other grounds such as hearsay. Authentication of exhibits takes time, and courts will appreciate any stipulation that will speed things up.

Exhibit Conferences

An exhibit conference can also be helpful to expedite trials, particularly when the opposing lawyer is unreasonable. If the court does not ordinarily conduct such a conference, file a motion asking the court to conduct one, pointing out how much time can be saved if the court deals with contested evidentiary issues prior to the trial. If the court agrees to conduct the conference, ask that both parties be required to exchange all exhibits seven days prior to the conference in order that each can be prepared to discuss them intelligently at the stipulation conference.

Stipulated Trials

While not frequently used, a stipulated trial would provide the court a written stipulation of all uncontested facts and copies of any relevant documents, and the lawyers would simply present arguments concerning the desired disposition. This procedure cannot be used where there are issues concerning a witness's credibility or for issues related to child custody. But for simple financial issues, where the basic facts are uncontested and the parties can reach a stipulation, it can be a convenient time saver.

Reserved Evidentiary Ruling
Either by stipulation or by court order, parties could conduct a trial admitting all exhibits and testimony without objection. All disputes concerning admissibility would be reserved until the conclusion of the case. At the conclusion of the case, the court would rule on any contested evidentiary issues raised by way of a motion to strike. By using this procedure, the proofs can be expedited, and objections that seem meritorious as the evidence comes in may seem less so in hindsight. With an experienced judge as fact finder, this procedure could significantly expedite the proofs.[2]

Concluding Comments

I started this book with an acknowledgement that many divorcing people prefer ADR systems today. Litigation is painful and expensive, and most people have been exposed to enough horror stories to realize that it should be avoided if possible. But, unfortunately, it is not always possible. As trial lawyers we have responsibilities to advocate for these suffering people in an ethical and civilized manner. Effective use of the rules of evidence is just one part of this equation, but a vital part. We all have a duty to know and apply the rules in an efficient way to ensure that—despite the high emotions of the parties—an enlightened and educated court process can solve their problems without undue hardship.

---

2.   1 McCormick on Evidence, § 60 at 300 (Kenneth S. Brown, ed., Thomson West, 6th ed. 2006).

Appendix

The Federal Rules of Evidence

Article I. General Provisions

Rule 101. Scope; Definitions

(a) *Scope.* These rules apply to proceedings in United States courts. The specific courts and proceedings to which the rules apply, along with exceptions, are set out in Rule 1101.

(b) *Definitions.* In these rules

    (1) "civil case" means a civil action or proceeding;

    (2) "criminal case" includes a criminal proceeding;

    (3) "public office" includes a public agency;

    (4) "record" includes a memorandum, report, or data compilation;

    (5) a "rule prescribed by the Supreme Court" means a rule adopted by the Supreme Court under statutory authority; and

    (6) a reference to any kind of written material or any other medium includes electronically stored information.

Rule 102. Purpose

These rules should be construed so as to administer every proceeding fairly, eliminate unjustifiable expense and delay, and promote the development of evidence law, to the end of ascertaining the truth and securing a just determination.

Rule 103. Rulings on Evidence

(a) *Preserving a Claim of Error.* A party may claim error in a ruling to admit or exclude evidence only if the error affects a substantial right of the party and:

    (1) if the ruling admits evidence, a party, on the record:

        (A) timely objects or moves to strike; and

        (B) states the specific ground, unless it was apparent from the context; or

    (2) if the ruling excludes evidence, a party informs the court of its substance by an offer of proof, unless the substance was apparent from the context.

(b) *Not Needing to Renew an Objection or Offer of Proof.* Once the court rules definitively on the record—either before or at trial—a party need not renew an objection or offer of proof to preserve a claim of error for appeal.

(c) *Court's Statement about the Ruling; Directing an Offer of Proof.* The court may make any statement about the character or form of the evidence, the objection made, and the ruling. The court may direct that an offer of proof be made in question-and-answer form.

(d) *Preventing the Jury from Hearing Inadmissible Evidence.* To the extent practicable, the court must conduct a jury trial so that inadmissible evidence is not suggested to the jury by any means.

(e) *Taking Notice of Plain Error.* A court may take notice of a plain error affecting a substantial right, even if the claim of error was not properly preserved.

Rule 104. Preliminary Questions

(a) *In General.* The court must decide any preliminary question about whether a witness is qualified, a privilege exists, or evidence is admissible. In so deciding, the court is not bound by evidence rules, except those on privilege.

(b) *Relevance That Depends on a Fact.* When the relevance of evidence depends on whether a fact exists, proof must be introduced sufficient to support a finding that the fact does exist. The court may admit the proposed evidence on the condition that the proof be introduced later.

(c) *Conducting a Hearing So That the Jury Cannot Hear It.* The court must conduct any hearing on a preliminary question so that the jury cannot hear it if:

(1) the hearing involves the admissibility of a confession;

(2) a defendant in a criminal case is a witness and so requests; or

(3) justice so requires.

(d) *Cross-Examining a Defendant in a Criminal Case.* By testifying on a preliminary question, a defendant in a criminal case does not become subject to cross-examination on other issues in the case.

(e) *Evidence Relevant to Weight and Credibility.* This rule does not limit a party's right to introduce before the jury evidence that is relevant to the weight or credibility of other evidence.

Rule 105. Limiting Evidence That Is Not Admissible against Other Parties or for Other Purposes

If the court admits evidence that is admissible against a party or for a purpose—but not against another party or for another purpose—the court, on timely request, must restrict the evidence to its proper scope and instruct the jury accordingly.

Rule 106. Remainder of or Related Writings or Recorded Statements

If a party introduces all or part of a writing or recorded statement, an adverse party may require the introduction, at that time, of any other part—or any other writing or recorded statement—that in fairness ought to be considered at the same time.

Article II. Judicial Notice

Rule 201. Judicial Notice of Adjudicative Facts

(a) *Scope.* This rule governs judicial notice of an adjudicative fact only, not a legislative fact.

(b) *Kinds of Facts That May Be Judicially Noticed.* The court may judicially notice a fact that is not subject to reasonable dispute because it:

    (1) is generally known within the trial court's territorial jurisdiction; or

    (2) can be accurately and readily determined from sources whose accuracy cannot reasonably be questioned.

(c) *Taking Notice.* The court:

    (1) may take judicial notice on its own; or

    (2) must take judicial notice if a party requests it and the court is supplied with the necessary information.

(d) *Timing.* The court may take judicial notice at any stage of the proceeding.

(e) *Opportunity to Be Heard.* On timely request, a party is entitled to be heard on the propriety of taking judicial notice and the nature of the fact to be noticed. If the court takes judicial notice before notifying a party, the party, on request, is still entitled to be heard.

(f) *Instructing the Jury.* In a civil case, the court must instruct the jury to accept the noticed fact as conclusive. In a criminal case, the court must instruct the jury that it may or may not accept the noticed fact as conclusive.

Article III. Presumptions in Civil Cases

Rule 301. Presumptions in Civil Actions Generally

In a civil case, unless a federal statute or these rules provide otherwise, the party against whom a presumption is directed has the burden of producing evidence to rebut the presumption. But this rule does not shift the burden of persuasion, which remains on the party who had it originally.

Rule 302. Applying State Law to Presumptions in Civil Cases

In a civil case, state law governs the effect of a presumption regarding a claim or defense for which state law supplies the rule of decision.

Article IV. Relevance and Its Limits

Rule 401. Test for Relevant Evidence

Evidence is relevant if:

(a) it has any tendency to make a fact more or less probable than it would be without the evidence; and

(b) the fact is of consequence in determining the action.

Rule 402. General Admissibility of Relevant Evidence

Relevant evidence is admissible unless any of the following provides otherwise:

- the United States Constitution;
- a federal statute;

- these rules; or
- other rules prescribed by the Supreme Court.

Irrelevant evidence is not admissible.

Rule 403. Excluding Relevant Evidence for Prejudice, Confusion, Waste of Time, or Other Reasons

The court may exclude relevant evidence if its probative value is substantially outweighed by a danger of one or more of the following: unfair prejudice, confusing the issues, misleading the jury, undue delay, wasting time, or needlessly presenting cumulative evidence.

Rule 404. Character Evidence; Crimes or Other Acts

(a)   Character Evidence.

   (1)   *Prohibited Uses.* Evidence of a person's character or character trait is not admissible to prove that on a particular occasion the person acted in accordance with the character or trait.

   (2)   *Exceptions for a Defendant or Victim in a Criminal Case.* The following exceptions apply in a criminal case:

   (A)   a defendant may offer evidence of the defendant's pertinent trait, and if the evidence is admitted, the prosecutor may offer evidence to rebut it;

   (B)   subject to the limitations in Rule 412, a defendant may offer evidence of an alleged victim's pertinent trait, and if the evidence is admitted, the prosecutor may:

   (i)   offer evidence to rebut it; and

   (ii)   offer evidence of the defendant's same trait; and

   (C)   in a homicide case, the prosecutor may offer evidence of the alleged victim's trait of peacefulness to rebut evidence that the victim was the first aggressor.

(3) *Exceptions for a Witness.* Evidence of a witness's character may be admitted under Rules 607, 608, and 609.

(b) Crimes, Wrongs, or Other Acts.

(1) *Prohibited Uses.* Evidence of a crime, wrong, or other act is not admissible to prove a person's character in order to show that on a particular occasion the person acted in accordance with the character.

(2) *Permitted Uses; Notice in a Criminal Case.* This evidence may be admissible for another purpose, such as proving motive, opportunity, intent, preparation, plan, knowledge, identity, absence of mistake, or lack of accident. On request by a defendant in a criminal case, the prosecutor must:

(A) provide reasonable notice of the general nature of any such evidence that the prosecutor intends to offer at trial; and

(B) do so before trial—or during trial if the court, for good cause, excuses lack of pretrial notice.

Rule 405. Methods of Proving Character

(a) *By Reputation or Opinion.* When evidence of a person's character or character trait is admissible, it may be proved by testimony about the person's reputation or by testimony in the form of an opinion. On cross-examination of the character witness, the court may allow an inquiry into relevant specific instances of the person's conduct.

(b) *By Specific Instances of Conduct.* When a person's character or character trait is an essential element of a charge, claim, or defense, the character or trait may also be proved by relevant specific instances of the person's conduct.

Rule 406. Habit; Routine Practice

Evidence of a person's habit or an organization's routine practice may be admitted to prove that on a particular occasion the person or organization acted in accordance with the habit or routine practice. The court may admit this evidence regardless of whether it is corroborated or whether there was an eyewitness.

Rule 407. Subsequent Remedial Measures

When measures are taken that would have made an earlier injury or harm less likely to occur, evidence of the subsequent measures is not admissible to prove:

- negligence;
- culpable conduct;
- a defect in a product or its design; or
- a need for a warning or instruction.

But the court may admit this evidence for another purpose, such as impeachment or—if disputed—proving ownership, control, or the feasibility of precautionary measures.

Rule 408. Compromise Offers and Negotiations

(a) *Prohibited Uses.* Evidence of the following is not admissible—on behalf of any party—either to prove or disprove the validity or amount of a disputed claim or to impeach by a prior inconsistent statement or a contradiction:

    (1) furnishing, promising, or offering—or accepting, promising to accept, or offering to accept—a valuable consideration in compromising or attempting to compromise the claim; and

    (2) conduct or a statement made during compromise negotiations about the claim—except when offered in a criminal case and when the negotiations related to a

claim by a public office in the exercise of its regulatory, investigative, or enforcement authority.

(b) *Exceptions.* The court may admit this evidence for another purpose, such as proving a witness's bias or prejudice, negating a contention of undue delay, or proving an effort to obstruct a criminal investigation or prosecution.

Rule 409. Offers to Pay Medical and Similar Expenses

Evidence of furnishing, promising to pay, or offering to pay medical, hospital, or similar expenses resulting from an injury is not admissible to prove liability for the injury.

Rule 410. Pleas, Plea Discussions, and Related Statements

(a) *Prohibited Uses.* In a civil or criminal case, evidence of the following is not admissible against the defendant who made the plea or participated in the plea discussions:

(1) a guilty plea that was later withdrawn;

(2) a nolo contendere plea;

(3) a statement made during a proceeding on either of those pleas under Federal Rule of Criminal Procedure 11 or a comparable state procedure; or

(4) a statement made during plea discussions with an attorney for the prosecuting authority if the discussions did not result in a guilty plea or they resulted in a later-withdrawn guilty plea.

(b) *Exceptions.* The court may admit a statement described in Rule 410(a)(3) or (4):

(1) in any proceeding in which another statement made during the same plea or plea discussions has been introduced, if in fairness the statements ought to be considered together; or

(2) in a criminal proceeding for perjury or false statement, if the defendant made the statement under oath, on the record, and with counsel present.

Rule 411. Liability Insurance

Evidence that a person was or was not insured against liability is not admissible to prove whether the person acted negligently or otherwise wrongfully. But the court may admit this evidence for another purpose, such as proving a witness's bias or prejudice or proving agency, ownership, or control.

Rule 412. Sex-Offense Cases: The Victim's Sexual Behavior or Predisposition

(a) *Prohibited Uses.* The following evidence is not admissible in a civil or criminal proceeding involving alleged sexual misconduct:

(1) evidence offered to prove that a victim engaged in other sexual behavior; or

(2) evidence offered to prove a victim's sexual predisposition.

(b) *Exceptions.*

(1) Criminal Cases. The court may admit the following evidence in a criminal case:

(A) evidence of specific instances of a victim's sexual behavior, if offered to prove that someone other than the defendant was the source of semen, injury, or other physical evidence;

(B) evidence of specific instances of a victim's sexual behavior with respect to the person accused of the sexual misconduct, if offered by the defendant to prove consent or if offered by the prosecutor; and

(C) evidence whose exclusion would violate the defendant's constitutional rights.

(2) Civil Cases. In a civil case, the court may admit evidence offered to prove a victim's sexual behavior or sexual predisposition if its probative value substantially outweighs the danger of harm to any victim and of unfair prejudice to any party. The court may admit evidence of a victim's reputation only if the victim has placed it in controversy.

(c) *Procedure to Determine Admissibility.*

    (1) Motion. If a party intends to offer evidence under Rule 412(b), the party must:

        (A) file a motion that specifically describes the evidence and states the purpose for which it is to be offered;

        (B) do so at least 14 days before trial unless the court, for good cause, sets a different time;

        (C) serve the motion on all parties; and

        (D) notify the victim or, when appropriate, the victim's guardian or representative.

    (2) Hearing. Before admitting evidence under this rule, the court must conduct an in-camera hearing and give the victim and parties a right to attend and be heard. Unless the court orders otherwise, the motion, related materials, and the record of the hearing must be and remain sealed.

(d) *Definition of "Victim."* In this rule, "victim" includes an alleged victim.

Rule 413. Similar Crimes in Sexual-Assault Cases

(a) *Permitted Uses.* In a criminal case in which a defendant is accused of a sexual assault, the court may admit evidence that the defendant committed any other sexual assault. The evidence may be considered on any matter to which it is relevant.

(b) *Disclosure to the Defendant.* If the prosecutor intends to offer this evidence, the prosecutor must disclose it to the defendant, including witnesses' statements or a summary of the expected testimony. The prosecutor must do so at least 15 days before trial or at a later time that the court allows for good cause.

(c) *Effect on Other Rules.* This rule does not limit the admission or consideration of evidence under any other rule.

(d) *Definition of "Sexual Assault."* In this rule and Rule 415, "sexual assault" means a crime under federal law or under state law (as "state" is defined in 18 U.S.C. § 513) involving:

    (1) any conduct prohibited by 18 U.S.C. chapter 109A;

    (2) contact, without consent, between any part of the defendant's body—or an object—and another person's genitals or anus;

    (3) contact, without consent, between the defendant's genitals or anus and any part of another person's body;

    (4) deriving sexual pleasure or gratification from inflicting death, bodily injury, or physical pain on another person; or

    (5) an attempt or conspiracy to engage in conduct described in subparagraphs (1)-(4).

Rule 414. Similar Crimes in Child-Molestation Cases

(a) *Permitted Uses.* In a criminal case in which a defendant is accused of child molestation, the court may admit evidence that the defendant committed any other child molestation. The evidence may be considered on any matter to which it is relevant.

(b) *Disclosure to the Defendant.* If the prosecutor intends to offer this evidence, the prosecutor must disclose it to the defendant, including witnesses' statements or a summary of the expected testimony. The prosecutor must do so at least 15 days before trial or at a later time that the court allows for good cause.

(c) *Effect on Other Rules.* This rule does not limit the admission or consideration of evidence under any other rule.

(d)   *Definition of "Child" and "Child Molestation."* In this rule and Rule 415:

    (1)   "child" means a person below the age of 14; and

    (2)   "child molestation" means a crime under federal law or under state law (as "state" is defined in 18 U.S.C. § 513) involving:

        (A)   any conduct prohibited by 18 U.S.C. chapter 109A and committed with a child;

        (B)   any conduct prohibited by 18 U.S.C. chapter 110;

        (C)   contact between any part of the defendant's body— or an object—and a child's genitals or anus;

        (D)   contact between the defendant's genitals or anus and any part of a child's body;

        (E)   deriving sexual pleasure or gratification from inflicting death, bodily injury, or physical pain on a child; or

        (F)   an attempt or conspiracy to engage in conduct described in subparagraphs (A)–(E).

Rule 415. Similar Acts in Civil Cases Involving Sexual Assault or Child Molestation

(a)   *Permitted Uses.* In a civil case involving a claim for relief based on a party's alleged sexual assault or child molestation, the court may admit evidence that the party committed any other sexual assault or child molestation. The evidence may be considered as provided in Rules 413 and 414.

(b)   *Disclosure to the Opponent.* If a party intends to offer this evidence, the party must disclose it to the party against whom it will be offered, including witnesses' statements or a summary of the expected testimony. The party must do so at least 15 days before trial or at a later time that the court allows for good cause.

(c)   *Effect on Other Rules.* This rule does not limit the admission or consideration of evidence under any other rule.

Article V. Privileges

Rule 501. Privileges in General

The common law—as interpreted by United States courts in the light of reason and experience—governs a claim of privilege unless any of the following provides otherwise:

- the United States Constitution;
- a federal statute; or
- rules prescribed by the Supreme Court.

But in a civil case, state law governs privilege regarding a claim or defense for which state law supplies the rule of decision.

Rule 502. Attorney-Client Privilege and Work Product; Limitations on Waiver

The following provisions apply, in the circumstances set out, to disclosure of a communication or information covered by the attorney-client privilege or work-product protection.

(a)   *Disclosure Made in a Federal Proceeding or to a Federal Office or Agency; Scope of a Waiver.* When the disclosure is made in a federal proceeding or to a federal office or agency and waives the attorney-client privilege or work-product protection, the waiver extends to an undisclosed communication or information in a federal or state proceeding only if:

(1)   the waiver is intentional;

(2)   the disclosed and undisclosed communications or information concern the same subject matter; and

(3)   they ought in fairness to be considered together.

(b) *Inadvertent Disclosure.* When made in a federal proceeding or to a federal office or agency, the disclosure does not operate as a waiver in a federal or state proceeding if:
  (1) the disclosure is inadvertent;
  (2) the holder of the privilege or protection took reasonable steps to prevent disclosure; and
  (3) the holder promptly took reasonable steps to rectify the error, including (if applicable) following Federal Rule of Civil Procedure 26(b)(5)(B).

(c) *Disclosure Made in a State Proceeding.* When the disclosure is made in a state proceeding and is not the subject of a state-court order concerning waiver, the disclosure does not operate as a waiver in a federal proceeding if the disclosure:
  (1) would not be a waiver under this rule if it had been made in a federal proceeding; or
  (2) is not a waiver under the law of the state where the disclosure occurred.

(d) *Controlling Effect of a Court Order.* A federal court may order that the privilege or protection is not waived by disclosure connected with the litigation pending before the court—in which event the disclosure is also not a waiver in any other federal or state proceeding.

(e) *Controlling Effect of a Party Agreement.* An agreement on the effect of disclosure in a federal proceeding is binding only on the parties to the agreement, unless it is incorporated into a court order.

(f) *Controlling Effect of This Rule.* Notwithstanding Rules 101 and 1101, this rule applies to state proceedings and to federal court-annexed and federal court-mandated arbitration proceedings, in the circumstances set out in the rule. And notwithstanding Rule 501, this rule applies even if state law provides the rule of decision.

(g) *Definitions.* In this rule:

(1) "attorney-client privilege" means the protection that applicable law provides for confidential attorney-client communications; and

(2) "work-product protection" means the protection that applicable law provides for tangible material (or its intangible equivalent) prepared in anticipation of litigation or for trial.

Article VI. Witnesses

Rule 601. Competency to Testify in General

Every person is competent to be a witness unless these rules provide otherwise. But in a civil case, state law governs the witness's competency regarding a claim or defense for which state law supplies the rule of decision.

Rule 602. Need for Personal Knowledge

A witness may not testify to a matter unless evidence is introduced sufficient to support a finding that the witness has personal knowledge of the matter. Evidence to prove personal knowledge may, but need not, consist of the witness' own testimony. This rule is subject to the provisions of Rule 703, relating to opinion testimony by expert witnesses.

Rule 603. Oath or Affirmation to Testify Truthfully

Before testifying, a witness must give an oath or affirmation to testify truthfully. It must be in a form designed to impress that duty on the witness's conscience.

Rule 604. Interpreter

An interpreter must be qualified and must give an oath or affirmation to make a true translation.

Rule 605. Judge's Competency as a Witness

The presiding judge may not testify as a witness at the trial. A party need not object to preserve the issue.

Rule 606. Who May Impeach a Witness

(a) *At the Trial.* A juror may not testify as a witness before the other jurors at the trial. If a juror is called to testify, the court must give a party an opportunity to object outside the jury's presence.

(b) *During an Inquiry into the Validity of a Verdict or Indictment.*

  (1) Prohibited Testimony or Other Evidence. During an inquiry into the validity of a verdict or indictment, a juror may not testify about any statement made or incident that occurred during the jury's deliberations; the effect of anything on that juror's or another juror's vote; or any juror's mental processes concerning the verdict or indictment. The court may not receive a juror's affidavit or evidence of a juror's statement on these matters.

  (2) Exceptions. A juror may testify about whether:

    (A) extraneous prejudicial information was improperly brought to the jury's attention;

    (B) an outside influence was improperly brought to bear on any juror; or

    (C) a mistake was made in entering the verdict on the verdict form.

Rule 607. Who May Impeach a Witness

Any party, including the party that called the witness, may attack the witness's credibility.

Rule 608. A Witness's Character for Truthfulness or Untruthfulness

(a) *Reputation or Opinion Evidence.* A witness's credibility may be attacked or supported by testimony about the witness's reputation for having a character for truthfulness or untruthfulness, or by testimony in the form of an opinion about that character. But evidence of truthful character is admissible only after the witness's character for truthfulness has been attacked.

(b) *Specific Instances of Conduct.* Except for a criminal conviction under Rule 609, extrinsic evidence is not admissible to prove specific instances of a witness's conduct in order to attack or support the witness's character for truthfulness. But the court may, on cross-examination, allow them to be inquired into if they are probative of the character for truthfulness or untruthfulness of:

    (1) the witness; or

    (2) another witness whose character the witness being cross-examined has testified about.

By testifying on another matter, a witness does not waive any privilege against self-incrimination for testimony that relates only to the witness's character for truthfulness.

Rule 609. Impeachment by Evidence of a Criminal Conviction

(a) *In General.* The following rules apply to attacking a witness's character for truthfulness by evidence of a criminal conviction:

    (1) for a crime that, in the convicting jurisdiction, was punishable by death or by imprisonment for more than one year, the evidence:

        (A) must be admitted, subject to Rule 403, in a civil case or in a criminal case in which the witness is not a defendant; and

(B)   must be admitted in a criminal case in which the witness is a defendant, if the probative value of the evidence outweighs its prejudicial effect to that defendant; and

(2)   for any crime regardless of the punishment, the evidence must be admitted if the court can readily determine that establishing the elements of the crime required proving—or the witness's admitting—a dishonest act or false statement.

(b)   *Limit on Using the Evidence after 10 Years.* This subdivision(b)appliesifmorethan10yearshavepassedsince the witness's conviction or release from confinement for it, whichever is later. Evidence of the conviction is admissible only if:

(1)   its probative value, supported by specific facts and circumstances, substantially outweighs its prejudicial effect; and

(2)   the proponent gives an adverse party reasonable written notice of the intent to use it so that the party has a fair opportunity to contest its use.

(c)   *Effect of a Pardon, Annulment, or Certificate of Rehabilitation.* Evidence of a conviction is not admissible if:

(1)   the conviction has been the subject of a pardon, annulment, certificate of rehabilitation, or other equivalent procedure based on a finding that the person has been rehabilitated, and the person has not been convicted of a later crime punishable by death or by imprisonment for more than one year; or

(2)   the conviction has been the subject of a pardon, annulment, or other equivalent procedure based on a finding of innocence.

(d)   *Juvenile Adjudications.* Evidence of a juvenile adjudication is admissible under this rule only if:

      (1)   it is offered in a criminal case;

      (2)   the adjudication was of a witness other than the defendant;

      (3)   an adult's conviction for that offense would be admissible to attack the adult's credibility; and

      (4)   admitting the evidence is necessary to fairly determine guilt or innocence.

  (e) *Pendency of an Appeal.* A conviction that satisfies this rule is admissible even if an appeal is pending. Evidence of the pendency is also admissible.

Rule 610. Religious Beliefs or Opinions

Evidence of a witness's religious beliefs or opinions is not admissible to attack or support the witness's credibility.

Rule 611. Mode and Order of Examining Witnesses and Presenting Evidence

  (a) *Control by the Court; Purposes.* The court should exercise reasonable control over the mode and order of examining witnesses and presenting evidence so as to:

      (1)   make those procedures effective for determining the truth;

      (2)   avoid wasting time; and

      (3)   protect witnesses from harassment or undue embarrassment.

  (b) *Scope of Cross-Examination.* Cross-examination should not go beyond the subject matter of the direct examination and matters affecting the witness's credibility. The court may allow inquiry into additional matters as if on direct examination.

  (c) *Leading Questions.* Leading questions should not be used on direct examination except as necessary to develop the witness's testimony. Ordinarily, the court should allow leading questions:

(1)   on cross-examination; and

(2)   when a party calls a hostile witness, an adverse party, or a witness identified with an adverse party.

Rule 612. Writing Used to Refresh a Witness's Memory

(a)   *Scope.* This rule gives an adverse party certain options when a witness uses a writing to refresh memory:

(1)   while testifying; or

(2)   before testifying, if the court decides that justice requires the party to have those options.

(b)   *Adverse Party's Options; Deleting Unrelated Matter.* Unless 18 U.S.C. § 3500 provides otherwise in a criminal case, an adverse party is entitled to have the writing produced at the hearing, to inspect it, to cross-examine the witness about it, and to introduce in evidence any portion that relates to the witness's testimony. If the producing party claims that the writing includes unrelated matter, the court must examine the writing in camera, delete any unrelated portion, and order that the rest be delivered to the adverse party. Any portion deleted over objection must be preserved for the record.

(c)   *Failure to Produce or Deliver the Writing.* If a writing is not produced or is not delivered as ordered, the court may issue any appropriate order. But if the prosecution does not comply in a criminal case, the court must strike the witness's testimony or—if justice so requires—declare a mistrial.

Rule 613. Witness's Prior Statement

(a)   *Showing or Disclosing the Statement during Examination.* When examining a witness about the witness's prior statement, a party need not show it or disclose its contents to the witness. But the party must, on request, show it or disclose its contents to an adverse party's attorney.

(b) *Extrinsic Evidence of a Prior Inconsistent Statement.* Extrinsic evidence of a witness's prior inconsistent statement is admissible only if the witness is given an opportunity to explain or deny the statement and an adverse party is given an opportunity to examine the witness about it, or if justice so requires. This subdivision (b) does not apply to an opposing party's statement under Rule 801(d)(2).

Rule 614. Court's Calling or Examining a Witness

(a) *Calling.* The court may call a witness on its own or at a party's request. Each party is entitled to cross-examine the witness.

(b) *Examining.* The court may examine a witness regardless of who calls the witness.

(c) *Objections.* A party may object to the court's calling or examining a witness either at that time or at the next opportunity when the jury is not present.

Rule 615. Excluding Witnesses

At a party's request, the court must order witnesses excluded so that they cannot hear other witnesses' testimony. Or the court may do so on its own. But this rule does not authorize excluding:

(a) a party who is a natural person;

(b) an officer or employee of a party that is not a natural person, after being designated as the party's representative by its attorney;

(c) a person whose presence a party shows to be essential to presenting the party's claim or defense; or

(d)   a person authorized by statute to be present.

Article VII. Opinions and Testimony

Rule 701. Opinion Testimony by Lay Witnesses

If a witness is not testifying as an expert, testimony in the form of an opinion is limited to one that is:

(a)   rationally based on the witness's perception;
(b)   helpful to clearly understanding the witness's testimony or to determining a fact in issue; and
(c)   not based on scientific, technical, or other specialized knowledge within the scope of Rule 702.

Rule 702. Testimony by Expert Witnesses

A witness who is qualified as an expert by knowledge, skill, experience, training, or education may testify in the form of an opinion or otherwise if:

(a)   the expert's scientific, technical, or other specialized knowledge will help the trier of fact to understand the evidence or to determine a fact in issue;
(b)   the testimony is based on sufficient facts or data;
(c)   the testimony is the product of reliable principles and methods; and
(d)   the expert has reliably applied the principles and methods to the facts of the case.

Rule 703. Bases of an Expert's Opinion Testimony

An expert may base an opinion on facts or data in the case that the expert has been made aware of or personally observed. If experts in the particular field would reasonably rely on those kinds of facts or data in forming an opinion on the subject, they need not be admissible for the opinion to be admitted. But if the facts or data would otherwise be inadmissible, the proponent of the opinion may disclose them to the jury only if their probative value in helping the jury evaluate the opinion substantially outweighs their prejudicial effect.

Rule 704. Opinion on an Ultimate Issue

(a) *In General—Not Automatically Objectionable.* An opinion is not objectionable just because it embraces an ultimate issue.

(b) *Exception.* In a criminal case, an expert witness must not state an opinion about whether the defendant did or did not have a mental state or condition that constitutes an element of the crime charged or of a defense. Those matters are for the trier of fact alone.

Rule 705. Disclosing the Facts or Data Underlying an Expert's Opinion

Unless the court orders otherwise, an expert may state an opinion—and give the reasons for it—without first testifying to the underlying facts or data. But the expert may be required to disclose those facts or data on cross-examination.

Rule 706. Court-Appointed Expert Witnesses

(a) *Appointment Process.* On a party's motion or on its own, the court may order the parties to show cause why expert witnesses should not be appointed and may ask the parties to submit nominations. The court may appoint any expert that the parties agree on and any of its own choosing. But the court may only appoint someone who consents to act.

(b) *Expert's Role.* The court must inform the expert of the expert's duties. The court may do so in writing and have a copy filed with the clerk or may do so orally at a conference in which the parties have an opportunity to participate. The expert:

(1) must advise the parties of any findings the expert makes;
(2) may be deposed by any party;
(3) may be called to testify by the court or any party; and
(4) may be cross-examined by any party, including the party that called the expert.

(c) *Compensation.* The expert is entitled to a reasonable compensation, as set by the court. The compensation is payable as follows:

(1) in a criminal case or in a civil case involving just compensation under the Fifth Amendment, from any funds that are provided by law; and
(2) in any other civil case, by the parties in the proportion and at the time that the court directs—and the compensation is then charged like other costs.

(d) *Disclosing the Appointment to the Jury.* The court may authorize disclosure to the jury that the court appointed the expert.

(e) *Parties' Choice of Their Own Experts.* This rule does not limit a party in calling its own experts.

Article VIII. Hearsay

Rule 801. Definitions That Apply to This Article; Exclusions from Hearsay

(a) *Statement.* "Statement" means a person's oral assertion, written assertion, or nonverbal conduct, if the person intended it as an assertion.

(b) *Declarant.* "Declarant" means the person who made the statement.

(c) *Hearsay.* "Hearsay" means a statement that:

(1) the declarant does not make while testifying at the current trial or hearing; and

(2) a party offers in evidence to prove the truth of the matter asserted in the statement.

(d) *Statements That Are Not Hearsay.* A statement that meets the following conditions is not hearsay:

(1) *A Declarant-Witness's Prior Statement.* The declarant testifies and is subject to cross-examination about a prior statement, and the statement:

(A) is inconsistent with the declarant's testimony and was given under penalty of perjury at a trial, hearing, or other proceeding or in a deposition;

(B) is consistent with the declarant's testimony and is offered to rebut an express or implied charge that the declarant recently fabricated it or acted from a recent improper influence or motive in so testifying; or

(C) identifies a person as someone the declarant perceived earlier.

(2) *An Opposing Party's Statement.* The statement is offered against an opposing party and:

(A) was made by the party in an individual or representative capacity;

(B) is one the party manifested that it adopted or believed to be true;

(C) was made by a person whom the party authorized to make a statement on the subject;

(D) was made by the party's agent or employee on a matter within the scope of that relationship and while it existed; or

(E) was made by the party's coconspirator during and in furtherance of the conspiracy.

The statement must be considered but does not by itself establish the declarant's authority under (C); the existence or scope of the relationship under (D); or the existence of the conspiracy or participation in it under (E).

Rule 802. The Rule against Hearsay

Hearsay is not admissible unless any of the following provides otherwise:

- a federal statute;
- these rules; or
- other rules prescribed by the Supreme Court.

Rule 803. Exceptions to the Rule against Hearsay—Regardless of Whether the

The following are not excluded by the rule against hearsay, regardless of whether the declarant is available as a witness:

(1)   *Present Sense Impression.* A statement describing or explaining an event or condition, made while or immediately after the declarant perceived it.

(2)   *Excited Utterance.* A statement relating to a startling event or condition, made while the declarant was under the stress of excitement that it caused.

(3)   *Then-Existing Mental, Emotional, or Physical Condition.* A statement of the declarant's then-existing state of mind (such as motive, intent, or plan) or emotional, sensory, or physical condition (such as mental feeling, pain, or bodily health), but not including a statement of memory or belief to prove the fact remembered or believed unless it relates to the validity or terms of the declarant's will.

(4)   *Statement Made for Medical Diagnosis or Treatment.* A statement that:

(A) is made for—and is reasonably pertinent to—medical diagnosis or treatment; and

(B) describes medical history; past or present symptoms or sensations; their inception; or their general cause.

(5) *Recorded Recollection.* A record that:

(A) is on a matter the witness once knew about but now cannot recall well enough to testify fully and accurately;

(B) was made or adopted by the witness when the matter was fresh in the witness's memory; and

(C) accurately reflects the witness's knowledge. If admitted, the record may be read into evidence but may be received as an exhibit only if offered by an adverse party.

(6) *Records of a Regularly Conducted Activity.* A record of an act, event, condition, opinion, or diagnosis if:

(A) the record was made at or near the time by—or from information transmitted by—someone with knowledge;

(B) the record was kept in the course of a regularly conducted activity of a business, organization, occupation, or calling, whether or not for profit;

(C) making the record was a regular practice of that activity;

(D) all these conditions are shown by the testimony of the custodian or another qualified witness, or by a certification that complies with Rule 902(11) or (12) or with a statute permitting certification; and

(E) neither the source of information nor the method or circumstances of preparation indicate a lack of trustworthiness.

(7) *Absence of a Record of a Regularly Conducted Activity.* Evidence that a matter is not included in a record described in paragraph (6) if:

(A) the evidence is admitted to prove that the matter did not occur or exist;

(B) a record was regularly kept for a matter of that kind; and

(C) neither the possible source of the information nor other circumstances indicate a lack of trustworthiness.

(8) *Public Records.* A record or statement of a public office if:

(A) it sets out:

    i.   the office's activities;

    ii. a matter observed while under a legal duty to report, but not including, in a criminal case, a matter observed by law-enforcement personnel; or

    iii. in a civil case or against the government in a criminal case, factual findings from a legally authorized investigation; and

(B) neither the source of information nor other circumstances indicate a lack of trustworthiness.

(9) *Public Records of Vital Statistics.* A record of a birth, death, or marriage, if reported to a public office in accordance with a legal duty.

(10) *Absence of a Public Record.* Testimony—or a certification under Rule 902—that a diligent search failed to disclose a public record or statement if the testimony or certification is admitted to prove that:

(A) the record or statement does not exist; or

(B) a matter did not occur or exist, if a public office regularly kept a record or statement for a matter of that kind.

(11) *Records of Religious Organizations Concerning Personal or Family History.* A statement of birth, legitimacy, ancestry, marriage, divorce, death, relationship by blood or marriage, or similar facts of personal or family history, contained in a regularly kept record of a religious organization.

(12) *Certificates of Marriage, Baptism, and Similar Ceremonies.* A statement of fact contained in a certificate:

(A) made by a person who is authorized by a religious organization or by law to perform the act certified;

(B) attesting that the person performed a marriage or similar ceremony or administered a sacrament; and

(C) purporting to have been issued at the time of the act or within a reasonable time after it.

(13) *Family Records.* A statement of fact about personal or family history contained in a family record, such as a Bible, genealogy, chart, engraving on a ring, inscription on a portrait, or engraving on an urn or burial marker.

(14) *Records of Documents That Affect an Interest in Property.* The record of a document that purports to establish or affect an interest in property if:

(A) the record is admitted to prove the content of the original recorded document, along with its signing and its delivery by each person who purports to have signed it;

(B) the record is kept in a public office; and

(C) a statute authorizes recording documents of that kind in that office.

(15) *Statements in Documents That Affect an Interest in Property.* A statement contained in a document that purports to establish or affect an interest in property if the matter stated was relevant to the document's purpose—unless later dealings with the property are inconsistent with the truth of the statement or the purport of the document.

(16) *Statements in Ancient Documents.* A statement in a document that is at least 20 years old and whose authenticity is established.

(17) *Market Reports and Similar Commercial Publications.* Market quotations, lists, directories, or other compilations that are generally relied on by the public or by persons in particular occupations.

(18) *Statements in Learned Treatises, Periodicals, or Pamphlets.* A statement contained in a treatise, periodical, or pamphlet if:
   (A) the statement is called to the attention of an expert witness on cross-examination or relied on by the expert on direct examination; and
   (B) the publication is established as a reliable authority by the expert's admission or testimony, by another expert's testimony, or by judicial notice. If admitted, the statement may be read into evidence but not received as an exhibit.
(19) *Reputation Concerning Personal or Family History.* A reputation among a person's family by blood, adoption, or marriage—or among a person's associates or in the community—concerning the person's birth, adoption, legitimacy, ancestry, marriage, divorce, death, relationship by blood, adoption, or marriage, or similar facts of personal or family history.
(20) *Reputation Concerning Boundaries or General History.* A reputation in a community—arising before the controversy—concerning boundaries of land in the community or customs that affect the land, or concerning general historical events important to that community, state, or nation.
(21) *Reputation Concerning Character.* A reputation among a person's associates or in the community concerning the person's character.
(22) *Judgment of a Previous Conviction.* Evidence of a final judgment of conviction if:
   (A) the judgment was entered after a trial or guilty plea, but not a nolo contendere plea;
   (B) the conviction was for a crime punishable by death or by imprisonment for more than a year;

 (C) the evidence is admitted to prove any fact essential to the judgment; and

 (D) when offered by the prosecutor in a criminal case for a purpose other than impeachment, the judgment was against the defendant. The pendency of an appeal may be shown but does not affect admissibility.

(23) *Judgments Involving Personal, Family, or General History, or a Boundary.* A judgment that is admitted to prove a matter of personal, family, or general history, or boundaries, if the matter:

 (A) was essential to the judgment; and

 (B) could be proved by evidence of reputation.

(24) [*Other Exceptions.*] [Transferred to Rule 807.]

Rule 804. Exceptions to the Rule against Hearsay— When the Declarant Is Unavailable as a Witness

(a) *Criteria for Being Unavailable.* A declarant is considered to be unavailable as a witness if the declarant:

 (1) is exempted from testifying about the subject matter of the declarant's statement because the court rules that a privilege applies;

 (2) refuses to testify about the subject matter despite a court order to do so;

 (3) testifies to not remembering the subject matter;

 (4) cannot be present or testify at the trial or hearing because of death or a then-existing infirmity, physical illness, or mental illness; or

 (5) is absent from the trial or hearing and the statement's proponent has not been able, by process or other reasonable means, to procure:

  (A) the declarant's attendance, in the case of a hearsay exception under Rule 804(b)(1) or (6); or

    (B) the declarant's attendance or testimony, in the case of a hearsay exception under Rule 804(b)(2), (3), or (4). But this subdivision (a) does not apply if the statement's proponent procured or wrongfully caused the declarant's unavailability as a witness in order to prevent the declarant from attending or testifying.

(b) *The Exceptions.* The following are not excluded by the rule against hearsay if the declarant is unavailable as a witness:

  (1) *Former Testimony.* Testimony that:

    (A) was given as a witness at a trial, hearing, or lawful deposition, whether given during the current proceeding or a different one; and

    (B) is now offered against a party who had—or, in a civil case, whose predecessor in interest had—an opportunity and similar motive to develop it by direct, cross-, or redirect examination.

  (2) *Statement under the Belief of Imminent Death.* In a prosecution for homicide or in a civil case, a statement that the declarant, while believing the declarant's death to be imminent, made about its cause or circumstances.

  (3) *Statement against Interest.* A statement that:

    (A) a reasonable person in the declarant's position would have made only if the person believed it to be true because, when made, it was so contrary to the declarant's proprietary or pecuniary interest or had so great a tendency to invalidate the declarant's claim against someone else or to expose the declarant to civil or criminal liability; and

    (B) is supported by corroborating circumstances that clearly indicate its trustworthiness, if it is offered in a criminal case as one that tends to expose the declarant to criminal liability.

   (4) *Statement of Personal or Family History.* A statement about:

      (A) the declarant's own birth, adoption, legitimacy, ancestry, marriage, divorce, relationship by blood, adoption, or marriage, or similar facts of personal or family history, even though the declarant had no way of acquiring personal knowledge about that fact; or

      (B) another person concerning any of these facts, as well as death, if the declarant was related to the person by blood, adoption, or marriage or was so intimately associated with the person's family that the declarant's information is likely to be accurate.

   (5) [*Other Exceptions.*] [Transferred to Rule 807.]

   (6) *Statement Offered against a Party That Wrongfully Caused the Declarant's Unavailability.* A statement offered against a party that wrongfully caused—or acquiesced in wrongfully causing—the declarant's unavailability as a witness, and did so intending that result.

Rule 805. Hearsay within Hearsay

Hearsay within hearsay is not excluded by the rule against hearsay if each part of the combined statements conforms with an exception to the rule.

Rule 806. Attacking and Supporting the Declarant's Credibility

When a hearsay statement—or a statement described in Rule 801(d)(2)(C), (D), or (E)—has been admitted in evidence, the declarant's credibility may be attacked, and then supported, by any evidence that would be admissible for those purposes if the declarant had testified as a witness. The court may admit evidence of the declarant's inconsistent statement or conduct, regardless of when it occurred or whether the declarant had an opportunity to explain or deny it. If the party against whom the statement was admitted calls the declarant as a witness, the party may examine the declarant on the statement as if on cross-examination.

Rule 807. Residual Exception

(a) *In General.* Under the following circumstances, a hearsay statement is not excluded by the rule against hearsay even if the statement is not specifically covered by a hearsay exception in Rule 803 or 804:

(1) the statement has equivalent circumstantial guarantees of trustworthiness;

(2) it is offered as evidence of a material fact;

(3) it is more probative on the point for which it is offered than any other evidence that the proponent can obtain through reasonable efforts; and

(4) admitting it will best serve the purposes of these rules and the interests of justice.

(b) *Notice.* The statement is admissible only if, before the trial or hearing, the proponent gives an adverse party reasonable notice of the intent to offer the statement and its particulars, including the declarant's name and address, so that the party has a fair opportunity to meet it.

Article IX. Authentication and Identification

Rule 901. Authenticating or Identifying Evidence

(a) *In General.* To satisfy the requirement of authenticating or identifying an item of evidence, the proponent must produce evidence sufficient to support a finding that the item is what the proponent claims it is.

(b) *Examples.* The following are examples only—not a complete list—of evidence that satisfies the requirement:

(1) *Testimony of a Witness with Knowledge.* Testimony that an item is what it is claimed to be.

(2) *Nonexpert Opinion about Handwriting.* A nonexpert's opinion that handwriting is genuine, based on a familiarity with it that was not acquired for the current litigation.

(3) *Comparison by an Expert Witness or the Trier of Fact.* A comparison with an authenticated specimen by an expert witness or the trier of fact.

(4) *Distinctive Characteristics and the Like.* The appearance, contents, substance, internal patterns, or other distinctive characteristics of the item, taken together with all the circumstances.

(5) *Opinion about a Voice.* An opinion identifying a person's voice—whether heard firsthand or through mechanical or electronic transmission or recording—based on hearing the voice at any time under circumstances that connect it with the alleged speaker.

(6) *Evidence about a Telephone Conversation.* For a telephone conversation, evidence that a call was made to the number assigned at the time to:

(A) a particular person, if circumstances, including self-identification, show that the person answering was the one called; or

(B) a particular business, if the call was made to a business and the call related to business reasonably transacted over the telephone.

(7) *Evidence about Public Records.* Evidence that:

(A) a document was recorded or filed in a public office as authorized by law; or

(B) a purported public record or statement is from the office where items of this kind are kept.

(8) *Evidence about Ancient Documents or Data Compilations.* For a document or data compilation, evidence that it:

(A) is in a condition that creates no suspicion about its authenticity;

(B) was in a place where, if authentic, it would likely be; and

(C) is at least 20 years old when offered.

(9) *Evidence about a Process or System.* Evidence describing a process or system and showing that it produces an accurate result.

(10) *Methods Provided by a Statute or Rule.* Any method of authentication or identification allowed by a federal statute or a rule prescribed by the Supreme Court.

Rule 902. Evidence That Is Self-Authenticating

The following items of evidence are self-authenticating; they require no extrinsic evidence of authenticity in order to be admitted:

(1) *Domestic Public Documents That Are Sealed and Signed.* A document that bears:

(A) a seal purporting to be that of the United States; any state, district, commonwealth, territory, or insular possession of the United States; the former Panama Canal Zone; the Trust Territory of the Pacific Islands; a political subdivision of any of these entities; or a department, agency, or officer of any entity named above; and

(B)   a signature purporting to be an execution or attestation.

(2) *Domestic Public Documents That Are Not Sealed but Are Signed and Certified.* A document that bears no seal if:

   (A)   it bears the signature of an officer or employee of an entity named in Rule 902(1)(A); and

   (B)   another public officer who has a seal and official duties within that same entity certifies under seal—or its equivalent—that the signer has the official capacity and that the signature is genuine.

(3) *Foreign Public Documents.* A document that purports to be signed or attested by a person who is authorized by a foreign country's law to do so. The document must be accompanied by a final certification that certifies the genuineness of the signature and official position of the signer or attester—or of any foreign official whose certificate of genuineness relates to the signature or attestation or is in a chain of certificates of genuineness relating to the signature or attestation. The certification may be made by a secretary of a United States embassy or legation; by a consul general, vice consul, or consular agent of the United States; or by a diplomatic or consular official of the foreign country assigned or accredited to the United States. If all parties have been given a reasonable opportunity to investigate the document's authenticity and accuracy, the court may, for good cause, either:

   (A)   order that it be treated as presumptively authentic without final certification; or

   (B)   allow it to be evidenced by an attested summary with or without final certification.

(4) *Certified Copies of Public Records.* A copy of an official record—or a copy of a document that was recorded or filed in a public office as authorized by law—if the copy is certified as correct by:

    (A) the custodian or another person authorized to make the certification; or

    (B) a certificate that complies with Rule 902(1), (2), or (3), a federal statute, or a rule prescribed by the Supreme Court.

(5) *Official Publications.* A book, pamphlet, or other publication purporting to be issued by a public authority.

(6) *Newspapers and Periodicals.* Printed material purporting to be a newspaper or periodical.

(7) *Trade Inscriptions and the Like.* An inscription, sign, tag, or label purporting to have been affixed in the course of business and indicating origin, ownership, or control.

(8) *Acknowledged Documents.* A document accompanied by a certificate of acknowledgment that is lawfully executed by a notary public or another officer who is authorized to take acknowledgments.

(9) *Commercial Paper and Related Documents.* Commercial paper, a signature on it, and related documents, to the extent allowed by general commercial law.

(10) *Presumptions under a Federal Statute.* A signature, document, or anything else that a federal statute declares to be presumptively or prima facie genuine or authentic.

(11) *Certified Domestic Records of a Regularly Conducted Activity.* The original or a copy of a domestic record that meets the requirements of Rule 803(6)(A)–(C), as shown by a certification of the custodian or another qualified person that complies with a federal statute or a rule prescribed by the Supreme Court. Before the trial or hearing, the proponent must give an adverse party reasonable written notice of the intent to offer the record—and must make the record and certification available for inspection—so that the party has a fair opportunity to challenge them.

(12) *Certified Foreign Records of a Regularly Conducted Activity.* In a civil case, the original or a copy of a foreign record that meets the requirements of Rule 902(11), modified as follows: the certification, rather than complying with a federal statute or Supreme Court rule, must be signed in a manner that, if falsely made, would subject the maker to a criminal penalty in the country where the certification is signed. The proponent must also meet the notice requirements of Rule 902(11).

Rule 903. Subscribing Witness's Testimony

A subscribing witness's testimony is necessary to authenticate a writing only if required by the law of the jurisdiction that governs its validity.

Article X. Contents of Writings, Recordings and Photographs

Rule 1001. Definitions That Apply to This Article

In this article:

(a) A "writing" consists of letters, words, numbers, or their equivalent set down in any form.

(b) A "recording" consists of letters, words, numbers, or their equivalent recorded in any manner.

(c) A "photograph" means a photographic image or its equivalent stored in any form.

(d) An "original" of a writing or recording means the writing or recording itself or any counterpart intended to have the same effect by the person who executed or issued it. For electronically stored information, "original" means any printout—or other output readable by sight—if it accurately reflects the information. An "original" of a photograph includes the negative or a print from it.

(e) A "duplicate" means a counterpart produced by a mechanical, photographic, chemical, electronic, or other equivalent process or technique that accurately reproduces the original.

Rule 1002. Requirement of the Original

An original writing, recording, or photograph is required in order to prove its content unless these rules or a federal statute provides otherwise.

Rule 1003. Admissibility of Duplicates

A duplicate is admissible to the same extent as the original unless a genuine question is raised about the original's authenticity or the circumstances make it unfair to admit the duplicate.

Rule 1004. Admissibility of Other Evidence of Content

An original is not required and other evidence of the content of a writing, recording, or photograph is admissible if:

(a) all the originals are lost or destroyed, and not by the proponent acting in bad faith;

(b) an original cannot be obtained by any available judicial process;

(c) the party against whom the original would be offered had control of the original; was at that time put on notice, by pleadings or otherwise, that the original would be a subject of proof at the trial or hearing; and fails to produce it at the trial or hearing; or

(d) the writing, recording, or photograph is not closely related to a controlling issue.

Rule 1005. Copies of Public Records to Prove Content

The proponent may use a copy to prove the content of an official record—or of a document that was recorded or filed in a public office as authorized by law—if these conditions are met: the record or document is otherwise admissible; and the copy is certified as correct in accordance with Rule 902(4) or is testified to be correct by a witness who has compared it with the original. If no such copy can be obtained by reasonable diligence, then the proponent may use other evidence to prove the content.

Rule 1006. Summaries to Prove Content

The proponent may use a summary, chart, or calculation to prove the content of voluminous writings, recordings, or photographs that cannot be conveniently examined in court. The proponent must make the originals or duplicates available for examination or copying, or both, by other parties at a reasonable time and place. And the court may order the proponent to produce them in court.

Rule 1007. Testimony or Statement of a Party to Prove Content

The proponent may prove the content of a writing, recording, or photograph by the testimony, deposition, or written statement of the party against whom the evidence is offered. The proponent need not account for the original.

Rule 1008. Functions of the Court and Jury

Ordinarily, the court determines whether the proponent has fulfilled the factual conditions for admitting other evidence of the content of a writing, recording, or photograph under Rule 1004 or 1005. But in a jury trial, the jury determines—in accordance with Rule 104(b)—any issue about whether:

(a)   an asserted writing, recording, or photograph ever existed

(b)   another one produced at the trial or hearing is the original; or

(c)   other evidence of content accurately reflects the content.

Article XI. Miscellaneous Rules

Rule 1101. Applicability of the Rules

(a)   *To Courts and Judges.* These rules apply to proceedings before:

(1)   United States district courts;

(2)   United States bankruptcy and magistrate judges;

(3)   United States courts of appeals;

(4)   the United States Court of Federal Claims; and

(5)   the district courts of Guam, the Virgin Islands, and the Northern Mariana Islands.

(b)   *To Cases and Proceedings.* These rules apply in:

(1)   civil cases and proceedings, including bankruptcy, admiralty, and maritime cases; criminal cases and proceedings; and

(2)   contempt proceedings, except those in which the court may act summarily.

(c)   *Rules on Privilege.* The rules on privilege apply to all stages of a case or proceeding.

(d)   *Exceptions.* These rules—except for those on privilege—do not apply to the following:

(1)   the court's determination, under Rule 104(a), on a preliminary question of fact governing admissibility;

(2)   grand jury proceedings; and

(3)   miscellaneous proceedings such as:

(A)   extradition or rendition;

(B)   issuing an arrest warrant, criminal summons, or search warrant;

(C) a preliminary examination in a criminal case;

(D) sentencing;

(E) granting or revoking probation or supervised release; and

(F) considering whether to release on bail or otherwise.

(e) *Other Statutes and Rules.* A federal statute or a rule prescribed by the Supreme Court may provide for admitting or excluding evidence independently from these rules.

Rule 1102. Amendments
These rules may be amended as provided in 28 U.S.C. § 2072.

Rule 1103. Title
These rules may be cited as the Federal Rules of Evidence.

Foundations

Common Foundations Necessary to Authenticate an Exhibit
Photographs • Identify the photograph • What does it depict? • The witness is familiar with the scene depicted. • That the scene depicted in the photograph fairly and accurately depicts the scene personally observed by the witness.

Common Foundations Necessary to Authenticate an Exhibit
Email   • Identify the email   • Identify the date of the email   • Identify the address of the sender or the recipient   • Have the witness indicate they recognize the email and how they received it   • Identify any personalized markings (corporate logo, e.g.)   • Identify contextual information (response to an earlier email).
Text message   • The context of the message: why it was sent, its purpose, earlier discussions on a topic of controversy, etc.   • Knowledge of the phone number sent to or received from;   • Identification of a photograph of the actual text that was sent;   • The process of taking the photograph (who took the photo, what camera was used, that it was an accurate reproduction of the actual text etc.)   • Use of a transcript of the actual text, including the procedures of making it (transcript was prepared based upon the actual text, reviewed by the sender and it accurately reflects the actual text);   • Testimony regarding any responsive text received or any verbal acknowledgement by the sender or recipient concerning the text.

Common Foundations Necessary to Authenticate an Exhibit

Writing: Identify the document

- What is it?
- Who prepared the document?
- When was it prepared?
- Basis of knowledge concerning its preparation
- Identification of any handwriting
- It is in the same condition as when prepared or received.

Business records

- Qualify the witness (custodian of the records, etc.)
- Identify the record (what is it?)
- The person who maintained the records had knowledge of the transactions or transmitted by someone with such knowledge.
- Record was made at or near the time of the underlying event or transaction recorded.
- It was the regular practice of the business to record this type of information
- This record was kept in the ordinary course of business.

Common Foundations Necessary to Authenticate an Exhibit
Website (including social media) • That the witness visited the website; • When the website was visited; • Information reflecting that the website had been maintained and was current, as opposed to stale sites not kept current (e.g. postings reflecting current information, dates, etc.) • How the site was accessed; • Description of the website accessed: identifying material on the website including names, addresses, logos, phone numbers, etc.; • Recognition of the website based upon past visits; • That the screenshot was printed from the website; • The date and time that the screenshot was captured; • That the screenshot in the printout is exactly the same as what the witness saw on the computer screen; • That the printout has not been altered or otherwise changed from the image on the computer screen.
Computer generated documents • Identify the computer where the document came from; • Where it was located on the computer (e.g., in the "My Document" folder on the computer) • The general topic of the document; • When it was prepared or discovered; • When it was printed; • That the printed copy is identical to the computer file; • That it is in the same condition as when it was printed; • That the document offered is the same one printed off the computer.

Common Foundations Necessary to Authenticate an Exhibit

Demonstrative exhibit

- The "item is a fair and accurate representation of relevant testimony or documentary evidence otherwise admitted in the case."
- Mark and identify the aid as a demonstrative exhibit;
- Have the witness testify that the demonstrative aid accurately represents something the witness is describing and that it will assist the court in understanding their testimony.

Summary of self-authenticated documents

- Domestic public documents under seal
- Domestic public documents not under seal
- Foreign public documents
- Certified documents of public records
- Official publications
- Newspapers and periodicals
- Trade inscriptions and the like
- Acknowledged documents
- Commercial paper and related documents
- Presumptions under acts of Congress
- Certified domestic records of regularly conducted activity
- Certified foreign records of regularly conducted activity

Common Foundations Necessary to Authenticate an Exhibit
Procedure for admission of exhibits • Have the proposed exhibit marked for identification purposes; • After marking the exhibit, show it to the opposing counsel; • Seek leave of court to approach the witness (where required); • Have the witness lay the appropriate foundation by their testimony to identify and authenticate the exhibit; • Tender the exhibit to the judge requesting that the exhibit be admitted
Foundation for a conversation • Who was present? • Where did the conversation occur? • If by phone, did the witness recognize the other person's voice? • Who else was present during the conversation? • What was the topic of the conversation? • Who spoke first? • What was said? • Was there a response to the comment?

Fact	Issue	How to Prove	Foundation/ Authentication	Objections & Response

Index

I